Cambridge Topics in Geography : second series

Editors Alan R. H. Baker, Emmanuel College, Cambridge
Colin Evans, King's College School, Wimbledon

The location in Britain

GW01466631

A. G. Hoare

Department of Geography, University of Bristol

Cambridge University Press

Cambridge
London   New York   New Rochelle
Melb

Published by the Press Syndicate of the University of Cambridge
The Pitt Building, Trumpington Street, Cambridge CB2 1RP
32 East 57th Street, New York, NY 10022, USA
296 Beaconsfield Parade, Middle Park, Melbourne 3206, Australia

© Cambridge University Press 1983

First Published 1983

Printed in Great Britain at the University Press, Cambridge

British Library Cataloguing in Publication Data

Hoare, A. G.
The location of industry in Britain
—(Cambridge topics in geography. 2nd series)
1. Industry, Location of—Great Britain
I. Title
338.6′042′0941   HC260.D5

ISBN 0 521 23123 X hard covers
ISBN 0 521 29827 X paperback

Library of Congress catalogue card number: 82 – 12884

To Kate

Contents

Clarks at Street, 1971 ▶
The family shoe firm of Clarks was founded in the village of Street on the edge of the Somerset Levels in 1825. Its original factory site has been extended onto adjacent land, as the company has grown in national stature. Street, very much a company town, has grown with it, through the immigration of Clarks' workers to the town and the Quaker firm's policy of providing schools, houses, and civic buildings for its workers' families. Since 1945, Clarks' expansion has taken it to over twenty towns in the west country and beyond, while Street's economy has also broadened somewhat. But the company is still closely involved with the arts, education and recreation provision locally and, in 1969, helped finance the relief road on the west (left) of the photo. Clarks' massive new warehouse complex dominates the centre left of the view.

Kindly supplied by C. and J. Clark Ltd.

Wiggins Teape paper mill, ▶
Fort William
In 1966, the Basingstoke-based paper-making giant, Wiggins Teape, opened an integrated pulp and paper mill on Loch Eil, near Fort William, with Ben Nevis as its backcloth. Half its costs were met by government sources as part of regional policy. Regionally, it proved a great success, creating 2000 jobs on site plus 'multiplier' work in forests and construction, reviving the Caledonian Canal and saving the West Highland railway. All government financial obligations have now been paid off, but since the mid-1970s the British paper-making industry as a whole has contracted severely. One reason is the general economic recession, and another is Britain's high energy prices, by international standards, to which the paper companies

and their dependent communities are very sensitive. As part of this, Wiggins Teape closed its increasingly uneconomic pulp operations at Fort William in 1980, although it continues making high quality paper there, now based on imported pulp.
Kindly supplied by Wiggins Teape Group Ltd

4

1 Introduction

Myths and legends

One sunny day in 1840 two officials of the Great Western Railway stopped for a picnic near the sleepy Wiltshire town of Swindon. Suddenly, one of them had an idea. 'The company needs a locomotive works,' he cried, 'let's find one for them. I'll toss my ham sandwich as far as I can, and where it lands can be the place to build.' So he threw with all his might, and at the spot where it landed the Directors of the GWR set about building their locomotive factory.

Thus was born, according to one version at least, what was to become perhaps the largest single manufacturing establishment in mid-nineteenth-century Europe.

For Mr Everyman 'industrial geography', if it means anything at all, is little more than a collection of such anecdotes. Yet while easy to salt away, such stories provide no in-depth understanding of the geography of industry in modern Britain. After all, their appeal lies partly in their eccentricity—ham-sandwich-throwing is *not* a widely accepted criterion for selecting factory locations. And can real decision-making be as simple and cavalier as this? Again, do geographers have no interest in industries once their initial sites have been settled—almost 150 years ago, in Swindon's case?

This introduction to the industrial geography of modern Britain is more representative of its scope and underlying processes than an anthology of anecdotes. Inevitably, though, it resorts to arguments and examples that are less romantic! This first chapter paints the background against which Britain's industrial geography has to be seen. First, though, what do we mean by 'industry' and 'geography'?

Definitions

'Industry'

Here, 'industry' will be equated with 'manufacturing', or 'secondary activity'—the processing of material inputs into new material goods. While this definition is far more restricted than in everyday parlance ('industry' equals 'work') or official usage (as in the 'Industry Training Boards' or the 'Department of Industry') the geography and experience of manufacturing in post-1918 Britain is sufficiently distinctive to justify such an apparently narrow one.

Hence our definition is based on the output of economic activity. There are, though, other bases for classifying the economy: job type (clerk, driver, canteen worker, machine operator. . .) and ownership type (locally-owned, British-owned, American-owned. . .) are but two. These others often cut across an 'output'-based classification. 'Output' classifications of the 'primary–secondary–tertiary' sort also raise practical problems, as a minority of firms are not obviously one thing or the other. And this minority includes most of the biggest ones. British Rail supplies

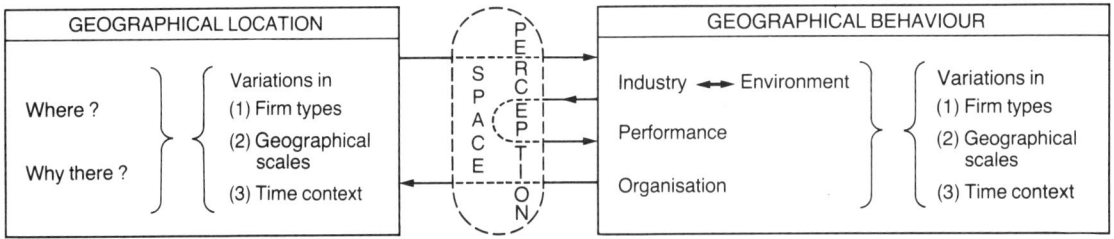

GEOGRAPHICAL LOCATION				GEOGRAPHICAL BEHAVIOUR	

Figure showing two boxes. Left box "GEOGRAPHICAL LOCATION": Where? / Why there? linked to Variations in (1) Firm types (2) Geographical scales (3) Time context. Center dashed oval: PERCEPTION OF SPACE. Right box "GEOGRAPHICAL BEHAVIOUR": Industry ↔ Environment / Performance / Organisation linked to Variations in (1) Firm types (2) Geographical scales (3) Time context.

Fig. 1.1 Two components of Industrial Geography. The go-between role of perception of space operates as when manufacturers look for new locations to suit the needs of their established business behaviour, and when they are reconsidering and possibly changing their behaviour from a fixed locational base.

transport services, but also manufactures rolling stock (as at Swindon). Marks and Spencer's retailing (tertiary) chain has extended 'backwards' by close association with clothing manufacturers and farmers. The manufacturers Dunlop Rubber acquired (primary) rubber estates in Malaysia and Sri Lanka before 1914, while takeovers among (secondary) brewers this century have increased the pool of (tertiary) sector pubs for the growing companies (Chapter 6).

'Geography'

The standpoint taken here is that 'geography' studies patterns and processes in space, a view which while not commanding total support among modern geographers has at least as many adherents as any other. 'Industrial geography' thus becomes the study of the spatial aspects of manufacturing activity. The scope of the academic field so defined is extensive, covering far more than just the initial decision on where to build a factory.

The scope of industrial geography

In fact, industrial geography has two different but inter-related sides to its character (Fig. 1.1). The more obvious is that of geographical location.

Here interest centres on the 'where?' and 'why there?' of manufacturing. In other words, geographers try to identify and explain the spatial positioning of industrial activity as such. Sometimes this is a 'snapshot' study of a given time, sometimes a study of change over time. Sometimes the emphasis is on all manufacturing, sometimes with particular sub-groups (steel firms, foreign firms, small firms, and so on). Equally, most studies focus on a particular 'spatial scale'—Britain as a whole, Scotland, Birmingham, Lambeth. . . Explaining these patterns involves not merely understanding initial location reasons but also subsequent changes in the locational mosaic and, more subtly, why there has often been no locational change despite the passing of time.

In the second interpretation, that of geographical behaviour, interest switches from why industry comes to be where it is to what it does when it gets there—to how it behaves. Fig. 1.1 suggests three aspects of geographical behaviour, any of which, again, can be studied for a range of firm types, spatial scales and times.

(a) **Industry ↔ environment interactions** Firms and their surrounding geographical environments interact. All manufacturers deliberately interact with selective parts of geographical space when obtaining their inputs, and when selling their products. At other times manufacturing firms generate unintentional environment spin-offs. Some of these may be potentially harmful to the environment (pollution being the obvious example) while others can be to its advantage, by contributing substantially to local authority rates and in several other ways. Thus the East Midlands Tourist Board has identified that region's heritage of old industrial sites and its modern industrial population as significant tourist attractions, with visits to the Crown Derby porcelain works booked up a year ahead. Spin-offs can work in the reverse way, too—from environment to industry: Nottingham Forest Football Club's success in the European Cup during 1978/9 brought an estimated £880,000 of new business for the city's industries, through a promotional campaign running alongside the football fixtures.

(b) Performance   Here the industrial geographer is interested in the spatial dimension of such economic indicators as profitability, technological innovation, production methods, labour productivity or employment growth.

(c) Organisation   Modern industry in Britain consists less and less of 'stand alone' plants, and more and more of multi-plant, multi-locational companies. A major academic growth area of recent years has been the study of geographical patterns associated with the running of groups of locationally separate plants under the umbrella of the one firm.

The distinction between geographical location and geographical behaviour is not a hard and fast one. Locations provide the bases from which behaviour radiates, while dissatisfaction with existing behaviour can lead to changes of location. A crucial intermediary between behaviour and location is the industrialist's perception of space. Like all of us, the industrialist reacts not to what things are like, but to what he thinks they are like, which is not necessarily the same thing. His perception of his existing location can cause him to change it, and his perception of alternatives directs his search for 'better' ones. This aspect of Britain's industrial geography is explored further in Chapter 3.

Industrial geography, industry and geography

Industrial geography is a hybrid subject, with a foot in each of two separate and wider fields of study (Fig. 1.2). The geographer approaching the subject from one of these is well aware that there is more to geography than industry, but can overlook the equally important implication that there is more to industry than geography. Indeed, some geographers drawing upon Marxist analysis based on class conflict have argued that studying the geography of industry in isolation from the wider issues of the investment and reinvestment of capital to make profits is a meaningless exercise (Walker and Storper 1981). By viewing industrial geography in the context of both of its parent studies we are in a better position to understand the importance of the spatial dimension to manufacturing firms, and also the significance of manufacturing for the wider study of geography.

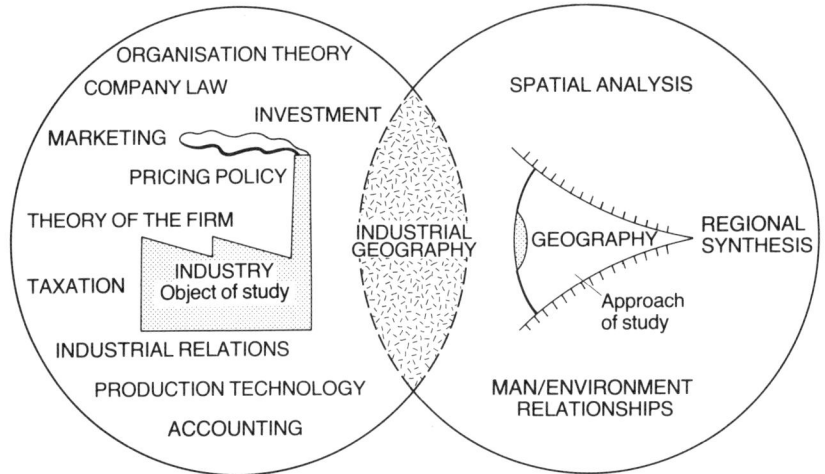

Fig. 1.2 Two perspectives on Industrial Geography. Geography provides a way of looking at manufacturing industry which focuses on just one aspect of industrial activity. Industrialists have to consider *all* aspects, and in this wider context the geographical components may have a low order of priority.

Industrial geography and the industrialist

We can categorise the decisions that industrial managers make in this way:

1 Non-where decisions. What to produce: shoes? ships? sealing wax? How to produce: labour-intensive methods? unionised labour? type of machinery? private or public ownership? How much to produce: 1 ? 100 ? 10,000 units a week?

2 Where decisions. How many plants (and how many locations)? Which towns? Which countries?

Every 'non-where' decision has its geographical spin-offs, and these fall under the 'geographical behavioural' half of Fig. 1.1. But these spin-offs will often be of only secondary importance to the industrialist. Thus a 'how' decision on a new process may lead him to buy from the sole UK supplier of the appropriate machine, wherever the latter is located, while the pollution produced by the 'what' and 'how much' decisions is happily flushed into the local environment with no thought for its wider social consequences.

Only in 'where' decisions—the geographical location part of Fig. 1.1— is space central to decision-making. Yet these are not as popular with industrialists as with geographers. Few industrialists have any specific geographical training, but many have the technical or financial background necessary for tackling the other decision options. 'Where' decisions are also the most costly and time-consuming to implement, and carry the greatest risk element.

Industrialists thus prefer to adopt the easier, short-term solutions of 'what', 'how' and 'how much' decisions, where they feel at home, rather than consider the costly uncertainties of 'where'. So if labour becomes scarce locally the manufacturer may prefer to switch to less labour-intensive methods or product lines, or 'bus in' workers from further afield, or even reduce output, rather than relocate in a labour-surplus area. The net result, then, is that location decisions are taken relatively infrequently and that this tendency is self-reinforcing.

It follows, too, that a good factory location is neither a sufficient nor a necessary condition for commercial success. While it is rarely easy to apportion blame for industrial failure or credit for prosperity, manufacturing plants may fall on hard times for 'non-where' reasons, irrespective of an apparently excellent location. Equally, other plants doggedly persist at 'bad' locations. In short, then, unfortunate 'non-where' decisions can fritter away prime locational potential, and fortunate ones more then compensate for apparently poor locations.

Industrial geography and the geographer

What, if anything, makes industrial geography distinct from those other brands of economic geography available? In the answer to this lies much of the practical significance of the study of industrial geography in modern Britain.

(a) Diversity   The various official classifications of economic activity in Britain (now known as the 'Standard Industrial Classifications' (SIC)) have consistently identified far more subdivisions of manufacturing than for primary and tertiary sectors (Table 1.1). Since manufacturing covers such a vast range of products as kilts, kites, kilns, kippers, kingpins, kitchen sinks and kidney machines it comes as no surprise that the geographical location and behaviour of Britain's manufacturers show an equivalent variety.

Table 1.1 Official classifications of the economy.

	Number of broad categories identified*			Number of detailed categories identified*		
	Primary sector	*Secondary (manufacturing) sector*	Tertiary sector	Primary sector	*Secondary (manufacturing) sector*	Tertiary sector
1931 Population Census classification	3	*11*	7	29	*263*	144
1948 SIC	2	*14*	7	9	*112*	39
1958 SIC	2	*14*	7	7	*109*	35
1968 SIC	2	*17*	7	8	*122*	50

*The broad and detailed categories of the S.I.C. systems are termed, respectively, 'Orders' and 'Minimum List Headings'.

(b) Freedom of manoeuvre   One popular way to classify economic location patterns is along a spectrum from resource- to market-orientation (Fig. 1.3). Primary resources must be gathered *in situ* (miners hew coal at the coal face, lumberjacks fell trees in forests). Conversely, service industries are usually market-oriented: housewives buy at their corner shop, their husbands patronise the local barber. In contrast, manufacturing is more flexible. Some industries are market-oriented, some concentrate on material locations, while for others intermediate locations are appropriate (Chapter 6). This flexibility arises because both the material inputs and material outputs of the manufacturing process can be transported through space.

(c) New goods for old   The transformation of material inputs into different material outputs serves further to distinguish manufacturing from other economic sectors, in two ways. First, manufacturing locations are responsive to two different sets of freight costs. Given the diversity of the

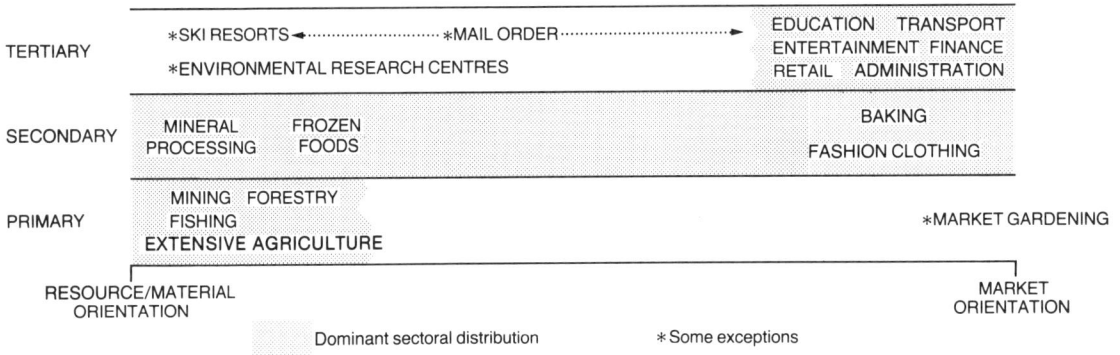

TERTIARY	*SKI RESORTS ◄ ·········· *MAIL ORDER ··········►	EDUCATION TRANSPORT ENTERTAINMENT FINANCE RETAIL ADMINISTRATION
	*ENVIRONMENTAL RESEARCH CENTRES	
SECONDARY	MINERAL FROZEN PROCESSING FOODS	BAKING FASHION CLOTHING
PRIMARY	MINING FORESTRY FISHING EXTENSIVE AGRICULTURE	*MARKET GARDENING

RESOURCE/MATERIAL ORIENTATION ⌐ ⌐ MARKET ORIENTATION

▓ Dominant sectoral distribution   *Some exceptions

Fig. 1.3 The dominant locational positions of economic activities in different sectors. Taken in aggregate, manufacturing firms spread themselves much more widely along the 'resource-market' spectrum than those in the other two sectors, although individual industries will have preference for certain parts of it. Try to fit into this diagram other examples you know something about: are there any manufacturing activities you would place half-way along, for example?

manufacturing section (subsection (a) above) some entrepreneurs are keen to minimise input costs, some to minimise output costs, while some occupy intermediate positions. This goes a long way to explain the position of a given firm on the material–market spectrum just described. Second, material transformation has anti-social side-effects—steam, smoke, solid and liquid waste, and noise. Such pollutants play a major part in the unsavoury public image of Britain's heavy manufacturing regions, and this explains why planning authorities take a close interest in the location and behaviour of industries within their jurisdiction (Chapter 3).

(d) Urban agglomeration   Britain's manufacturers are gregarious creatures. Table 1.2 shows how, at the county scale, manufacturing employment is more clustered geographically than that of other sectors, than total employment or than population. Furthermore, counties with high dependence upon manufacturing tend to be urban (high-density) ones, with the notable exception of Greater London. In contrast, agriculture, predictably enough, is important in rural counties, while service employment seems largely unrelated to population density, especially when the 'special case' of London is again ignored (Fig. 1.4).

Table 1.2 British employment structure: geographical concentration, 1976. *Source*: compiled from Lee (1979).

	Percentage of G.B. total included				
	Population	Total employment	Agriculture	*Manufacturing*	Services
Including Greater London					
Leading 5 counties	31.3	36.6	21.4	*39.0*	38.7
10	44.7	49.0	37.0	*49.3*	57.1
20	63.2	66.8	58.7	*69.7*	68.2
30	75.9	78.7	73.7	*81.2*	79.6
Excluding Greater London					
Leading 5 counties	24.4	27.2	21.6	*31.0*	25.9
10	39.2	41.5	37.3	*45.2*	40.5
20	59.6	61.8	59.3	*63.4*	61.4
30	73.6	75.6	74.4	*79.9*	75.4

(e) Longevity   Manufacturing has probably provided at least one-third of national employment since at least 1841. The laws of chance suggest that a long established manufacturing sector will contain a sizeable number of long established firms and premises. Fig. 1.5a shows the date of establishment of a sample of 200 large British manufacturers and an equivalent number of service firms. Some 70% of the former were established before 1900 and, on balance, form slightly the older group.

% Employment in services (1976)

72.40 ·E.Sussex Greater London·
·S.Glamorgan

% 57.05 ·Merseyside

West Midlands

41.70 ·Derbyshire

7.50 888.84 1770.18 2651.52 3532.86 4414.20
Persons per sq.km

% Employment in agriculture (1976)

14.40 ·Powys
·Dumfries & Galloway

% 7.25

Greater London

Merseyside West Midlands

0.10 Midlands

7.50 888.84 1770.18 2651.52 3532.86 4414.20
Persons per sq.km

Note:2(3...)=2(3...)coincident dots

% Employment in manufacturing (1976)

48.60 West Midlands·

% 32.85 ·Merseyside

Highlands Greater London
·S.Glamorgan

17.10

7.50 888.84 1770.18 2651.52 3532.86 4414.20
Persons per sq.km

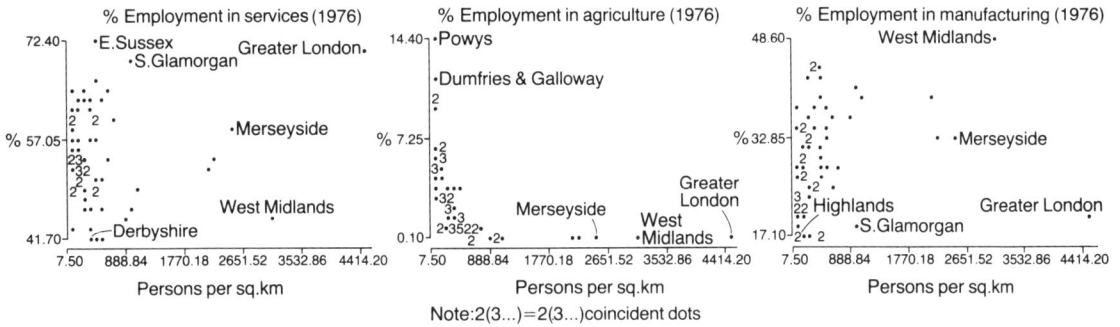

Fig. 1.4 The relative importance of employment in 3 economic sectors when compared with population density. The 'manufacturing' case shows a broad 'positive' relationship with population density, but it is a far from perfect relationship. Why is Greater London so much out of line?

Fig. 1.5 (a) Dates of company establishment of a sample of large present-day manufacturers and service firms in the United Kingdom, and (b) dates of beginning work at their then-current premises for a sample of manufacturers and service firms surveyed in west London in 1969. Post-war office growth in the sector of London between Westminster and Heathrow Airport at a time when factory expansion in the capital was severely limited by local and central planning controls (see Chapter 3) underlies the much greater difference between the curves in (b) than in (a). *Sources:* (a) *Key Business Enterprises* (Dun and Bradstreet Ltd, London, 1980); (b) Author's field survey.

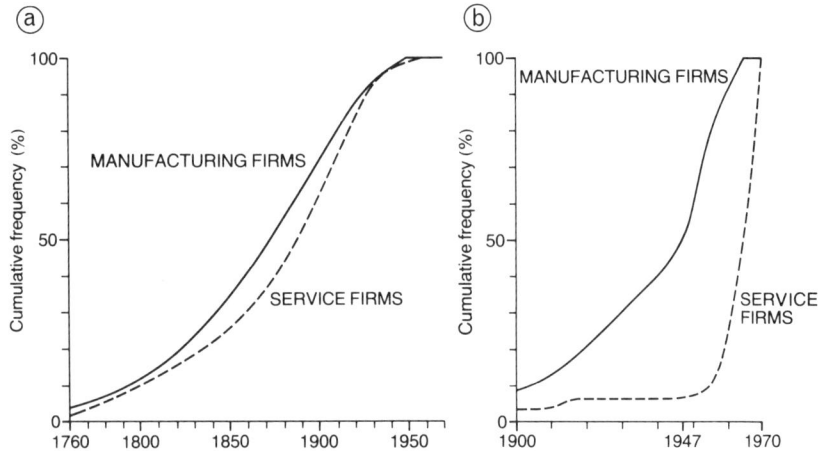

(a)

(b)

Few of them will still be in their original premises, but a second sample, drawn from west London in 1968/9 (Hoare 1974) also shows a difference, and now a very marked one, between the age of 'present' premises of manufacturers and service companies (Fig. 1.5b). Manufacturing premises are clearly older, with some 50% predating the introduction of effective town planning legislation in England in 1947. The practical implications of this longevity are taken up in Chapter 3.

(f) Firms of many parts Longevity provides an opportunity for growth, and some firms have certainly grown very big indeed. Since 1945 in particular growth has resulted in firms adding to their numbers of premises. And the range of functions undertaken at these locations, within the umbrella of a single firm is far wider than applies with non-manufacturing firms (Fig. 1.6). As well as enjoying 'economies of scale' (i.e. unit cost reductions through a high quantity of production) through overall company growth manufacturers also benefit from intra-company scale economies by concentrating functions at particular sites. Some of the possible company structures that may evolve are illustrated in Fig. 1.6.

The locational requirements and the geographical behaviour of these diverse functions can be very different. Factories may demand access to material sources, providing much local employment but also considerable pollution; the research centre may require close proximity to an 'information environment', while being benign to the physical one; while the warehouse values good motorway access and provides only modest amounts of employment. A location that suits and tolerates one function need not suit and tolerate them all.

11

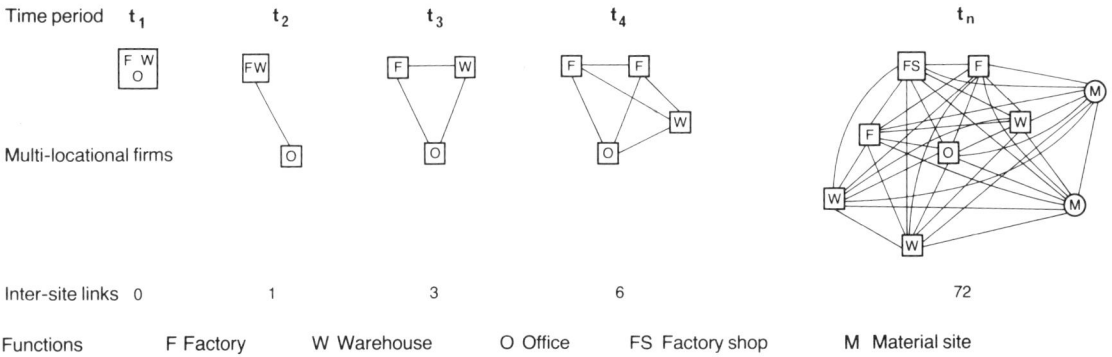

Time period	t_1	t_2	t_3	t_4	t_n

Multi-locational firms

Inter-site links	0	1	3	6	72

Functions   F Factory   W Warehouse   O Office   FS Factory shop   M Material site

Fig. 1.6 A growing multi-locational manufacturing firm. 'Functional splitting' accompanying company growth allows the peculiar locational needs of different functions more easily to be met, but this must be traded off against the cost of inter-site transfer of goods, staff and information.

But the progressive splitting of different functions among different locations increases the strain on the company's internal communication. If a company grows as in Fig. 1.6, if each unit needs contact with all others, and if each link is of equal importance, then the number of internal links grows proportionally faster than the number of units. Clearly, large multi-locational manufacturers must reconcile the advantages of 'function splitting' with the strains imposed on internal company contact.

(g) **Manufacturing and the economic base**   Much of the geographical interest in manufacturing lies in the ripples it sets up elsewhere in the economy. Manufacturing firms are often part of the 'basic', or 'export', sector of a geographical area. This is the sector that generates jobs and money in that area by selling in 'outside' markets. Note that the 'area' can be of any size, from the district of a town, to a region, to a country as a whole or even a group of countries.

The area's export-generated activity recirculates within it, in a multitude of ways (Fig. 1.7), as money is spent and respent, and as more jobs create more jobs. Thus, the overall dependence of the area upon its export firms is greater than the jobs and income tied up in these firms alone. The relationship between the export and the 'dependent' sector (called also the 'non-export' and, perhaps confusingly, the 'service' sector) represents the economic base multiplier. In the 'jobs' case this multiplier for a given area A is measured thus:

$$\text{Export base multiplier for A} \quad = \quad \frac{\text{Total jobs in A}}{\text{'Export' activity jobs in A}}$$

If, then, A has 10,000 workers in export activities out of a total workforce of 15,000, the economic base multiplier will be $15,000/10,000 = 1.5$. This gives a rough indication of the overall impact upon jobs in A should the export sector expand (500 new export jobs will stimulate about 250 more in their wake), while its decline has a converse effect as the multiplier goes into reverse.

But 'rough' is the operative word. The whole basic/export notion is fraught with problems, such as the practical methods by which the export sector and the multiplier can be measured (see, for example, Glasson 1978, pp. 81–7). Accepting these, though, available data show manufacturing as more 'basic' than British economic activity as a whole.

12

Fig. 1.7 'Internal' recycling of export earnings within a geographical area. This leads to a further increase in total earnings through the 'multiplier' mechanism. We could redraw this diagram, substituting 'jobs' for 'income', although this would almost certainly change the size of the multiplier. Why should this be?

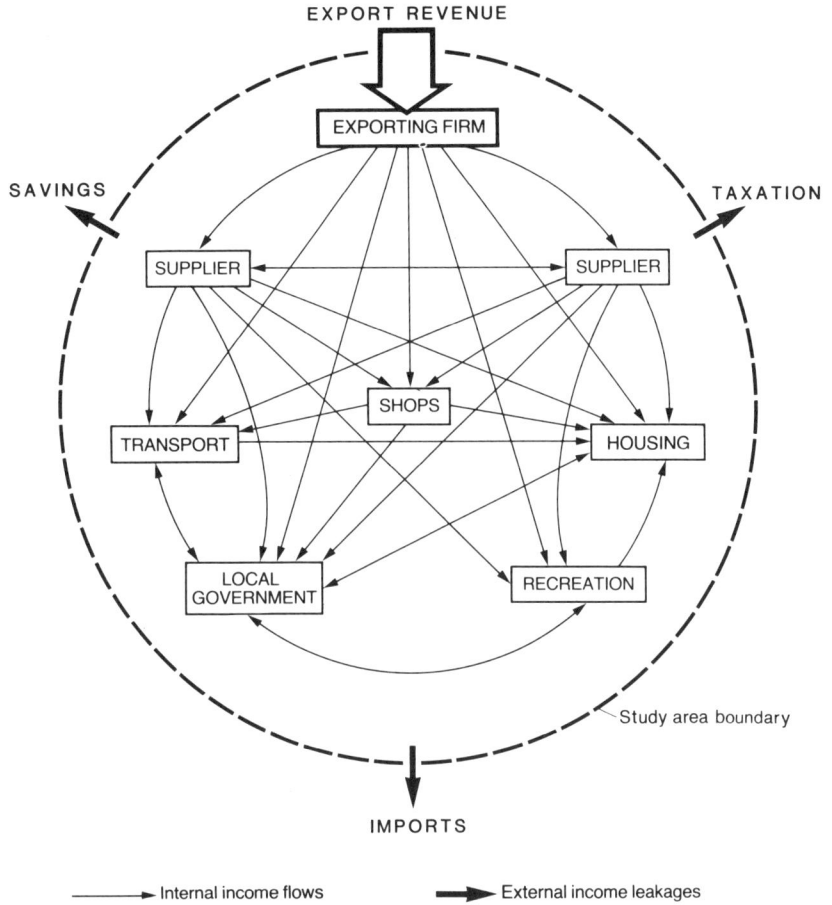

EXPORT REVENUE

EXPORTING FIRM

SAVINGS   TAXATION

SUPPLIER   SUPPLIER

SHOPS

TRANSPORT   HOUSING

LOCAL GOVERNMENT   RECREATION

Study area boundary

IMPORTS

→ Internal income flows   ➡ External income leakages

Table 1.3 UK export generation: manufactures and services, 1976. *Sources:* various official statistics.

	Exports (£m.)	UK employment (000) 1976	
	(a)	(b)	(a)/(b)
Manufactures	21,347	7,245.8	2.95
Invisibles	13,461	12,880.5[1]	1.05

[1]Service-sector employment excluding construction, gas, water, electricity.

Table 1.4 Market concentrations of London firms. *Source:* compiled from London Employment Survey (Greater London Council).

	Percentage of firms with more than 60% markets in specified areas			
	Within 3 miles	Greater London	South-East England	UK
Manufacturing	15.8	45.9	60.5	87.2
Services	65.3	76.0	83.4	88.1
Construction	23.4	77.2	90.6	96.7

Table 1.3 presents a somewhat unconventional view of Britain's overseas trade. While, in absolute net terms, Britain's 'visible' trade (which includes manufacturers) is in deficit and the tertiary-sector 'invisibles' in surplus, yet when their respective employment strengths are taken into account, manufacturing emerges as by far the greater export generator. An extensive survey in Greater London in 1966 showed manufacturing's 'basic' orientation was also apparent at sub-national geographical scales (Table 1.4). In fact, of the four spatial scales shown, the national one

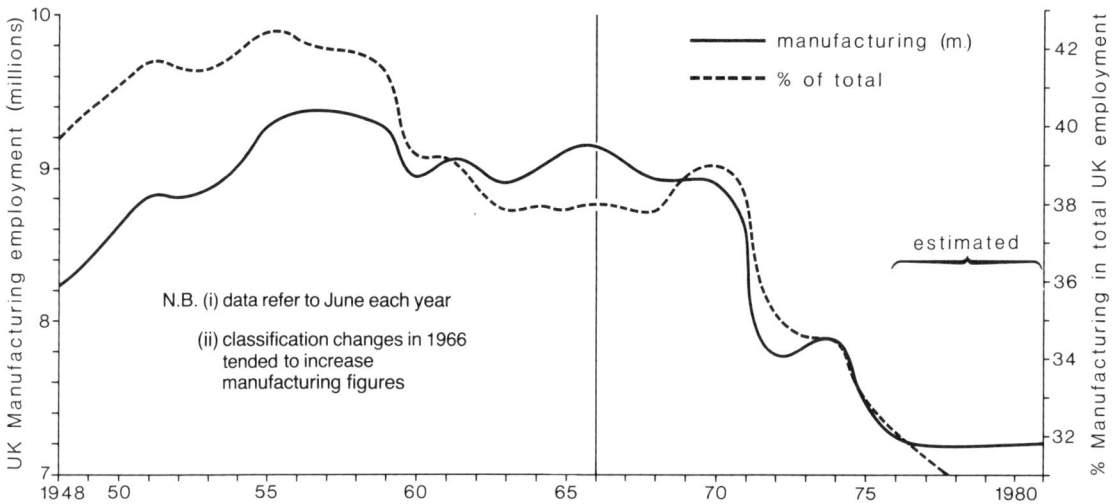

Fig. 1.8 Relative and absolute levels of United Kingdom manufacturing employment, 1945-80. The shake-out of industrial jobs after 1966 (when manufacturers found it no longer attractive to hoard labour in the hopes of business picking up) is readily apparent, despite classification changes. As the overall number of jobs in the national economy is broadly constant, the two 'curves' keep in close harmony. *Sources:* (i) Department of Employment and Productivity (1971) *British Labour Statistics: historical abstract 1886-1968* (HMSO, London); (ii) Department of Employment (various dates) *British Labour Statistics Year Books* (HMSO, London); (iii) 1981 estimates from *Department of Employment Gazette,* May 1975.

finds the export performance of manufacturing and other sectors at their most similar. Britain's manufacturing sector thus provides the major pillars upon which the economies and societies of districts, towns and regions are built. (See also p. 4.)

This same message comes across from sketchy evidence of the dependence of communities upon particular parts of the manufacturing sector, upon particular firms, or even upon particular projects in a particular firm. In 1977 a CBI study of 5 large industrial companies in north-west England estimated that each of their 53,000 regional workers provided work for one other worker in the region in 'service' sectors (a base multiplier of 2.0)—40,000 supplying their annual input purchases of £367m., and a further 12,500 in retailing. In the same region manufacturing decline has thrown the multiplier into reverse. The 1979 closure of the Asda superstore at Kirkby (Merseyside), after just 4 years of operation, was blamed on the decline in spending power due to the recent closure of several local factories. Similarly, the collapse of Rolls Royce in 1971, because of its overdependence on one contract, for RB 211 aero-engines, spelt immediate disaster for the Derby and Ilkeston Window Cleaning Company, just one of its 2,000 suppliers, whose entire monthly income of £3,000 came from work at the firm's Derby head offices, while fears of further economic ramifications caused panicky depositors to queue for 2 days outside the Derbyshire Building Society to withdraw their savings.

Manufacturing in Britain since 1918

Of the many changes that the nation's manufacturing has undergone since 1918 (see, for example, George 1974; NIESR 1977; Phillips and Maddock 1973; Pollard 1969), three are of particular interest geographically.

Manufacturing's role in the economy

Taking the most commonly used economic indicator, employment, Fig. 1.8 shows manufacturing trends since 1948, before which corresponding statistics simply do not exist. While some years are exceptions, the general pattern is clear enough, with a relative decline in manufacturing since

Fig. 1.9 Changes in the United Kingdom manufacturing contribution of 17 industries, 1907-70. The two axes show changes as measured by jobs and by 'net output' (the value of goods produced minus that of input materials and fuels). Thus 'food, drink, tobacco' increased its national job share from 8.7% to 9.9% (+1.2% points) but reduced its net output share from 14.6% to 12.7% (−1.9% points). Source: Calculated from Business Statistics Office (no date) Historical record of the Census of Production 1907 to 1970 (HMSO, London).

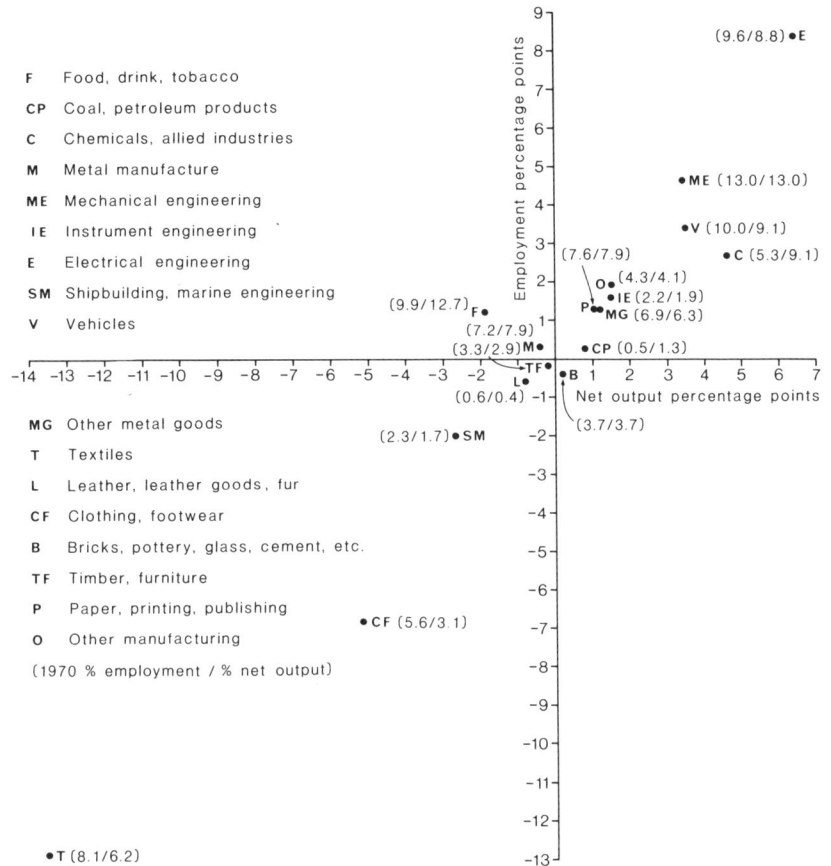

F   Food, drink, tobacco
CP   Coal, petroleum products
C   Chemicals, allied industries
M   Metal manufacture
ME   Mechanical engineering
IE   Instrument engineering
E   Electrical engineering
SM   Shipbuilding, marine engineering
V   Vehicles

MG   Other metal goods
T   Textiles
L   Leather, leather goods, fur
CF   Clothing, footwear
B   Bricks, pottery, glass, cement, etc.
TF   Timber, furniture
P   Paper, printing, publishing
O   Other manufacturing

(1970 % employment / % net output)

1956 coupled with an absolute one since about 1970. Indeed, the overall loss of manufacturing jobs—often referred to as the process of 'deindustrialisation'—has gone so far that an article in *The Times* of 18 March 1982 could claim that 'Britain today has ceased to be an industrial nation.' In the absence of any smooth take-up of the labour released by manufacturing's decline the outcome is increased social distress, notably through unemployment, as when a massive shake-out of labour from industry in the mid-1960s heralded a 'once-and-for-all' increase in registered unemployment of some 250,000.

This distress is geographically discriminating too, partly as some areas are more manufacturing-oriented than others, and partly as some industrial areas have declined faster than others (Chapter 4). The relevance of this for the welfare geography of Britain, and the government's response to it, are discussed in later chapters.

Changes within the manufacturing sector

(a) Industrial structure   The make-up of Britain's manufacturing sector has also changed in terms of the end-product goods produced, and its restructuring allows us to identify three groups of industries. The first (engineering, vehicles, the lighter metal trades, paper- and chemical-based products, and the 'others') has expanded both in employment and output, the second, more 'traditional', group (shipbuilding, textiles, clothing, leather- and wood-based manufacture) declined in both, while the third,

Fig. 1.10 Growth paths for expanding industrial firms. Three 'internal' paths involve no absorption of pre-existing companies, unlike the 'external' path of take-overs and mergers. In practice, over a long period most large companies will show elements of a number of different growth paths.

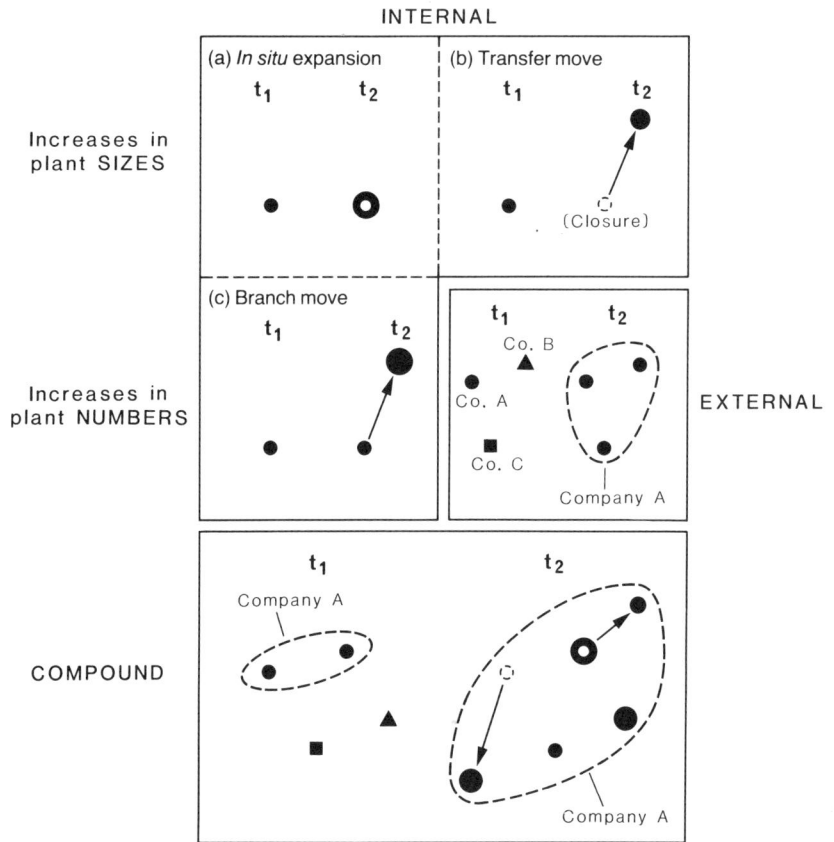

INTERNAL

(a) *In situ* expansion

t_1 t_2

Increases in plant SIZES

(b) Transfer move

t_1 t_2

(Closure)

(c) Branch move

t_1 t_2

Increases in plant NUMBERS

t_1 t_2

Co. B

Co. A

Co. C

Company A

EXTERNAL

COMPOUND

t_1 t_2

Company A

Company A

residual, group shows conflicting trends on the two indices (Fig. 1.9).

Since different industries have different locational needs and generate different geographical patterns, so this restructuring adds another 'spatial' component to those of overall manufacturing decline. Indeed, one school of thought relates the changing economic fortunes of Britain's regions to the geographical impacts within the country of such national-level structural changes (Chapter 4).

(b) Job types   Since 1918 non-production (largely 'white-collar') manufacturing jobs have risen markedly compared to shop-floor, production ('blue-collar') jobs, partly as machinery has been easier to substitute for labour in this latter category. Thus 'administrative, technical and clerical' workers grew from 10% of all British manufacturing jobs in 1924 to 28% in 1975 (Crum and Gudgin 1977). Given the varied locational requirements of the production and non-production units within large companies and the increased role played by multi-locational companies (below, (c)) some geographical effects within Britain of this changing balance of job types are only to be expected.

(c) Industrial concentration   The last 60 years have seen a rapid rise in the industrial control exercised by a few giant companies. In 1900 Britain's largest 100 manufacturing firms produced 15% of national industrial output, and the biggest of them employed 5,000 workers. By the 1970s the largest 100 controlled 50% of output and the biggest, ICI, employed some 200,000. A number of routes are open to such growing

Table 1.5 The role of big plants in GB manufacturing, 1935–63. *Source:* George (1974, p.34).

Plant employment	% total manufacturing employment		
	1935	1951	1963
11 – 49	13.9	11.5	9.0
50 – 99	11.7	10.4	8.3
100 – 299	26.2	22.2	20.3
300 – 499	12.8	11.6	11.4
500 – 999	13.9	13.6	14.6
1,000 – 1,499	6.3	7.2	8.2
≥ 1,500	15.2	23.6	28.2

firms; some result in increased plant size, some in increased plant numbers, and some in both (Fig. 1.10). Since 1935 big plants have certainly grown in size both absolutely and in comparison with small ones (Table 1.5). However, recent analysis of the top end of the industrial size spectrum has shown that the dramatic growth of the biggest industrial companies since 1950 has come about through increase in plant numbers (Prais 1976). Between 1958 and 1972 the average number of plants owned by the top 100 companies soared from 27 to 72, while for all industrial companies the average number of plants per firm rose from 2.4 to 3.7 over 1958–68. Finally, 'external' rather than 'internal' growth routes have been the more important in this rise of plant numbers (Fig. 1.10), with the 1960s in particular witnessing a 'merger boom' of unprecedented proportions in British manufacturing.

The role of government

Increased governmental influence in manufacturing affairs has been a final important trend, and one taking a number of forms (Corden and Fels 1976). Central government has acted to provide financial support for industry as a whole, and for certain sections of it (for example, cotton after 1959), to assume ownership of manufacturing activity directly (outright nationalisation) or at second hand (as through the National Enterprise Board), to provide promotional, information and forecasting services, and variously to constrain and to encourage mergers, depending on where the public interest was felt to lie. All these must affect geographical location and behaviour, though in ways often very hard to unravel, so intertwined are the roles of 'the market' and 'the ministry'. The most obvious effect on manufacturing location directly is through regional policy, a topic we return to in Chapter 3. (See also p. 4.)

Bristol: industrial relocation, before and after
The 'old' factory of what is now Imperial Tobacco was opened by W.D. and H.O. Wills in 1886 in Bristol's Victorian suburb of Bedminster, a relocation forced by expansion from central Bristol where tobacco had been brought by the River Avon direct to waterside wharfs. But with subsequent growth, the multi-storeyed, landlocked factory itself proved inflexible and constraining, enforcing a 5 km. move to the 'new' site at suburban Hartcliffe in 1973. This is now the biggest cigarette factory in Europe, its 56 acre site being designed to high environmental standards and for a production regime and a volume of car and lorry traffic never dreamed of by Wills' Victorian decision-makers. Hartcliffe proved easily accessible to the company's workforce, many of whom by now lived in new housing estates nearby. It now also houses Imperial Tobacco's head offices, although the parent company, the Imperial Group, is London-based. The 1886 building continued to serve as the offices for other parts of the Group.

Kindly supplied by Imperial Tobacco Ltd., Bristol.

18

2 The driving forces

Introduction

Against the background of Chapter 1, the remaining five chapters examine Britain's industrial geography since 1918: Chapters 2 and 3 discuss the processes underlying the spatial patterning of manufacturing activity, while the following three consider the geographical patterns so generated.

Manufacturers are in business to make money. They make money by converting a set of 'inputs' into manufactured items which are then sold in the market. In the shorthand of the economist, then, manufacturers aim to match 'supply' (of inputs) with 'demand' (for goods). These are the essential components of manufacturing activity. It follows that they represent the 'driving forces' behind the geography of manufacturing activity as well.

Other forces also impinge upon manufacturing industry, and upon its geography, too – forces which while not essential to the very existence of that activity are nevertheless so important in Britain as to affect strongly the way manufacturing and its geography develop. These 'constraints' are of three sorts. First, manufacturers have to be seen as part of larger 'organisations', be they social, political or commercial ones. Secondly, 'behavioural' influences on manufacturers' actions result from their being fallible, prejudiced and emotional human animals rather than cold, economic calculating machines. Finally, constraints emerge as manufacturing patterns develop through time.

These driving forces and constraints are shown diagramatically in Fig. 2.1. The next chapter explores the importance for manufacturing geography in Britain of the constraints, while the rest of this one shows the corresponding effects of the driving forces. Some of these are best seen through the geography of supply, some through the geography of demand, while others work through both.

The geography of supply

Manufacturers need a variety of inputs for production, and these are often classified broadly as materials, land (or 'space'), labour and capital (or 'finance'), although we shall use a rather finer subdivision. Most of these inputs can be important geographically in three different ways.

(a) **Variations in quantity**   A manufacturer needs inputs in specified amounts, perhaps 350 acres of land, 1,000 workers each working day, 500 tonnes of coal per week, and £2m. for new plant over the next two years. The available quantity of inputs will often vary from place to place. This is partly because of the 'at source' geography of supplies: there is a lot of coal underground at Selby, less at Pontypridd, and none at Guildford. It also depends on the mobility of the input requirements. Hence the manufacturer can probably accumulate his 1,000 workers at a major

Fig. 2.1 Driving forces and constraints. This framework, developed fully in Chapter 2 and 3, takes as its basis the fundamental role of 'demand' and 'supply' in all forms of economic activity, and hence in the spatial (geographical) aspects of *one* sector of that economy. But their influence is moderated by other 'constraining' forces which can sometimes restrict the spatial possibilities raised by supply and demand and sometimes can extend them.

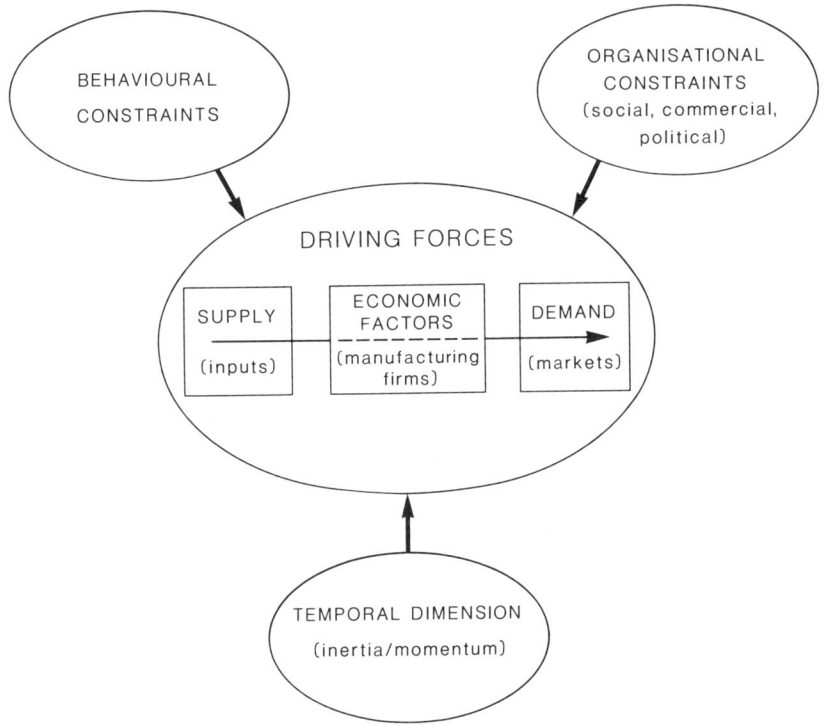

transport and commuting centre like Cardiff, but less easily in the South Wales valleys with their much more constricted route networks.

(b) Variations in absolute cost   A given quantity of supply costs more in one place than another, whether it is the cost of the labour (wages), the land (rents and rates), the capital (interest) or the price of the coal. Again, both 'at source' and 'mobility' factors are at work here, although it may be difficult for the manufacturer to isolate the importance of each. How much of the wage paid in Cardiff, for example, will be to cover commuting costs from the valleys, and what part of the price of coal in Guildford is the delivery charge from Selby?

(c) Relative cost (quality) variations   The manufacturer has also to consider the 'value for money' of his inputs at different locations. The price and availability of his coal needs may be identical in Durham and Widnes, but the calorific value of the coal may differ substantially. Typists may accept the same wage in Bognor as in Bangor, but produce twice as much work per day in the one as in the other.

The inputs

(a) Raw materials and fuels   Fig. 2.2 shows Britain's major mineral and fuel resources. In a well-surveyed country like Britain the potential quantity of these in particular areas is fairly well-known, although even here the size of some resources is in considerable doubt: estimates made in 1973-4 of usable reserves of North Sea Oil, for example, ranged from 25,000m. tonnes to 138,000m. tonnes (Chapman 1976). However, the actual quantities the same sources supply may fall well short of their

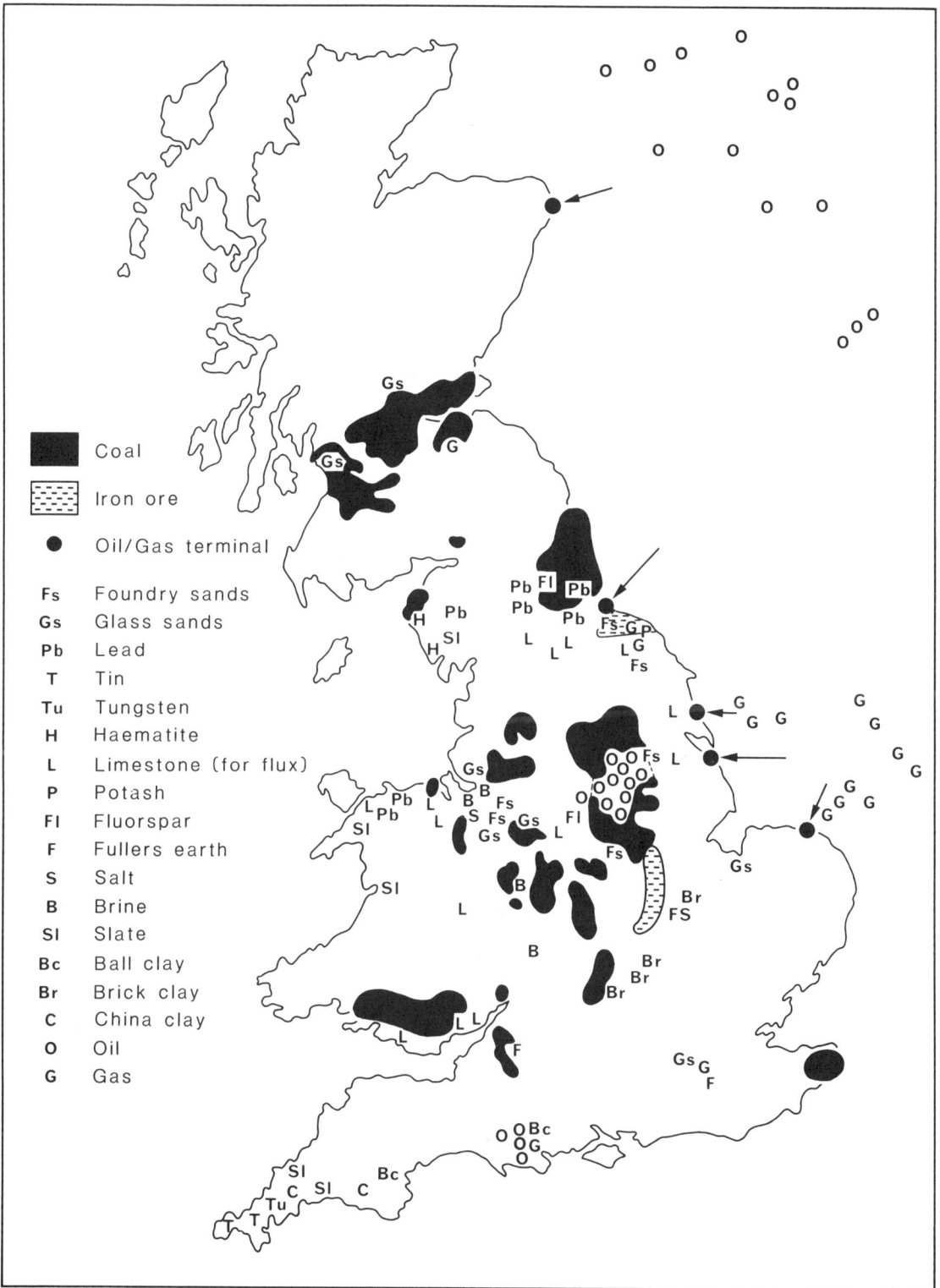

Key (legend):

- ■ Coal
- ▦ Iron ore
- ● Oil/Gas terminal
- **Fs** Foundry sands
- **Gs** Glass sands
- **Pb** Lead
- **T** Tin
- **Tu** Tungsten
- **H** Haematite
- **L** Limestone (for flux)
- **P** Potash
- **Fl** Fluorspar
- **F** Fullers earth
- **S** Salt
- **B** Brine
- **Sl** Slate
- **Bc** Ball clay
- **Br** Brick clay
- **C** China clay
- **O** Oil
- **G** Gas

Fig. 2.2 Mineral and fuel deposits in Britain and offshore. While many parts of Britain seem well positioned for industrial activity based on processing one resource or another, the questions of whether and where such developments arise in practice are far more complicated.

potential, being dependent on a variety of economic, technological and planning considerations (Blunden 1975).

Long-established manufacturing concerns dependent upon these resources include glass at St Helens (based on the Shirdley Hill sands), the Cheshire–Merseyside chemical complex (using Cheshire salt and Lancashire coal), the processing of Fullers Earth at Redhill (Surrey) and of slates in Wales and Cumbria, and the close geographical association in Britain as a whole between cement manufacture and chalk deposits. As will be shown later, there are good economic reasons why materials with a low value-to-weight ratio such as these should be processed at or near their source locations. However, industry is less strongly tied to minerals and fuels than before. There is no clearer example than coal. Once the uncrowned king of Britain's nineteenth-century industrial geography, it is monarch no more. Some 65% of coal mined in Britain in 1980 was converted into a highly mobile secondary energy source, electricity, and of 75 industries identified in an official survey in 1968 only 6 spent more on coal than on electricity. Only in aluminium does electricity itself exert any real locational pull today: the pre-1939 Kinlochleven plant is sited near an HEP scheme, and the 1960s processors at Lynemouth (Northumberland) and Holyhead (Anglesey) are next door to modern power stations (Watts 1970). Many mineral deposits now have an equally modest locational pull. Only 3 of Britain's 78 deposits of commercial silica have generated local glassworks, St Austell's important china clay deposits have never stimulated local processing, and some newer cement works are sited away from major chalk deposits (Blunden 1975). The 1965 plant at Southam (Warwickshire), for example, uses chalk slurry brought 92 km by pipeline. The reasons for this general state of affairs lie partly in improved transport, partly in the high landscape quality of many resource areas, making planning permission for processing plants difficult to obtain, and partly in the inheritance of plant elsewhere which cannot easily be written off just because new resource areas are coming on stream.

'At source' costs (sometimes called 'pit-head' costs) can vary substantially, as among Britain's coalfields. Here the early development of easily won (and cheap) coal in Wales, Scotland and the North East puts them now at a disadvantage compared with the newer fields of South Yorkshire, Derbyshire and Nottinghamshire, where extensive, thick, uniform and unfractured seams encourage large-scale, low-cost mechanisation. Turning to delivered cost variations, the standard tariff for industrial consumers of natural gas, for example, varied from 5.01p per therm in the North West to 10.16p in Wales (May 1974), while that for industrial oils shows a neat spatial pattern reflecting distance from major refining centres. In a few cases such differentials have a dramatic effect: the closure of the Invergordon aluminium smelter on the Cromarty Firth (announced in December 1981), involving the loss of 900 jobs, was blamed on high energy costs from the local Scottish Hydroelectricity Board.

Some material supplies vary in quality too, as does coal through variations in its chemical composition. Anthracite from South Wales and coking and gas coals from Durham have seen a relative decline in their markets this century, as compared with coal from Yorkshire and the East Midlands, which is better suited for conversion to electricity. Similarly,

Welsh slate, which is uniform in colour and fine-grained, has suffered the decline of its traditional roofing market, while newer, speciality markets of slate for cladding, fencing and paving have benefited the thicker, multi-coloured slates of Cumbria.

Finally, the brick clays from the Oxford Clay measures illustrate how quantity, quality and cost considerations all interact (Gleave 1965; Blunden 1975). Bricks ('flettons') made from these deposits have increased their share of the British market steadily to 43% in 1970. One reason lies in the quality of the clays. Their high water content (18-20%) makes them easily workable, their carbonaceous content (of 5-7%) reduces the coal needed for firing, and they have few other impurities to cause shrinkage or cracking in the bricks. As a result, the quantity of Oxford Clays required to make a given number of bricks is only some 25% that of coal measures clays. Their consistent chemical and geological properties also make the Oxford Clays highly suitable for mechanised extraction, thus greatly reducing 'pit-head' unit costs compared with competitive brickworks elsewhere. Such low-cost methods are achieved only in the large brickworks made possible by the extensive Oxford Clay deposit. The precise locations of the major brick producers on major railway crossings provide a further cost advantage, while the policy of the major producer in charging a uniform price in all markets allows it to undercut higher-cost, lower-quality producers in their own localities.

(b) Other primary material inputs: agriculture, fishing and forestry   These are important for a relatively small group of industries. Physical controls such as climate, soil and relief affect the quantity aspect of supply, and through it the processing locations of such relatively low value : high weight inputs. The fact that some are also perishable further encourages processing near the input source, to minimise any loss in quality before processing takes place. Fish-based products are thus manufactured at major fishing ports, while many East Anglian farmers supply peas and beans under contract to freezer companies, such as Birds Eye, within 90 minutes of picking. Sometimes existing growers may draw in manufacturers to these localities, but at others existing manufacturers progressively widen their supply areas among surrounding farmers. Either way, though, the supply must be reliable: the British Sugar Corporation closed its Cupar (Fife) refinery in 1971 because the uncertainties of the local climate led to fluctuating levels of beet output from neighbouring farms.

(c) Land   Manufacturers may require 'land' as vacant space or with premises standing upon it. Either way, land is immobile. Industrialists with particular land requirements have to select one of the set of locations meeting their specifications. As industry is not a major consumer of space this may not seem a severe constraint at first glance. Even so, the need of manufacturing for land has become both more demanding since 1918 and more difficult to meet. Not only has manufacturing output increased but so have the space needs per unit of output, with modern flow-line, single-storey production methods, stringent health and safety regulations, and affluent employees requiring space for car-parking. Thus between 1960 and 1969 the average new factory floorspace per worker rose from 60 to 70 square metres (Keeble 1976). Some locations, such as the inner cities

Fig. 2.3 (a) Average rental values for factory premises in Great Britain, 1980. Note the pressure on space in the South East of England and the general decline of values away from this core area. Aberdeen is an exception—a remote but high-value county—based on the North Sea Oil boom. (b) Simplified industrial estate rental values for South Wales/Severnside, 1969. Although an historical pattern (in both the currency and the level of rents shown!), the clear urban peaks in the surface will probably apply to rental values today, for sites both on and off industrial estates. *Sources:* (a) Cambridge Information and Research Services Ltd (1980); (b) Bale (1976).

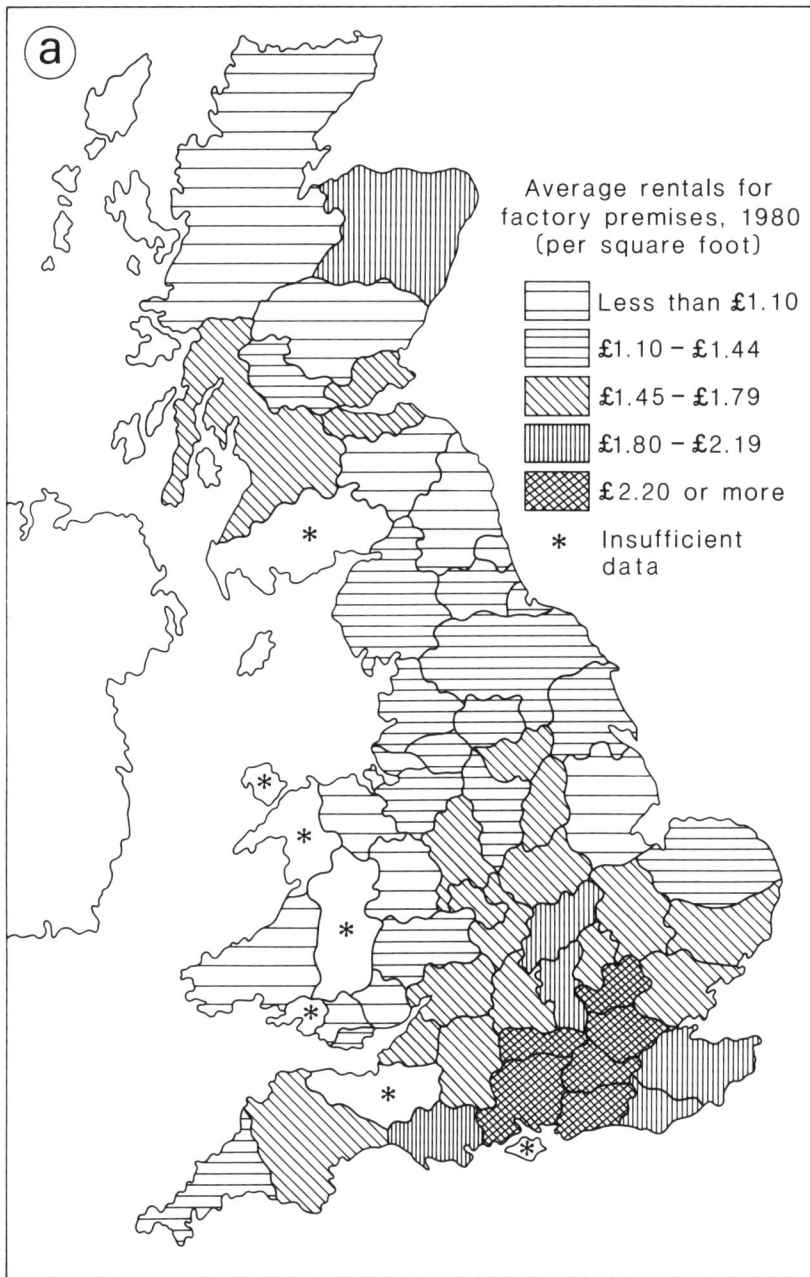

(a)

Average rentals for factory premises, 1980 (per square foot)

- Less than £1.10
- £1.10 – £1.44
- £1.45 – £1.79
- £1.80 – £2.19
- £2.20 or more
- * Insufficient data

and the South Wales valleys, simply cannot supply land in this quantity.

Planning controls on land use in Britain mean that what is physically available may not be actually available for manufacturing use (Chapter 3). Central and local planning authorities can also positively affect the geography of supply by building 'advance' factories to standard designs. The availability of vacant sites and factories may also be independent of political control. In the western Home Counties, where planning policy has generally been to restrict industrial growth, Lewis (1971) still found that the major reason behind the movement of 43 firms into the area between 1945 and 1966 was the availability of sites and premises at reasonable cost. This often involved the reuse of wartime factories and hangars as by Fords (Langley) and Smiths (Witney).

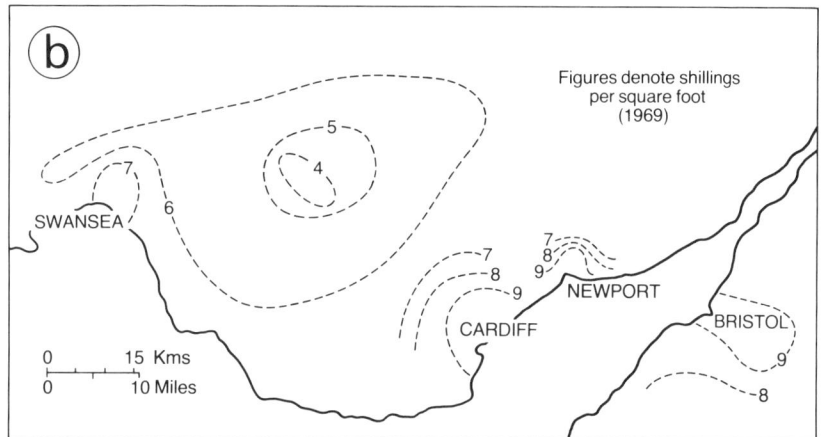

The conventional view on land costs is that, regionally, the contour map of industrial rents is highest in the South East, and, sub-regionally, displays peaks in major urban centres (Fig. 2.3). Large, single-storey manufacturing plants often cannot afford such high central rents in competition with more intensive multi-storey users such as offices and department stores, and hence are forced to the suburbs, where rents are lower.

Land quality is also important: 10 acres renting at £x annually may be less of a bargain compared with a similar site at £2x if the first requires draining, levelling, infilling and piling. Yet this is often necessary on extensive estuary sites. The Llanwern steel works, for example, required nearly 10m. tons of ballast to raise it above flood level, while developing low-lying estuarine lands on the other side of the Severn at Avonmouth has involved Bristol City Council in raising the average level of the land by 4 ft to protect against flood damage and maintain efficient surface drainage. It also enforces a reassessment of land drainage and coastal embankment systems designed for former agricultural users rather than potential industrial ones. Scenically attractive sites may receive planning permission conditional on expensive landscaping by the occupier. Quality considerations affect industrial premises too. Inner-city sites often mean dingy, cramped, multi-storey converted premises, inefficient for work and unattractive for staff, while suburban greenfield sites allow firms to build for what they need. This consideration among others led the Wills cigarette factory to move from its 1880s works in inner Bristol to the outer suburbs in 1973. Shortage of floorspace in built-up areas may also force firms to fragment their operations among a number of separate sites. Here an 'out-of-town' move brings them all back under one roof, to the benefit of intra-firm communication. (See also p. 18.)

(d) The environment Despite modern industry's ability to adjust its internal environment through humidifiers, air conditioning, water treatment and the like, the environment still has a role to play. 'We needed. . . clean air to avoid contamination of our product,' reported the Managing Director of Wrigley's chewing gum factory, explaining its 1970 move from Wembley to Plymouth, while manufacturers around Heathrow Airport find noise and vibrations caused by low-flying aircraft a major problem. The senior executive of one firm (which moved to Wales partly for this reason) expressed a common view:

'We will not have to suffer [at the new site], and suffer it really is, the noise of aircraft passing over our premises. I have calculated that conversations are stopped for 25 seconds every time a large jet aircraft takes off over the plant... It particulary upsets our research areas and can affect sensitive instruments and generally interrupt activities. This is a major consideration when looking for sites in a Development Area and I believe there is no intention at all to have an airport anywhere near where we are locating.'

Water, both for process use and waste disposal is also important for a number of industries. Reasons for the concentration of distilleries in the Spey valley are shrouded in Scottish mist, but one alleged factor is the particular properties of streams flowing off peat lying on top of granite. But to keep this factor in perspective, less than 5% of Rees' (1969) sample of manufacturers in south-east England regarded water as of first-order importance in their own location decisions, in contrast to responses of over 35% for 'land' (see also Chapter 6).

(e) Capital   Leaving regional policy finance on one side, the selective geographical availability of capital is less important than in the past. Some now major corporations began with their founders successfully garnering funds from friends and local contacts, but their present-day finance comes from their own accumulated profits, and from the 'money market' which in turn draws and disburses finance over a wide geographical area. Decisions about the provision of industrial capital are often taken centrally within the appropriate financial institution, irrespective of where the investment will be located.

Even so, Keeble (1976) quotes a case of higher interest rates being charged for 'risky' development in the North and Wales (9%) than in the South East (7¾%), and official planning reports in the Northern region blame its disappointing number of new firms on the reluctance of regional financial bodies to handle high-risk ventures. Conversely, financial directors of large manufacturing concerns often need access to the City of London to raise cash and credits, and oversee foreign exchange dealings:

'... many companies feel that it is essential to have a continuing presence and ear to the ground in London, otherwise they may lose £100,000 in an afternoon' (Crum and Gudgin 1977, p.127).

This last, though, concerns just part of the largest companies. On balance, inter-source variations of capital seem more important than geographical ones. One British dump truck manufacturer was able to secure bank loans only after being guaranteed financial backing by the Department of Industry, and has received its most recent credit from the London branch of a US bank, at an interest rate 6% below that offered by British banks (Northcott 1977). Industrial capital is very mobile, not just nationally but also internationally.

(f) Enterprise   The same goes for 'enterprise', the decision-making stratum of senior executives. Top management, like top footballers, stride the international stage as long as money and conditions are right. This merely represents the extreme case of the tendency for geographical mobility of labour to rise with its qualifications and experience (Toyne 1974, p. 137). Some considerations increase the supply of mobile

| (a) By region | | % 1978 females | (b) By selected local authorities in South West Region | | |
% 1978 males aged 15-64		aged 15-64*	% 1971 males aged 15-64	% 1971 females aged 15-60	
Northern	63.4	62.4			
Yorkshire/Humberside	64.9	61.4			
West Midlands	66.2	62.3			
East Anglia	65.5	61.6	Bath CB	64.9	54.2
South East	65.7	62.3	Bristol CB	65.7	55.7
			Cheltenham MB	64.7	56.4
South West	65.1	60.7	Clevedon UD	60.9	49.2
West Midlands	65.6	62.8	Dulverton RD	62.5	54.9
North West	61.2	61.3	Gloucester CB	61.9	55.1
Wales	64.8	61.7	Weston-super-Mare MB	59.1	51.9
Scotland	64.7	62.0			
Northern Ireland	62.1	59.8			
United Kingdom	65.1	62.0			

*1978 Females proportion for 15-60 not available

Table 2.1 Percentage of total population in working age-groups. *Sources:* Regional Statistics 1980, No. 15 (CSO); 1971 Population Census.

enterprise that a geographical area can attract, and some reduce it. In locations where expanding industries predominate, ambitious employees of existing companies may decide to set up on their own, and will often do so locally at first, for reasons discussed in Chapter 3. But where stagnant, declining industries dominate, scope for such new enterprise is severely limited. The size distribution of existing factories also seems important: proportionately more new firms are created by former employees of small firms than of large (Gudgin *et al.* 1979). A locality may also be able to draw in entrepreneurial talent for 'behavioural' reasons considered later, while strong family responsibilities and other ties to the local community dampen the long-distance mobility of decision-makers, as they do throughout the labour spectrum.

(g) Labour   Although lower proportionately than two decades ago, wages and salaries will represent about half the value of 'net output' (the value of output minus material and fuel costs) of British manufacturing. Labour represents, too, an important, spatially-varying input, if an elusive one.

At face value, labour quantity equates with working-age populations (16-64 for men, 16-59 for women), and this certainly varies as a percentage, locally and regionally (Table 2.1). However, not all of these groups will be available for work in reality, a fact not least due to the 'housewife' component. Thus female numbers seeking work fall well below the '16-59' potential, and the ratio between those in or seeking work, and those potentially eligible for work—the 'Female Activity Rate'—also varies regionally and locally (Table 2.2).

Seasonal variations in labour availability are also important. Tourist resorts have less full-time labour available than their demographic profiles suggest, but this may actually attract firms for whom a winter peak of labour demand dovetails with summer tourism employment. Such was one advantage of Torbay for Suttons Seeds following its move from Reading.

For many firms registered unemployment is an attractive measure of labour availability, though this too is often misleading (Boon 1974). By excluding some housewives who are interested in work (Taylor 1968) and including those of both sexes not interested in or capable of work, the official figures could both understate and overstate the supply (Armstrong and Taylor 1978, Ch. 5). Regional unemployment

Table 2.2 Female activity rates. *Sources:* Regional Statistics 1980, No. 15 (CSO); 1971 Population Census.

(a) By region, 1975

North	43.6%
Yorkshire/Humberside	45.7%
East Midlands	46.0%
East Anglia	44.5%
South East	47.2%
South West	40.8%
West Midlands	47.8%
North West	48.0%
Wales	39.8%
Scotland	45.8%
Great Britain	45.8%

(b) By selected local authorities in South West region, 1971

Bath CB	34.5%
Bristol CB	33.8%
Cheltenham MB	35.2%
Gloucester CB	32.6%
Weston-super-Mare	26.3%

Table 2.3 Different perspectives on regional unemployment: average monthly unemployment, 1976. *Sources:* various.

	Registered unemployed		Registered unemployed persons/sq. mile
Region	% labour force	Number (000)	
Northern Ireland	10.3 (1)	54.9 (10)	10.1 (8)
North	7.5 (2)	100.8 (7)	13.5 (6)
Wales	7.4 (3)	77.7 (8)	9.7 (9)
North West	7.0 (4.5)	197.3 (2)	62.5 (1)
Scotland	7.0 (4.5)	152.9 (3)	5.0 (11)
South West	6.4 (6)	101.9 (6)	11.2 (7)
West Midlands	5.9 (7)	134.5 (4)	26.8 (3)
Yorkshire/Humberside	5.6 (8)	114.7 (5)	20.9 (4)
East Anglia	4.9 (9)	33.8 (11)	7.4 (10)
East Midlands	4.8 (10)	74.0 (9)	15.7 (5)
South East	4.2 (11)	315.1 (1)	29.8 (2)
United Kingdom	5.8	1,358.8	14.5

Note: figures in brackets show regional ranks.

percentages are even more dangerous. Table 2.3 shows that a very different geographical picture can emerge once percentages are converted into more meaningful figures on absolute numbers and areal density.

Mobility, from place to place and job to job, also affects labour supply.

(i) Geographical mobility: commuting   Where daily commuting is extensive, employees have a wide choice of work and employers of labour. Public transport helps channel such flows upon major employment centres. Predictable differences occur: white-collar staff travel farther than blue, senior staff farther than junior, men farther than women, and car-owners farther than non-car-owners. Should prevailing commuting patterns fail to produce enough workers, employers can give them a nudge through private bus services.

(ii) Geographical mobility: permanent migration   Long-distance (inter-regional) migration is relatively more important among younger and better-educated workers. A survey of 935 manufacturing employees in south-west England found that of those who had moved to the region to take up jobs 20% had A-level qualifications or above, and 54% some 'trade' qualification, compared to just 5% and 38% respectively for those in the survey born and bred in the region (Nelson and Potter 1982). Figure 2.4 shows the regional net gainers and losers between 1960 and 1971.

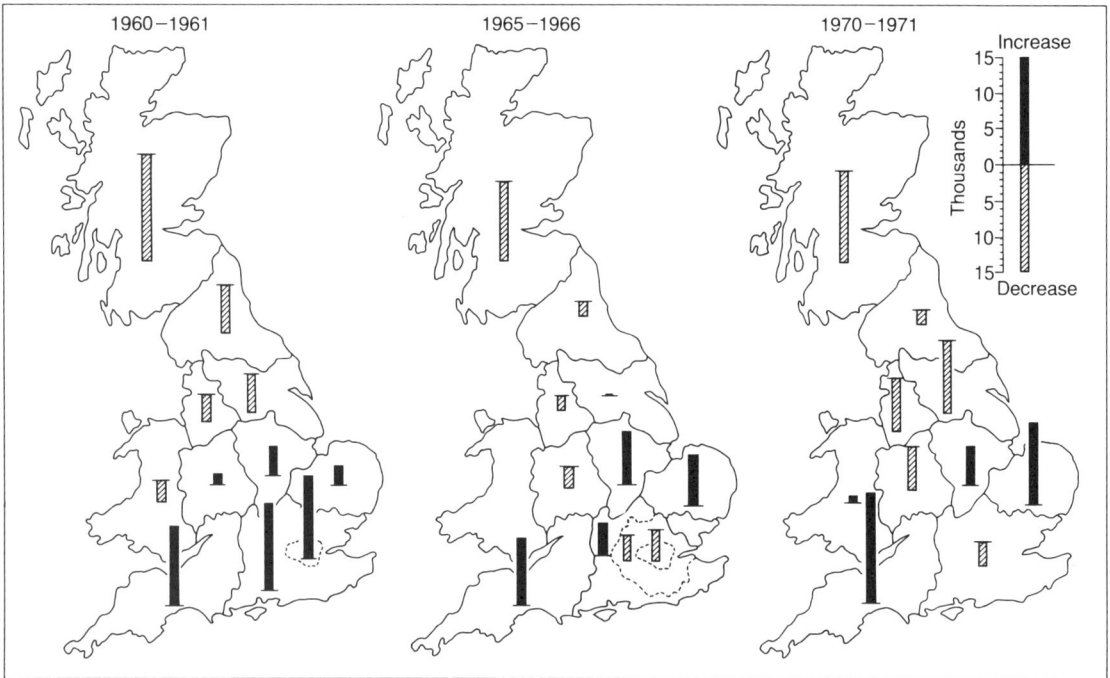

Fig. 2.4 Net balance of inter-regional migration of those in working age groups in Great Britain, 1960-71. A generally favourable balance in the south and east compared to the north and west is readily apparent (although London itself is an exception after 1965), but these absolute figures cannot show the *relative* impact these flows will make. East Anglia and the East Midlands had the same total 1965-6 influx, for example, but the former had less than half the resident workforce of the latter. *Source:* based on House (1977).

Some regions are consistent gainers, some consistent losers, some change fo the worse (notably the South East) while Wales improves its position. Such inter-regional trends conceal intra-regional ones, and here urban-to-rural household migration is a dominant theme, especially of the better qualified. Equivalent industrial migration flows from inner urban areas can be stimulated by this reduction of labour quality and quantity, so fuelling a cycle of disadvantage for inner cities (Chapter 5). Permanent migration is usually the result of a myriad individual decisions, but can also be organised on an aggregate basis, as with movement to the New and Expanded Towns (Chapter 5) or the recruitment of Scottish workers in the 1930s for the Corby steelworks (Chapter 6). (There is an equally organised return movement every weekend to watch the Rangers.) Both sorts of movement respond to housing availability. Some companies find this a significant problem, and authorities seeking new industrial investment publicise the availability of houses to suit all tastes and pockets. The 'niceness' of the local environment is a further potent factor here (Chapter 3).

(iii) Occupational mobility   Firms can also poach labour. Areas with an abundance of non-industry-specific skills offer most scope for this: the shorthand typist works for anyone, but the saggarmaker's bottom-knocker needs retraining for work outside the pottery industry. Some areas have a local tradition of labour playing musical chairs among employers to make the most of bonuses and other 'perks' on offer (Northcott 1977).

With so many factors influencing wage rates and fringe benefits, a geographical dimension to labour cost is hard to isolate. However, when the role of industrial structure is filtered out, the South East and the nineteenth-century industrial regions appear as high-wage areas, although the details vary from industry to industry (Fig. 2.5). Such differences are probably of lessening importance. As wage rates are increasingly

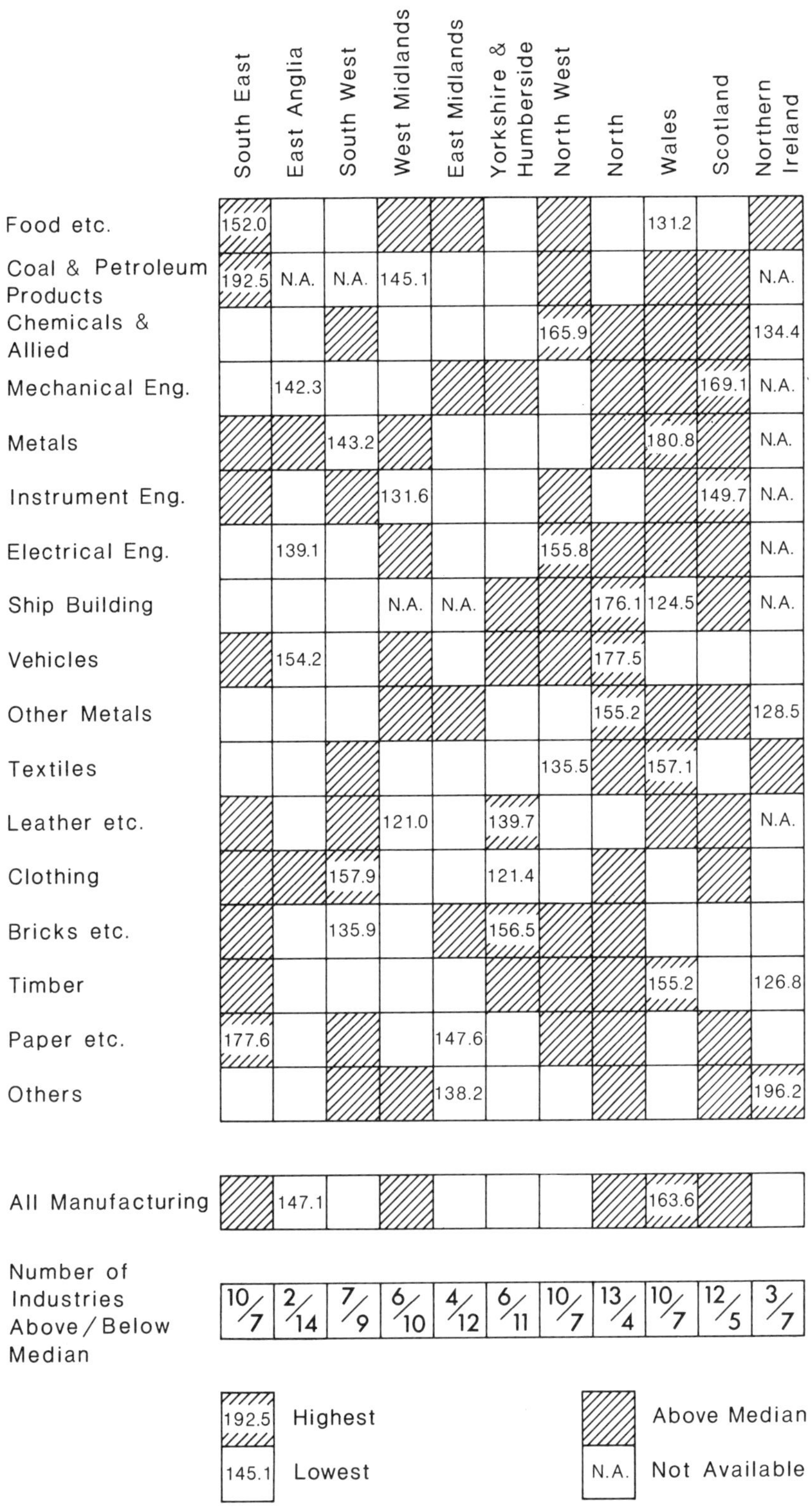

Fig. 2.5 Regional average wage rates in October, 1976, for full-time male manual workers (values in new pence per hour). The general impression is one of complexity: no region is above or below average consistently over all 17 industries. The relative importance of each industry matters as far as the regional average is concerned, so the West Midlands is above average overall, yet has a majority of below-average scores among the 17 industries. *Source:* Department of Employment (1978) *British Labour Statistics Year Book 1976* (HMSO, London).

	South East	East Anglia	South West	West Midlands	East Midlands	Yorkshire & Humberside	North West	North	Wales	Scotland	Northern Ireland
Food etc.	152.0									131.2	
Coal & Petroleum Products	192.5	N.A.	N.A.	145.1							N.A.
Chemicals & Allied						165.9					134.4
Mechanical Eng.		142.3								169.1	N.A.
Metals			143.2							180.8	N.A.
Instrument Eng.			131.6							149.7	N.A.
Electrical Eng.		139.1					155.8				N.A.
Ship Building				N.A.	N.A.			176.1	124.5		N.A.
Vehicles		154.2						177.5			
Other Metals								155.2			128.5
Textiles							135.5			157.1	
Leather etc.				121.0		139.7					N.A.
Clothing			157.9			121.4					
Bricks etc.			135.9			156.5					
Timber										155.2	126.8
Paper etc.	177.6					147.6					
Others							138.2				196.2
All Manufacturing		147.1								163.6	

	South East	East Anglia	South West	West Midlands	East Midlands	Yorkshire & Humberside	North West	North	Wales	Scotland	Northern Ireland
Number of Industries Above / Below Median	10/7	2/14	7/9	6/10	4/12	6/11	10/7	13/4	10/7	12/5	3/7

Legend:
- 192.5 Highest
- 145.1 Lowest
- (hatched) Above Median
- N.A. Not Available

negotiated on an inter-plant, inter-firm, inter-area basis, pronounced wrinkles in the map of labour costs should be ironed out. Intra-regional wage differences can also be significant. In the South East they encourage migration from London: on moving from Central London to Swindon,

	Absences from work as % workers, 1971 (In sample week)	Stoppages of work due to industrial disputes (Days lost per 1,000 workers)	Full-time students, 1972, As % 18-20-aged residents (Male)	(Female)	Labour productivity (net manufacturing output per employee), 1968 (£)
North	18.7	329.9	3.46	2.12	1,956
Yorkshire and Humberside	17.5	352.6	3.08	2.65	1,791
East Midlands	14.4	158.1	4.02	3.09	1,849
East Anglia	15.8	147.4	3.73	3.28	1,949
South East Greater London	15.6	328.5	5.91	4.49	2,166
South East Rest of SE	16.4				2,140
South West	17.4	99.4	5.21	3.22	1,923
West Midlands	19.9	521.3	1.15	3.33	1,841
North West	20.0	650.2	3.87	2.95	1,938
Wales	20.4	371.2	2.31	2.31	2,078
Scotland	15.8	369.3	3.55	3.27	1,861
Northern Ireland	N/A	433.5	N/A	N/A	1,651

Table 2.4 Selected measures of regional labour quality. *Source:* Keeble (1976, pp. 65, 218).

for example, Burmah Oil's combined savings on property and wages in the first year (1973-74) was £0.5m.

Regional variations in labour quality are at least as important as those of cost. Data in Table 2.4 suggest declining standards away from the South East, although a recent study of firms who have relocated (and are thus in a good position to judge inter-regional differences at first hand) shows the peripheral regions in a better light over work attitudes, adaptability, relations with management and turnover. Wiggins Teape's intra-regional move from London to Basingstoke also resulted in a halving of staff turnover, although the loss of the city's hustle and bustle also seemed to reduce productivity! (*Sunday Times*, 9 January 1977). At the increasingly important international scale, though, labour quality in Britain compares badly with overseas. In 1971 the Ford Motor Company in Detroit ruled out Britain as a location for a new plant, estimating some jobs took 90% longer to complete here than on the Continent, while 9 years later its British Chairman complained

'We are not making the progress we should in productivity. It is sheer intransigence to change—it is conservatism' (*The Times*, 20 February 1980).

Overall, the geography of labour is one of swings and roundabouts, with variations in quantity, quality and cost often directly opposing each other.

(h) The information environment Some of a manufacturer's information needs are bound up with obtaining other supplies and serving markets, but there are others less relevant to the everyday thrust of business activity which are still essential for longer-term success. Research and development is an obvious example. Many large companies do their own 'R & D' (Oakey *et al.* 1980), but most also have recourse to outside expertise in universities, governmental or independent institutions. These research centres have a south-eastern bias (Buswell and Lewis 1970; Hall 1970) (Fig. 2.6), partly for reasons of the supply of skilled labour, and environmental appeal (Chapter 3). Away from London R & D links have stimulated industrial development around Edinburgh, Oxford and Cambridge universities (Chapter 6), in the last case taking the form of a science park on the city outskirts. Industrial liaison companies have been

Fig. 2.6 (a) Some major research centres in the United Kingdom of a 'non-industry-specific' variety. London's dominance is plain for all to see. (b) Industrial research associations associated with research for specific industries. Still a London-region dominance, but to a lesser extent than in (a). Sheffield's importance as a research base for special steels (see Chapter 6) stands out too, while you can probably guess whch of the centres relate to the pottery, linen and shipbuilding industries. *Sources:* (a), (b) *Industrial Research in the United Kingdom* (Longman, 1980); (b) *Register of Consulting Scientists* (Fulmer Research Institute, Stoke Poges, 1978).

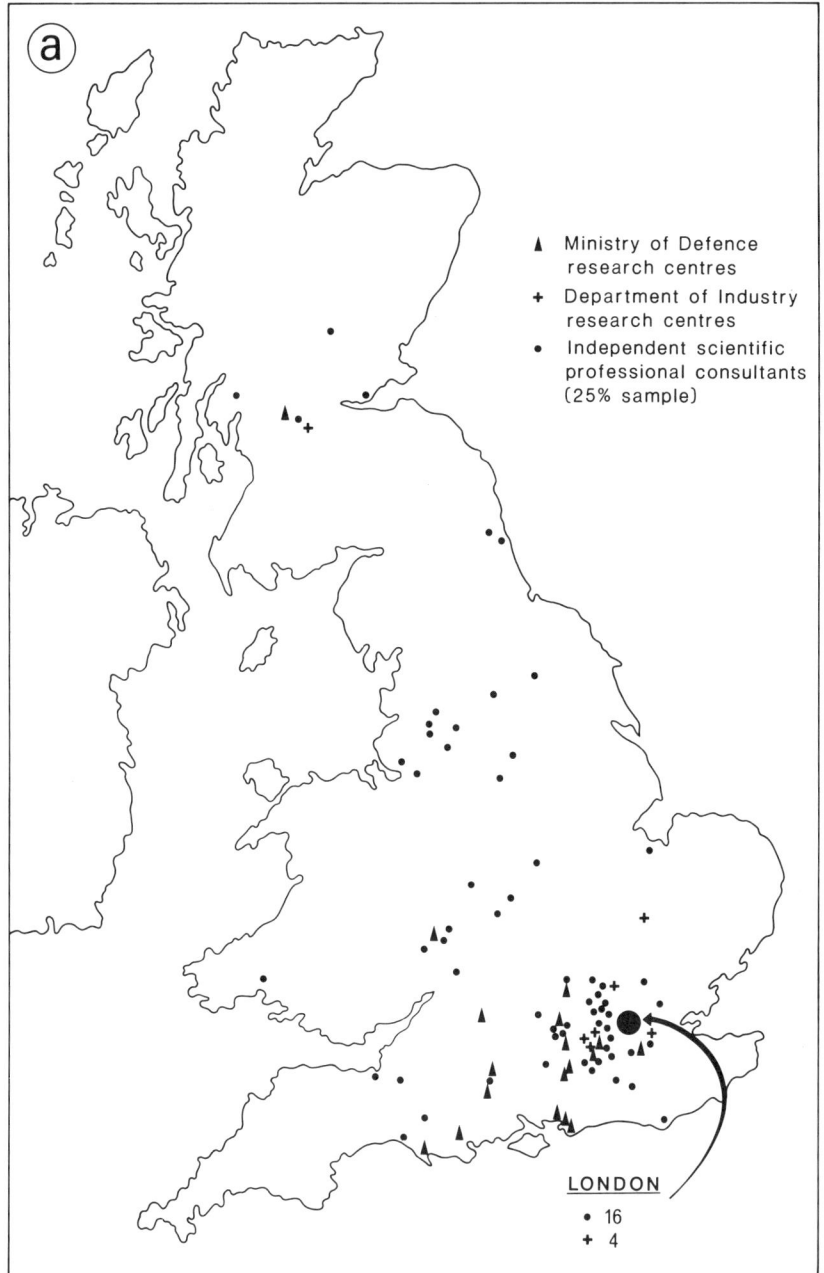

▲ Ministry of Defence research centres
+ Department of Industry research centres
• Independent scientific professional consultants (25% sample)

LONDON
• 16
+ 4

set up, as by Loughborough, Leeds, Lancaster and Bath universities, to place such ties between academic research and manufacturing application on a more formal footing.

Firms depend on other sorts of information too. Government's growing interest in all aspects of business, complex commercial legal and tax systems, and discussions with trades unions, patent officials, advertising and accountancy companies all require firms to contact a host of outside bodies. This usually means contact with large cities, and with London in particular. Thus Sir Derek Ezra neatly justified the National Coal Board's resolve to retain its London head office:

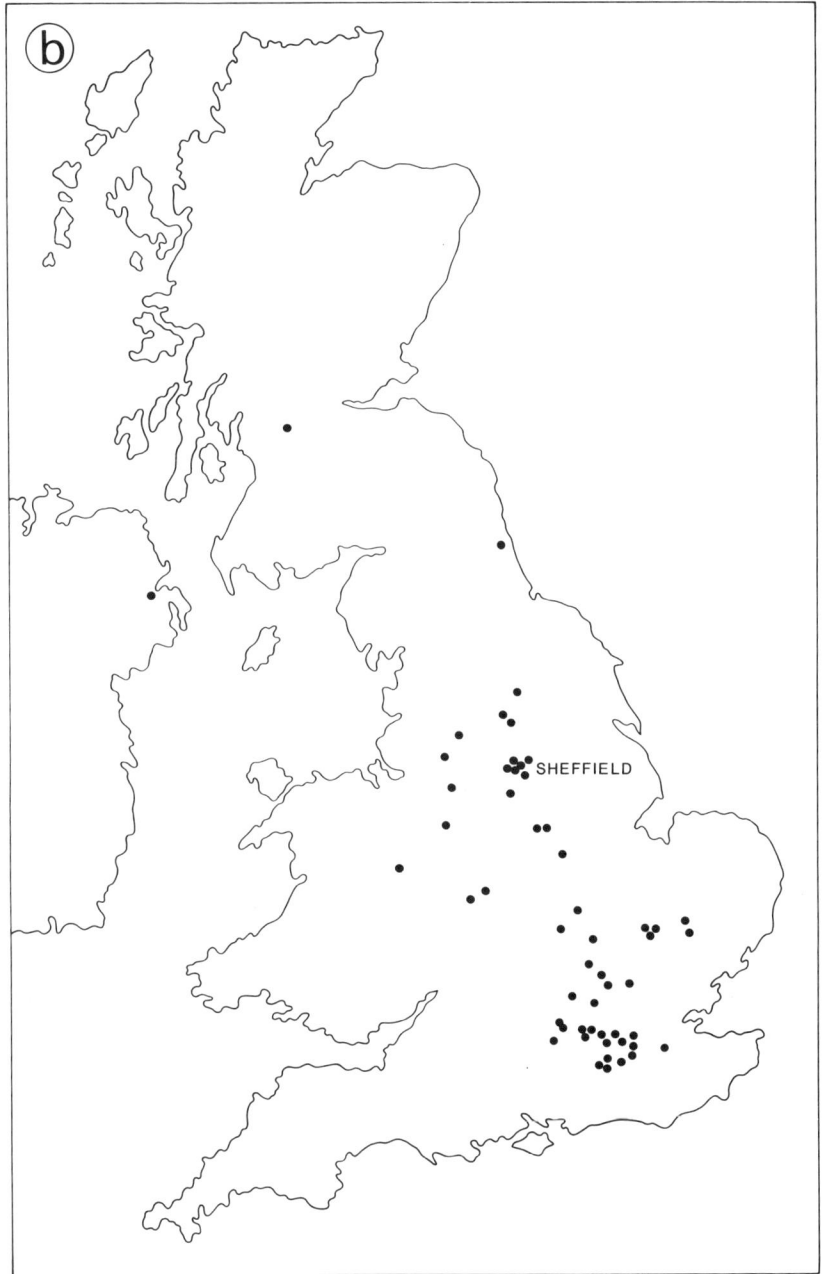

'Our Board members have to be in London for daily meetings with government departments. They need financial advice at a moment's notice so we need our finance team. Then we need our industrial relations people, there have to be press statements so we need a press office, and so it goes on' (*Sunday Times*, 9 January 1977).

The geography of demand

Of the two driving forces of the economy, industrial surveys suggest demand is the more important, yet it is also the one we know less about.

	Markets in UK					
	Intermediate demand			Final demand		
	Primary sector	Manufacturing sector	Utilities and services	Consumer and public authority	Investments and stocks	Exports
All manufacturing	2.5	36.8	11.0	24.7	8.5	16.4
Soft drinks	5.0	3.2	0	85.8	1.5	4.3
Cement	3.3	32.2	58.4	2.9	0.5	2.6
Clothing	—	9.5	4.4	69.5	1.4	14.4
Machine tools	0.7	17.4	1.0	1.1	50.4	29.1
Aerospace	0	28.7	1.9	44.3	—	24.6
Pumps, valves and compressors	1.3	43.0	6.1	1.5	18.5	25.3
Iron castings	0	82.8	14.2	0.9	—	2.3

Notes: —denotes negligible.

'Intermediate demand' refers to markets that in their turn are concerned with production of items for final demand.

Table 2.5 Percentage by value of types of markets served by UK manufacturers, 1968. *Source:* calculated from CSO (1973).

Table 2.6 Markets and suppliers as location considerations.

(a) E.W. Lewis (1971): Survey of 86 manufacturers in Western Home Counties
'What are the most important advantages of your present location?'
(A list of 15 were prompted).

	Number	**All positive responses**	
		Rank (out of 15)	% all positive responses
Access to raw materials and components	41	3	9.3
Access to London and Midlands markets	66	1	15.1

(b) London Employment Survey (1967) (See Hoare 1973): Survey of 35,000 manufacturers in Greater London
Respondents rating factor 'important' in their being in London and 'essential' to staying there.

	% respondents	Rank order of importance out of 15 factors
Access to suppliers of goods and materials	38.9	3
Access to buyers of your products or services	55.3	1

A later section in this chapter considers the most important of the markets to which British manufacturers sell output, namely other British manufacturers (Table 2.5) while this one examines controls upon the geography of demand considered more generally. But this is something of an academic minefield!

What is clear is that British industrialists repeatedly cite market access as of prime geographical significance to them in assessing their locations (Table 2.6). Note, though, that the various market categories of Table 2.5 cannot separately be identified from Table 2.6. Note too that 'access to markets' could refer to any of a host of spatial scales (local, regional, national, international) and either to access between the freight depots of producers and customers or to contact between the offices engaged in buying and selling, which may be a very different thing geographically (Fig. 1.6). As a recent study of manufacturers' London offices remarks:

Fig. 2.7 Derivation of the spatial revenue surface for possible production sites, based on (a) the geography of potential customers and pricing policy, and (b) the price elasticity of demand for the goods being sold. Hence we can predict (c) the amount of revenue earned at each distance from the factory and (d) the total revenue, by summing over all distances in (c). Other complications discussed in the text could be added to this graphical analysis.

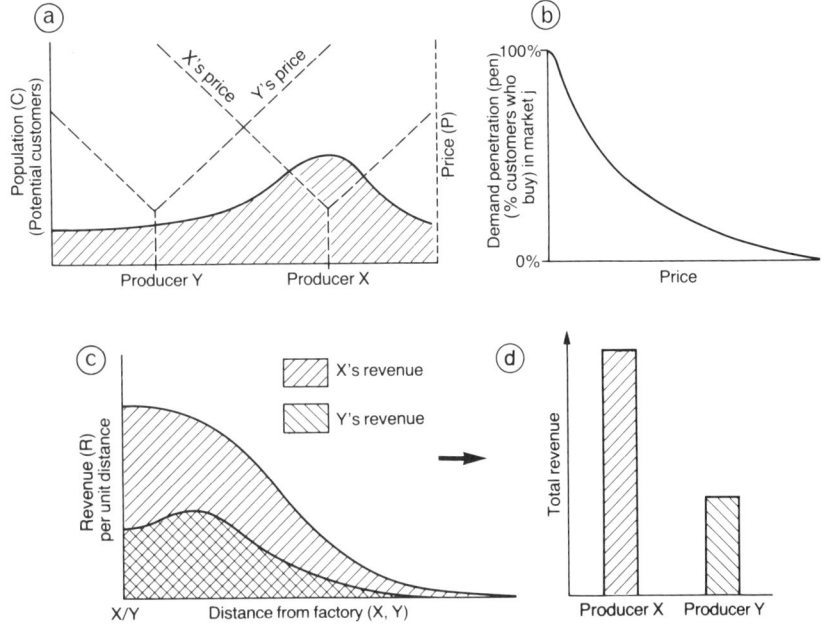

'Corporations involved in selling large quantities of bulk commodities... may feel that the presence of important purchasing companies in London requires a high-level sales presence in the head office... if you are selling cans or bottles by the million to food processors you need to be near the executives who buy them' (Crum and Gudgin 1977, p. 127).

Once we ask also 'what is the geography of demand?' for any particular industrial product, then the problems multiply. Geographers rarely have access to confidential data on past sales performance, or the resources to carry out massive market-probing surveys like that responsible for Table 1.4. And, anyway, the past is less of a sure guide to the present, and the present to the future on the demand side, where sales are liable to intense competition and fluctuations, than on the supply side.

What can be done is to isolate a set of factors which, in combination, underlie spatial variations in demand and revenue. First, note that manufacturers m's revenue over a set of j markets (R_m) can be modelled in this way:

$$R_m = \sum_{j=1}^{j=n} (P_j S_j) \quad \text{when } P_j = \text{price in } j \quad \sum_{j=1}^{j=n} = \text{sum of all } j \text{ cases}$$

$$S_j = \text{sales in } j \qquad n = \text{number of } j \text{ markets}$$

and that:

$$S_j = M_j \cdot \text{pen}_j \quad \text{when } M_j = \text{potential customers in } j$$
$$\text{pen}_j = \% \text{ of potential customers who actually buy ('penetration') in } j$$

What, then, determines P_j and S_j in each j market? Pricing policy is discussed later, but assume now that m charges a price that reflects his production and delivery costs, so P_j increases with distance from his factory (Fig. 2.7a). The value of S_j then depends on the size of the 'potential' demand at j, and the proportion of those who actually buy.

35

(a) Potential demand (M$_j$) For consumer markets this is j's population weighted, as necessary, by other controls such as income, demographic structure (relevant, say, for sales of prams, tights or bath chairs) or possible regional tastes, as are hinted at in Table 2.7.

(b) Penetration (pen$_j$) Here, five factors are important.

(i) Price elasticity of demand This controls the way sales vary with price. A typical negative relationship between the two, as in Fig. 2.7b, causes pen$_j$ to fall with distance from the factory, under price conditions specified.

(ii) Local preference Some customers may buy from local suppliers to preserve 'local' jobs and incomes ('Buy British' campaigns cash in on this desire, though on a national scale), some as a safeguard if purchase is faulty (it is easier to harangue a local supplier than one at the other end of the country).

(iii) Place reputation If a particular place has a 'name' for a particular product all its relevant manufacturers will benefit (Chapter 3).

(iv) Advertising and marketing strategies Manufacturers may deliberately trial-market new products in selective regions (advertising on the local ITV network, for example) or otherwise aim to ensnare new centres within the existing market net.

Table 2.7 Regional variations in consumption patterns: average per caput biscuit consumption per week, 1973-4; percentage of sample purchasing pens, August 1972. *Source:* Mintel (April 1977, May 1977, August 1978).

Region	Chocolate (oz)	Non-chocolate (oz)	% Chocolate
South East/East Anglia	0.95	4.67	16.8
South West	1.17	4.58	20.3
West Midlands	0.96	4.09	19.0
East Midlands	0.98	4.34	18.4
Wales	1.23	4.30	22.2
North West	1.16	4.17	21.8
Yorkshire/Humberside	1.13	4.60	19.7
North	1.70	4.72	26.4
Scotland	2.10	4.74	29.7
Great Britain	1.18	4.54	20.6

Region	% Ball-points	% Felt-tipped	Ball point/ felt-tipped
London and South	32	10	3.2
East Anglia and Midlands	33	11	3.0
Wales and West	30	19	3.3
Lancashire	38	10	3.8
Yorkshire and North East	33	10	3.3
Scotland	30	6	5.0

(v) Competitor behaviour The pen$_j$ value for m will also respond to the location, price, advertising and marketing strategies of his competitors.

Diagramatically, the outcome may be as in Figure 2.7. In practice, though, most of the determinants of R_m defy easy quantification, so

Fig. 2.8 Market potential surface for sales to domestic consumers, 1976. Here we assume a producer aims to sell his products throughout mainland Britain, rather than concentrating on certain local or regional markets. The London-Lancashire consumer axis, long a feature of Britain's economic geography, stands out (it used to be called the 'the coffin'). Were the producer to focus on sales to other *manufacturers* (see Table 2.5 for more on this) we should have to adjust the P_j term, and this would affect the resultant surface.

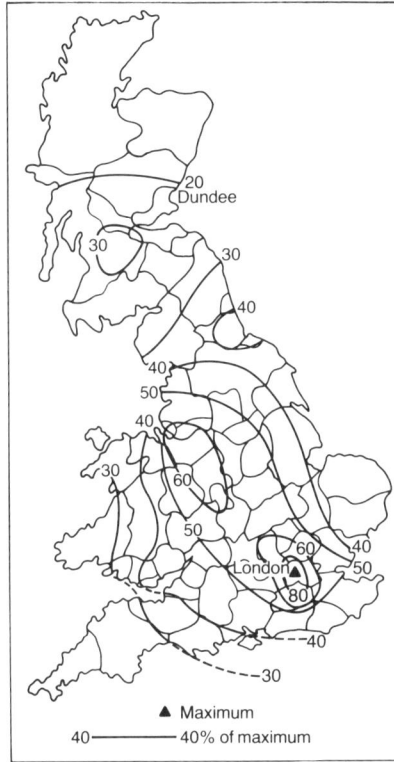

Fig. 2.9 Delivery cost surface for sales to domestic consumers, 1976. As in Fig. 2.8, we assume the producer attempts to sell throughout Great Britain but, unlike 2.8, price does not vary spatially and hence affect purchasing behaviour. In both cases, though, we could introduce a variety of other measures of 'distance' into the formulae, and add in competing producers with different locational options for their factories.

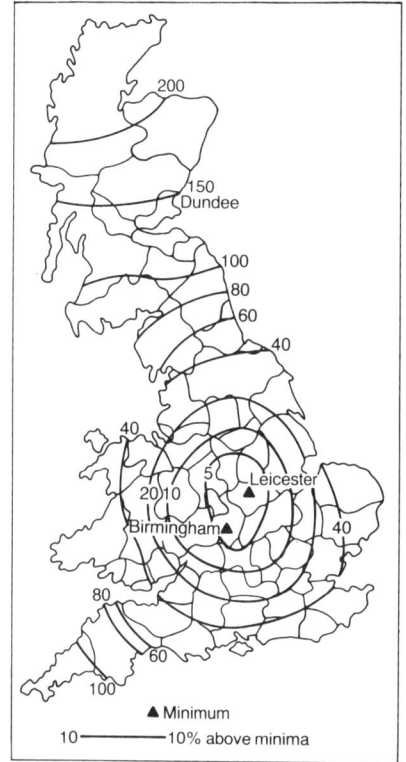

geographers often bypass these problems by using two alternative models (Harris 1954). The first, the Market Potential Model, has this form:

$$R_m = \sum_{j=1}^{j=n} (M_j/d_{\mathrm{mj}}{}^{\alpha})$$

when d_{mj} = distance between m and j
α = a constant exponent

M_j again represents potential custom at j, and the 'friction of distance' $(d_{mj}{}^{\alpha})$ element embodies the decline of pen$_j$ with distance from m, in response to the factors just examined. In the simplest case, where $\alpha = 1$, a town of 10,000 at a distance of 5 km from the factory provides more revenue than a similar one 50 km away in the ratio of 10,000/5 : 10,000/50 = 10 : 1, while if $\alpha = 2$ this becomes 10,000/25 : 10,000/2,500 = 100 : 1. Note that this model cannot predict the precise levels of monetary revenue over the j markets, merely the relative revenue levels from different 'base' (factory) locations. Applying 1976 county population data to this model shows the favoured position of south-eastern locations (Fig. 2.8). Manufacturing for the national market from Dundee produces only 20% of the revenue obtainable from London.

If, instead, m charges a uniform price throughout Britain, price elasticity can be ignored. His concern is now to minimise his total delivery costs (TC_m), defined by the Minimum Transport Cost model as

$$TC_m \quad \sum_{j=1}^{j=n} (M_j\, d_{jm})$$

37

Using the same data as before Fig. 2.9 shows the optimal location has shifted to the Midlands from London. The Dundee location now incurs transport costs 150% greater than the minimum at Birmingham or Leicester.

So far, the international dimension to markets has been ignored. For many firms, though, markets must be seen on a continental or inter-continental scale. Incorporating western Europe into either of these same two models heightens the South East's pull compared to other parts of the country. But it may also discourage manufacturers from locating in Britain at all. In the words of the project planning manager of General Motors European Component Operations:

'International marketing men do not like the idea of supplying the mainland of Europe from an island, particularly an island with a bad industrial relations track record for supply reliability. The marketing preference is to supply the island from the mainland. It is less expensive, less trouble and more reliable' (*The Times*, 10 May 1980).

For world-wide markets the choice of locations is obviously wider still, but within Britain the geography of international transport terminals again underlines the South East's strength.

Factors affecting supply and demand

Transport

Transport plays some part in the costs of many of the manufacturer's supplies and, through the prices that he in turn charges, in his own revenue. Whether for assembling inputs or delivering outputs, transport cost has two elements. These are the 'fixed' cost element, not dependent upon the length of haul (such as the costs of loading, unloading and paper-work) and the 'distance' cost (fuels, drivers' wages, and other running costs) that does increase with length of haul. The precise form these elements assume in any particular case depends partly on the method of transport used and the nature of the cargo.

(a) **Transport method** Fig. 2.10 shows the different costs of moving a given shipment from Bristol by competing media (road and rail) and competing carriers. Substantial differences can arise for the same haul, and the rank position of the competitors shows many 'cross-overs'. However, many British industries carry their own freight, amounting to 42% of the cost to manufacturers of internal freight transport in 1963 (Edwards 1970). Here, too, variations in cost arise, depending on the transport network used. Thus drivers' wages, payable on an hourly basis, and fuel costs, partly dependent on journey speed, go farther (literally) on a motorway journey than over B class roads.

(b) **Goods** Goods carried affect movement costs through the handling of bulky, fragile or dangerous cargoes, and the insurance and security of valuable ones. Cargo weight is particularly important: a major survey of freight costs within Britain showed this 'explained' 80% of variation in transport cost among 2,483 consignments (Bayliss and Edwards 1970). If the weight of material inputs exceeds that of the end-products, transport costs thus encourage manufacture near material sources (for example, as

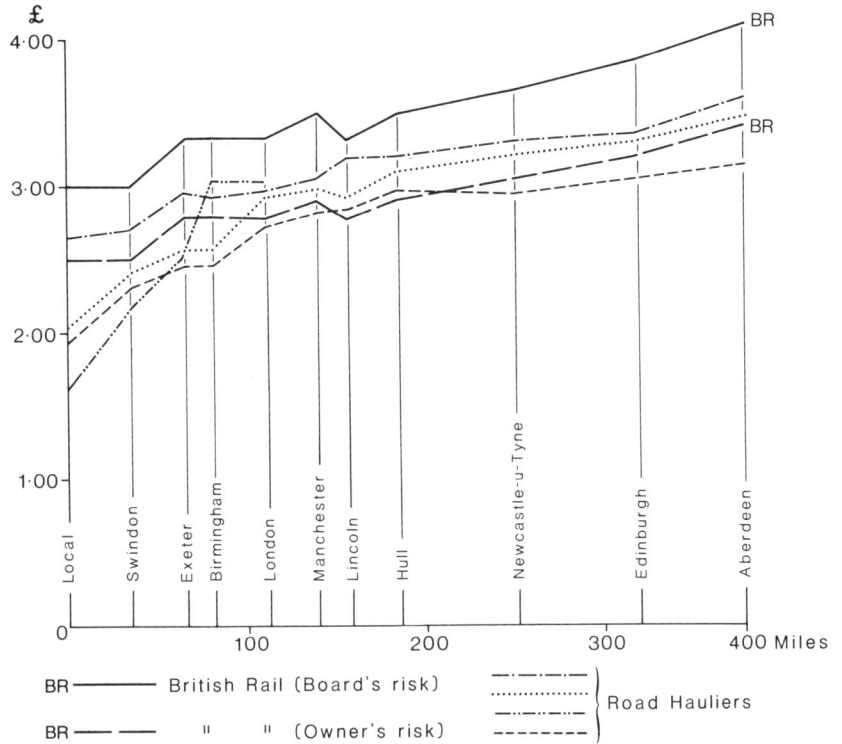

Fig. 2.10 Freight charges for a 10-kg package from Bristol, 1980, as quoted by a set of road and rail carriers. Transport charges are not a simple matter of distance (note the Lincoln 'dip'), while the relative attractiveness of different carriers varies with distance, hence the 'cross-overs'. *Source:* various commercial freight schedules.

BR ——————— British Rail (Board's risk)

BR — — — — "   " (Owner's risk)

Road Hauliers

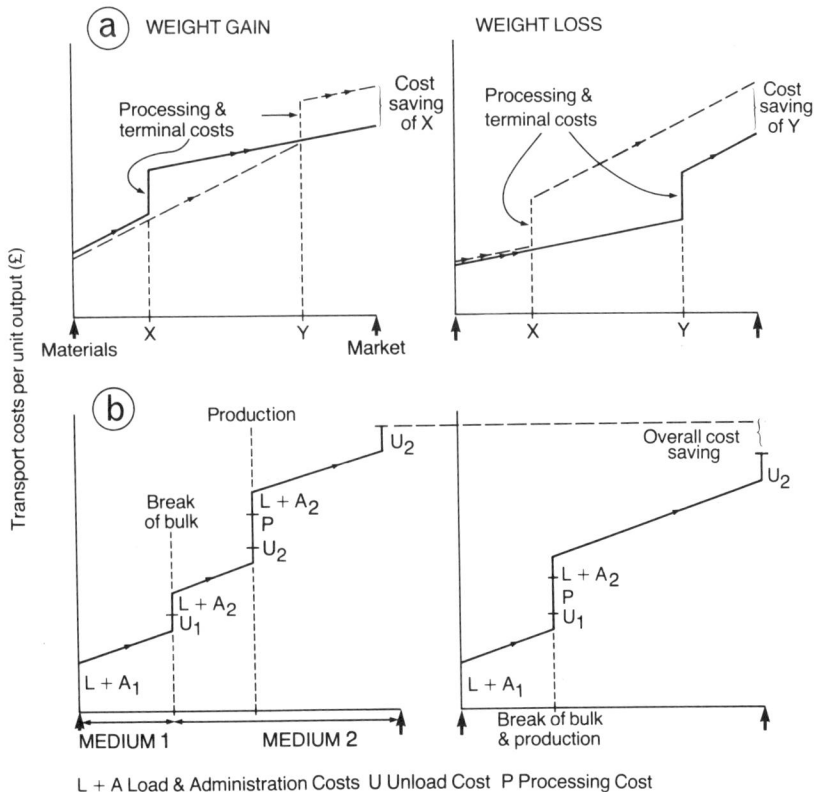

Fig. 2.11 (a) The effects of gain and loss in weight of transported goods upon total transport costs and hence factory location. See Chapter 6 for brewing (weight gain) and steel (weight loss) examples. Other things being equal (they never are!), these should be drawn respectively to market and material production sites. (b) Break-of-bulk locations can attract factory locations by saving the equivalent of one set of terminal costs. This is less relevant to goods than travel in containers or roll-on-roll-off vehicles, easy to switch between transport media.

L + A Load & Administration Costs U Unload Cost P Processing Cost

39

with sugar refining, steel and newsprint manufacture) while in the opposite 'weight-gain' cases (like brewing and baking) the pull is towards the market. Fig. 2.11 shows how such weight gains and losses affect the relationship between assembly and delivery costs and so the pulls of material and market.

Three further aspects of transport cost are important. First, when freight passes from one medium to another (as at a port, air terminal or rail depot) additional fixed cost elements are incurred. Where freight is a large part of industrial costs this can stimulate location at the interchange point, as here this break-of-bulk charge can be absorbed into the production process. Paper and cement firms favour waterside locations for this reason. Secondly, when manufacturers 'buy in' transport from specialist hauliers their transport costs are the prices those hauliers charge. Rather than calculating anew a charge for each shipment, hauliers prepare a schedule of freight rates for given origin–destination pairings. (Strictly speaking, these are what Fig. 2.10 shows.) As long as total revenue exceeds total costs over all the hauls they make a profit, and customers can cost their transport needs in advance. Thus rates normally increase with distance in a 'stepped' fashion. Thirdly, specialist transport carriers have a geography of their own. London manufacturers can more easily find a carrier supplying their precise needs at the 'right price' than can those in Cornwall. The London carrier is also more able to acquire a return load, making the cost to his manufacturer client for the outward run commensurately lower.

Transport costs should be kept in perspective. In 1963 British manufacturers' transport costs were only some 6% of net output, and in only 23 out of 123 industries did this rise above 10% (Edwards 1970). Furthermore, the fixed cost element (which, remember, is not distance-dependent) is about 70% of the transport costs of the average internal industrial haul (Chisholm and O'Sullivan 1973).

Finally, there is more to transport than cost. Manufacturers with access to efficient transport facilities benefit from savings in time, and a more reliable service. Farmers with perishable produce are found close to processing plants, and evening newspaper producers (whose product is also highly perishable) need quick access to their readers. A Barnstaple glove manufacturer who moved from London had to raise his stocks by 20% owing to unreliable deliveries of supplies to Devon, while Perdio Ltd closed its Sunderland factory in 1968 after just 3 years as the 480-km delivery of components from the Midlands was taking up to 10 days. More generally, the quality of domestic and international transport services varies widely throughout Britain, with the pinnacle being in London. These affect passenger transport as much as freight. Among manufacturers around Heathrow Airport, for example, 44% regarded the airport as of some value for passenger purposes, compared to 34% for freight (Hoare 1974). Multinational companies value airport accessibility for their dispersed operations to aid efficient supervision. Equally, London's nodality in terms of internal transport means that head office staff there are within a return daily trip of branches throughout Britain. An amazing number of towns and regions away from the South East try to sell themselves through publicity brochures as 'central' to the motorway system, often stressing the speed (rather than cost) savings this brings (Burgess 1982).

Fig. 2.12 Time–space options
for two companies planning
visits to business contacts.
The more centrally located
company benefits in three
distinct ways over his
'peripheral' rival. The 'space'
axis could represent London,
or the West Midlands, or
Britain as a whole, or . . .

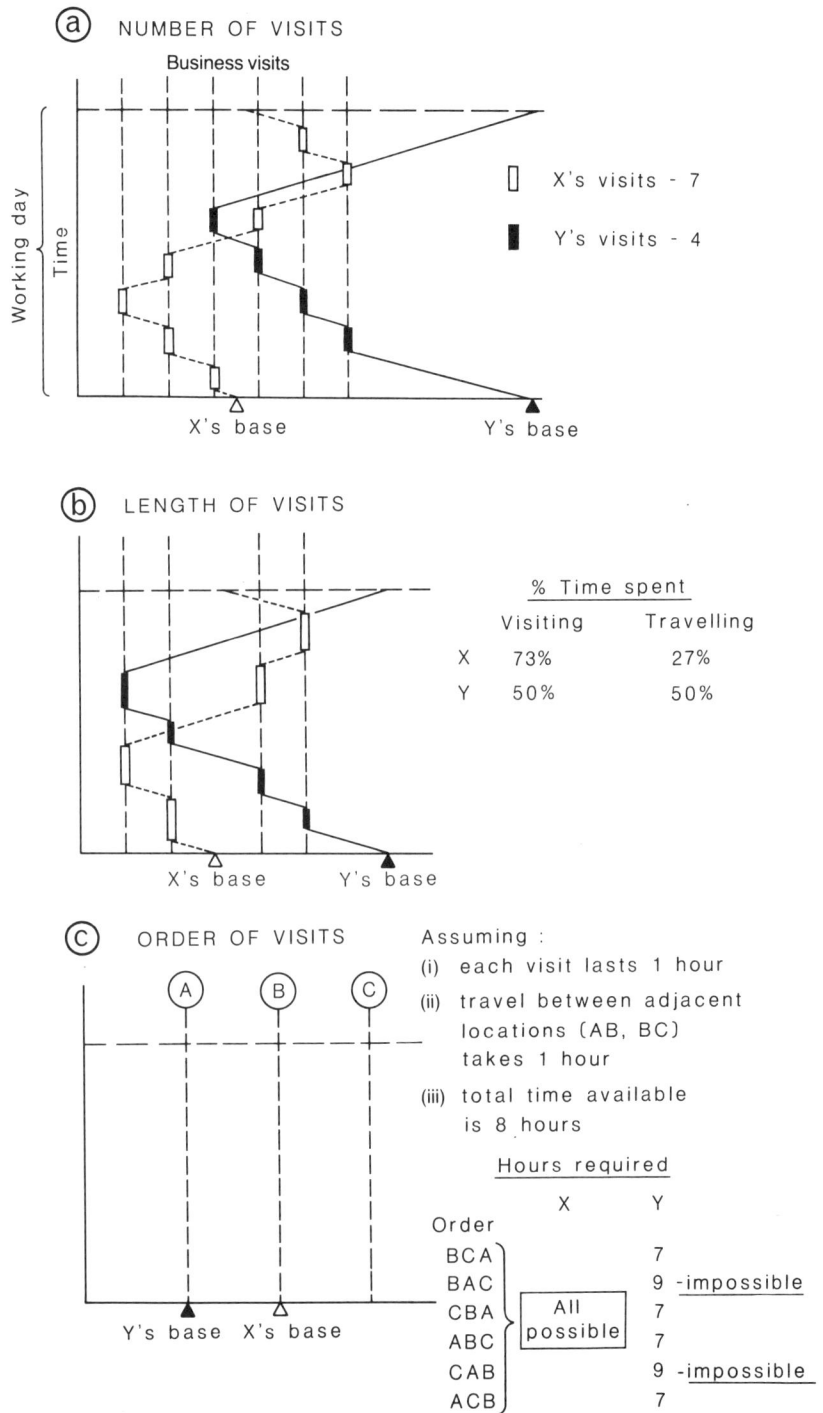

(a) NUMBER OF VISITS

Business visits

Working day / Time

☐ X's visits - 7
■ Y's visits - 4

X's base   Y's base

(b) LENGTH OF VISITS

	% Time spent	
	Visiting	Travelling
X	73%	27%
Y	50%	50%

X's base   Y's base

(c) ORDER OF VISITS

Assuming :
(i) each visit lasts 1 hour
(ii) travel between adjacent locations (AB, BC) takes 1 hour
(iii) total time available is 8 hours

(A) (B) (C)

Y's base   X's base

Hours required

Order	X	Y	
BCA		7	
BAC		9	-impossible
CBA	All possible	7	
ABC		7	
CAB		9	-impossible
ACB		7	

Time geography: time as a scarce resource

These well-worn notions of centrality and time-saving have recently been
dressed in fresh clothes by intriguing work on 'time geography' (Thrift
n.d.). Here all human activities, including economic ones, are seen as
occupying blocks of 'time-space' (Fig. 2.12). The industrialist needs to
occupy certain spaces during his working time. Some must be occupied at

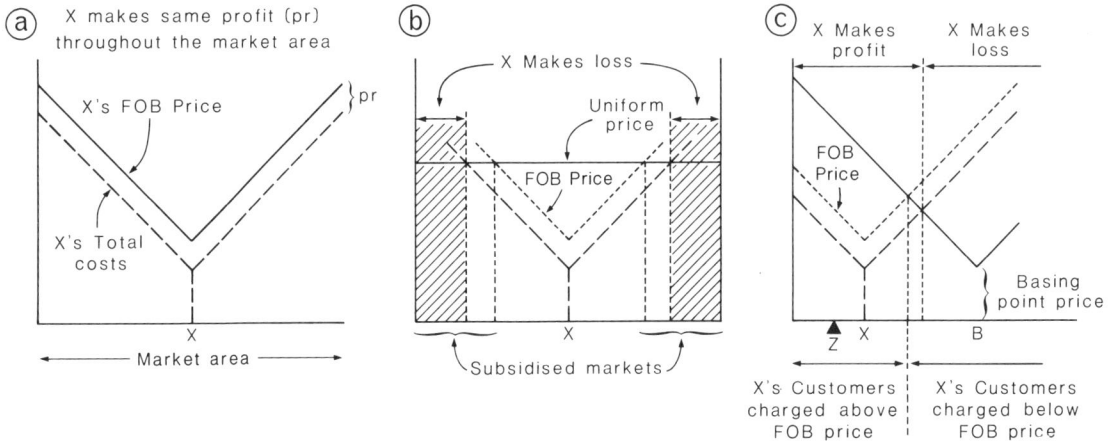

ⓐ X makes same profit (pr)
throughout the market area

X's FOB Price

}pr

X's Total
costs

X

◄——— Market area ———►

ⓑ

◄—— X Makes loss ——►

Uniform
price

FOB Price

X

Subsidised markets

ⓒ

X Makes profit | X Makes loss

FOB
Price

Basing
point price

Z X | B

X's Customers
charged above
FOB price | X's Customers
charged below
FOB price

Fig. 2.13 Pricing options for manufacturers. In many cases firms are free to switch between (a) and (b) or adopt parts of each, as circumstances decree. In (c), though, producers are tied to the pricing system of their industry's governing body. Periodic changes will occur in the number and location of the basing points used, though whether the basing-point system is to the customer's benefit is a moot point.

particular times (a meeting at his accountants is scheduled for 2.30) while others are more flexible ('drop in some time before lunch, old man'). He also needs to travel through 'time-space' between meetings and his speed depends on available transport.

As both time and space are scarce resources (there are only 8 hours in the businessman's working day) he must pack his activities into time-space efficiently. In Fig. 2.12 the more central manufacturer can make more contacts (a), longer contacts (b), and has flexibility over the order of his contacts (c). In these diagrams speed of time-space travel (i.e. available transport) is held constant, but the argument could easily be recast by comparing an industrialist close to speedy transport (motorways, high-speed trains) with one less fortunate. The 'speedy' businessman would have the same advantages as the 'central' one. In modern Britain this underscores the importance of city-centre locations and transport nodality for senior manufacturing executives, for whom such outside contacts are central to their working lives.

Pricing policy

Prices affect both a manufacturer's costs and revenues. His material costs are the prices suppliers charge him. If he is a large customer, he can haggle over these (as the British Steel Corporation does with the National Coal Board), but otherwise he buys at the 'list price'. Equally, he presents his own list prices to potential customers.

Three spatial pricing policies apply to Britain (Fig. 2.13). In the 'free-on-board' (FOB) system, prices reflect transport costs to market. So the manufacturer buying FOB benefits from being close to his suppliers, while if selling FOB he loses revenue in distant markets, assuming demand is price-elastic. Under the 'uniform' system the manufacturer has no reason in price terms to be near suppliers or customers, as distant hauls are subsidised by closer ones. With the 'basing point' system the customer at Z pays the price at the basing point, B, plus the transport cost from there to Z. He gains no price benefit from buying locally (from X). Evidence quoted by Chisholm (1966), though now rather dated, suggests uniform pricing is dominant, at least for sales within Britain. FOB pricing can still be found, while the steel industry uses basing point pricing (Heal 1974).

	% by value from UK economy			
	Primary sector	Manufacturing sector	Remainder*	Imports
All manufacturing	9.0	54.9	17.8	18.3
Grain milling	19.5	11.7	20.3	48.5
Paper and board	5.5	24.7	25.1	44.7
Woollens and worsteds	1.4	57.6	11.5	29.4
Toilet preparations	0	58.7	34.8	6.5
Motor vehicles	1.0	85.4	8.6	5.8

*Public utilities, construction and services.
Note: Data include input from the same industrial sector.

Table 2.8 Input sources of UK manufacturing, 1968. *Source:* calculated from CSO (1973).

Industrial linkages

The popular image of factories as engaged in converting fuels and a few unprocessed raw materials into a range of household goods is wide of the mark. We have seen already how British manufacturers sell mostly to themselves (Table 2.5) and Table 2.8 shows the same holds on the input side. Fig. 2.14 portrays the complexity of such flows among just one small part of the British manufacturing sector, while Fig. 2.15 does the same for a hypothetical individual plant. Clearly, in these sorts of examples the labels 'supplier' and 'customer' become very blurred. Accompanying these 'visible' material flows among manufacturers are various invisible movements of information, advice and instruction, and both sorts of flow also can involve the movement of staff of the inter-linked companies. Figs. 2.14 and 2.15 give no hint of whether the flows shown are long or short. With certain headline-catching projects such as Concorde or the US Space Shuttle they can be international. However, the tendency often will be for them to be short, and thus contribute to industrial agglomeration.

Why should this be? Transport cost is not likely to be very important, but the 'time' and 'reliability' aspects of short hauls probably are. Efficient access between customer and supplier means that unforeseen problems and needs, the emergencies common to all manufacturing operations, can be sorted out quickly. Hence, the need to 'keep in touch'. As well, some industries such as fashion clothing and shoes benefit from being on hand to gauge the fluctuating pulse of the market. Psychology is also important. The remote company fears its customers will overlook it when placing orders, and its suppliers will be less keen to keep its business or will reduce the quality of service offered.

These are not just empty fears. One firm moving from Birmingham the 48 km to Telford found a former supplier took to dumping its order by the roadside at the Birmingham city boundary (Edge 1973), while Wiggins Teape at Basingstoke felt itself remote from the London circuit.

'[The financial director] worries for the firm's sake he might be left off lunch lists altogether now he is out in the country... One Arab customer refused point-blank to go to Basingstoke. So now there is an office suite and an overseas liaison officer resident in the West End' (*Sunday Times*, 9 January 1977).

Convincing examples of agglomeration through linkage come from petro-chemical complexes. Thus the numerous by-products of modern, large capacity oil refineries are often redistributed as manufactured inputs on

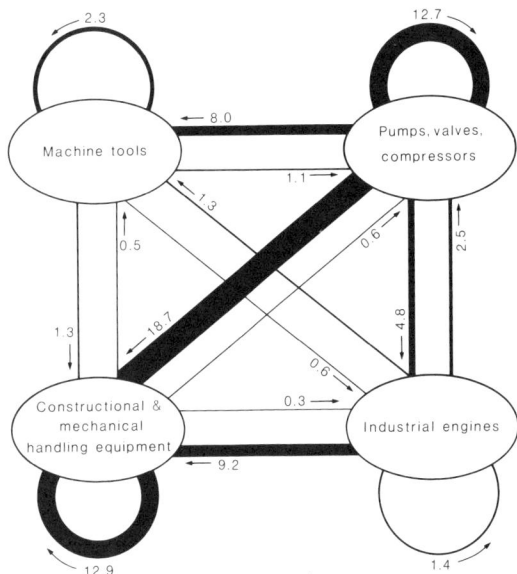

Figures in £m.

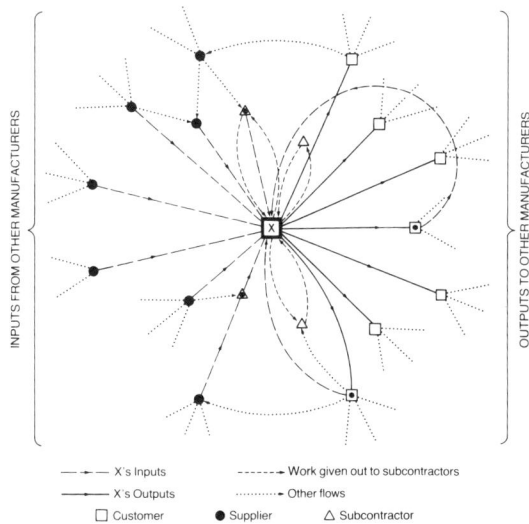

- →— X's Inputs
- —●— X's Outputs
- □ Customer
- ----→ Work given out to subcontractors
- ·········· Other flows
- ● Supplier
- △ Subcontractor

Fig. 2.14 Value of material flows among four industries in the United Kingdom, 1968. All are 'MLH' categories within the Mechanical Engineering 'Order' of the Standard Industrial Classification (see Table 1.1). Each industry makes some use of all the others, even if most pairs of flows are lop-sided, and two industries buy substantially from their own member firms. *Source:* based on Central Statistical Office (1973) *Input–Output tables for the United Kingdom 1968* (HMSO, London).

Fig. 2.15 Hypothetical pattern of industrial linkages affecting one manufacturing plant. In practice, the real-world picture for manufacturers is much more involved than this (as with car firms of Chapter 6). As many of the links also involve movements of supervisory staff and data (invoices, specifications. . .) and can turn 'critical' without warning as emergencies arise, it is a brave manufacturer who moves away from a tight knot of suppliers and customers.

adjacent sites, with the interdependencies being enhanced by some return flows to the refinery. However, most of the 'classic' examples of spatial agglomeration through linkage—such as the inner London clothing and Birmingham jewellery quarters (Martin 1966; Hall 1962; Wise 1950)—are nineteenth-century vestiges. Their present-day relevance, and that of local linkage ties as a whole, has been increasingly thrown in doubt.

Some fashion industries have successfully decamped to the peripheries—the influx of knitted fabrics to South Wales is one example—while field surveys in London and Birmingham show that modern industrial linkages are often not as locally oriented as previously thought (Taylor and Wood 1973; Keeble 1969). Local ties vary widely among industries and firms, and not always in a consistent pattern. Thus while some twentieth-century growth industries seem among the most locally oriented in London and elsewhere (Lever 1972), in Birmingham's metal working sector growing, successful firms have thrown off their local linkage ties, leaving these to their smaller, less dynamic counterparts.

Finally, it may be that the importance of linkages as a geographical binding force is only partly related to the quantity of flows between supplier and customer. Large flows may be regular, well-scheduled ones, with the need for close contact coming more from irregular, occasional, stop-gapping flows. Industries surveyed in London which stressed the need for being close to their linkage partners were certainly slow to decentralise out of the capital, yet no tendency was also found for pairs of linked industries, between which material flows were extensive, also to be located unduly close to each other (Hoare 1975).

3 Constraints

Introduction

Chapter 2 has perhaps conjured up the picture of an industrial landscape populated by single-plant firms, each enthusiastically readjusting its geographical location and behaviour in response to the dictates of supply and demand, but unfettered by any other, 'extraneous', pressures. But this would be a false picture: John Donne's early seventeenth-century tenet that 'no man is an island, entire of itself' is equally true of the late twentieth-century industrial plant. Already, some of the wider constraints have been hinted at in Chapter 2, and this chapter develops them more fully, under the three general headings of Behaviour, Organisation and Time. Many geographers would argue that spatial differences of costs and revenue in modern Britain are relatively small, and becoming smaller, while these constraints are becoming ever more significant.

Behavioural constraints

Some text-books might have us believe that all decisions taken by the industrial firm are directed towards the 'optimal end' of maximum profit, and that it has all the 'optimal means' necessary to achieve that goal, namely complete and accurate information about its business environment and the ability to process that knowledge perfectly into practical decisions. An alternative, 'behavioural' view of business activity is that neither of these two conditions applies in practice, so profit-maximisation is unlikely to occur, other than by chance. To understand this alternative approach to industrial geography involves us in a set of interconnected ideas, mostly imported into geography from other academic disciplines. Fig. 3.1 suggests one way of summarising these notions spatially.

In the first three diagrams ((a) – (c)) the industrialist can still be assumed to be seeking maximum profit, with optimal 'ends' and 'means'. In (a) he thus simply locates at the maximum profit location (P). In (b) and (c), while the profit-making geographical surface still peaks at P he consciously locates at I. These apparently perverse decisions might result from a simple extension of the optimising argument over an extended time period. Thus the manufacturer may plan to double his output at some future date (t_2) which requires a quantity of immobile inputs available only at I (diagram (b)). Alternatively, the financial cost of moving from a previous optimum at I to the current one at P may exceed the profits foregone at I (i.e. $c > f$ in diagram (c)), when evaluated over the foreseeable future.

But other reasons for remaining at I involve our discarding the whole idea of profit maximisation. Diagrams (d) – (g) show four other possibilities which individually can produce a 'suboptimal' outcome. As, in reality, this quartet can coexist, suboptimality becomes all the more likely.

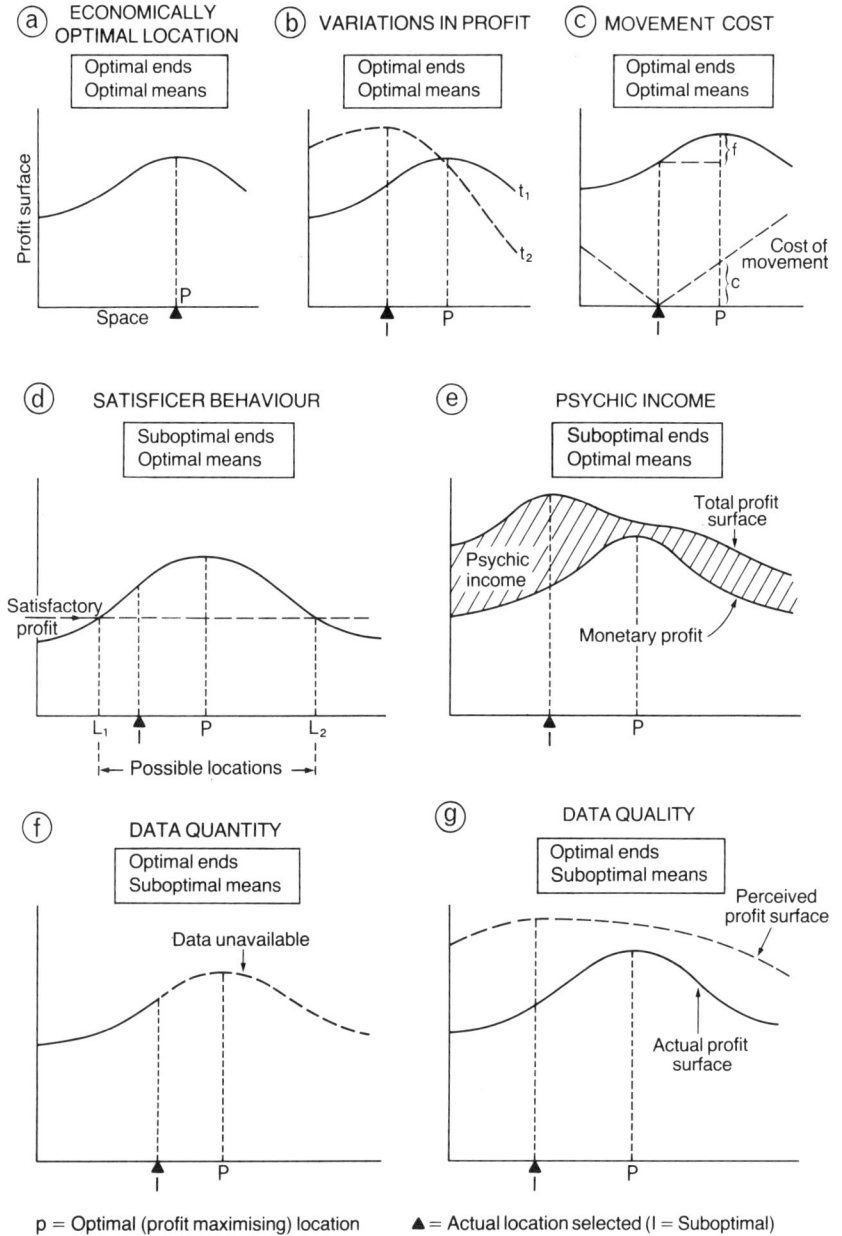

Fig. 3.1 Optimality and suboptimality in industrial location. A manufacturer's location can be modelled in optimal economic terms (as in Chapter 2) through the simple static case (a) or through dynamic modifications (b) and (c). But other reasons for the separation of his location (at l) from the economic optimum at P involve a set of behavioural ideas discussed in the text (diagrams (d) – (g)). Real-world locations are likely to involve elements of all four of these behavioural cases.

p = Optimal (profit maximising) location   ▲ = Actual location selected (l = Suboptimal)

The satisficer model (Fig. 3.1d)

Table 3.1 shows the remarkably diverse business objectives identified in a recent sample of British manufacturing firms. Under 20% cite 'profit maximisation' as the first objective of their management. Some of the other motivations (such as 'sales growth', or 'market share') might (generously) be interpreted as those of 'optimisers', but the locations they direct firms to need not necessarily be those also optimal on profit criteria. Interestingly, the majority of surveyed firms had at least three business objectives, of which profit maximisation represents only about 10%. The very existence of a number of commercial goals makes it improbable that manufacturers can pursue each of these optimally within any one locational strategy.

Table 3.1 Management
objectives: 'What was the
firm's first objective in
general management?'
Source: Centre for Inter-Firm
Comparison (1977).

	Objectives			
	1st	2nd	3rd	Total
Maximum return on assets	20	5	2	27
Adequate returns on assets	33	11	3	47
Growth in sales volume	9	25	10	44
Increased market share	1	13	7	21
Remain independent	11	15	15	31
Survival	11	10	7	28
Others	19	17	21	57

Less ambitious aims of 'adequate returns', 'independence' or, simply, 'survival' are rated above optimal ones by the sample, suggesting we should view these industrialists as 'satisficers' rather than 'optimisers', happy with their geographical lot as long as it yields satisfactory returns. Rather than single-track optimisers firms now emerge as multi-track satisficers (Fig. 3.1d). This broadens the range of locations that firms can occupy, depending on how a firm chooses to define what is 'satisfactory'. Each firm will have its own ideas on this, and each will adjust its satisfaction level up or down as circumstances change. A specified satisfaction level less than the level of optimum profit will give a range of locational options ($L_1 - L_2$) at which the firm could be happy (Fig. 3.1d). Any firm initially located at I will remain there as long as returns do not sink below the prevailing satisfaction level. Only then will it evaluate alternative locations against the cost, sweat and bother of moving. Given the multitude of factors influencing the geography of profit (Chapter 2), detailed changes in the location of the optimum profit point over fairly short periods can be both commonplace and beyond the manufacturer's control. The prospect of endlessly chasing a peripatetic profit optimum around the industrial landscape will add further to the appeal of the satisficer option!

Psychic income (Fig. 3.1e)

A related explanation of a firm's persisting at suboptimal locations comes from 'psychic income'—the 'revenue' it receives over and above that revealed in the balance sheets. Often referred to as the 'golf course' effect, the psychic income derived from a location is really a composite of a number of benefits that decision-makers and their families gain from proximity to friends, to a pleasant living environment and to familiar surroundings where they feel 'at home'. Eversley (1965) argues that the manufacturer might rationalise his decision to stay put in just these 'psychic' terms:

'I live in a nice house in a nice district. I paid very little for it 20 years ago. If I move it will cost a lot to get anything that suits me as well. My daughters go to a nice school where they learn to speak good English, and my son meets nice girls at his country club. My wife can get up to London/Birmingham in half an hour to go shopping at Harrods/Rackhams. I can meet my clients at a decent club to which I belong and can take them out to lunch or dinner at a very good hotel or restaurant. If I want to go on holiday, I can be at Heathrow or Gatwick by 9 and in Majorca by noon. If I am not feeling well, I can call in a white specialist at any time who will treat me like someone of importance. If I need counsel, I can have him at his leisure in his chambers.

Fig. 3.2 An index of the 'level of living' in England and Wales for 1961. Based on population census data for 145 administrative areas this index was derived by reducing 53 original variables to 4 key diagnostic ones. (See the 'source' for more details.) The best and worst areas turn out to be Buckinghamshire and Gateshead respectively. *Source:* Knox (1973)

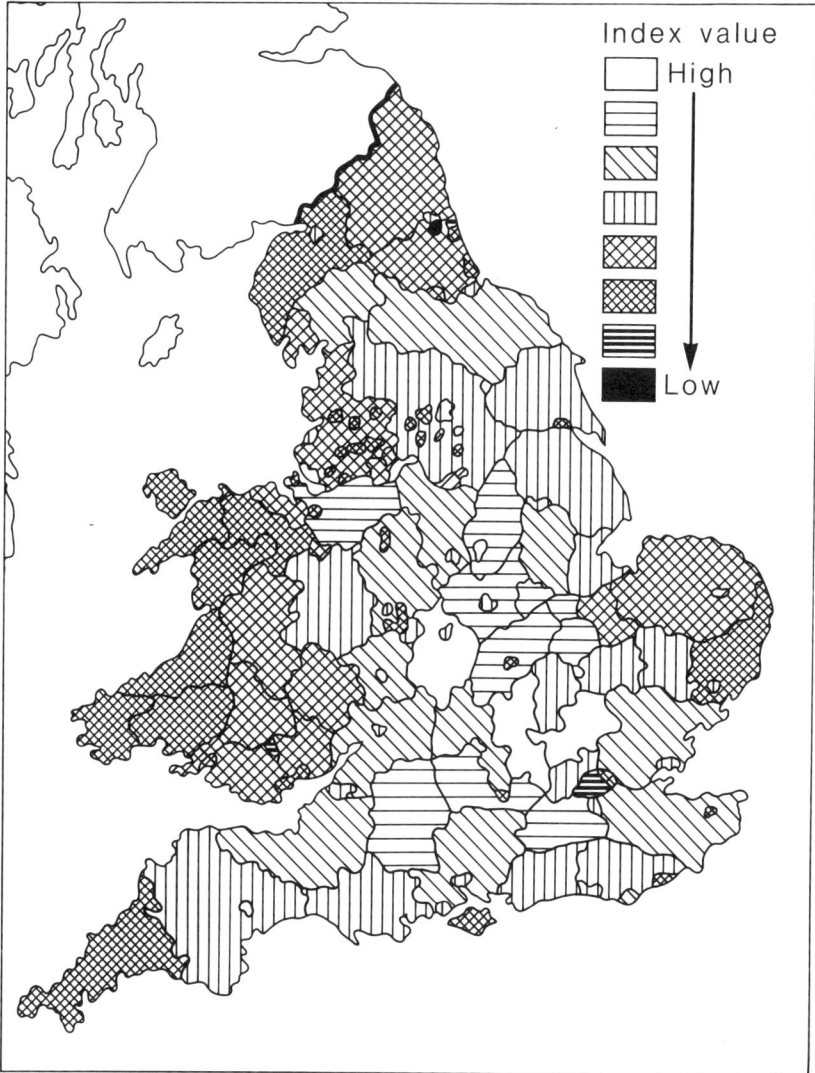

We have less than 20 inches of rainfall here and it never gets really cold, except maybe once in a while. The oil lorry never fails to call. There are plenty of taxis in the street if it does come on to rain. I belong to a good golf club, my wife to a good bridge club, my daughter to a good amateur theatre company, and my son plays polo. My daughter is quite unlike me and my wife when we were young. All our friends live round here. The village shop stocks the things we now like. The garage has a Jaguar specialist (or: there is a Rolls/Bentley appointed retailer in the next town).'

If views like these are widespread, small wonder that firms are reluctant to move. And even if they do, psychic income is still relevant. As there is no logical reason why the geography of psychic and monetary income should be similar, a manufacturer who seeks to maximise total revenue (monetary and psychic) may settle where monetary profit is sub-optimal (Fig. 3.1e). While psychic income defies easy measurement, attempts by geographers to measure its close relations, the 'quality of life', or 'levels of living' in Britain suggest a geographical pattern with two ingredients (Fig. 3.2): first, a regional gradient in favour of the South and Midlands, and second, an urban/rural distinction in favour of the latter (Knox 1973). Changing the particular methods of measuring 'levels of living' changes the resultant pattern. For firms concerned with entertaining their business contacts, 'quality of life' is associated more with top-class hotels, restaurants, theatres and night clubs, and in these respects the geographical pattern rapidly becomes one of London versus the rest.

These arguments might seem 'unbusinesslike' and almost flippant, yet there is substantial evidence to support them. In 1966 22% of London's manufacturing respondents identified that city's hotels and entertainment facilities as 'important' to their being in the capital (Hoare 1973), while decentralised firms have found out-of-town locations less satisfactory in this regard (*Sunday Times*, 9 January 1977). An investigation of factories that had moved to Devon and Cornwall (usually from the South East) since 1939 found that 30% of manufacturers gave the 'attractiveness of the area to key workers and management' as the main reason for their choice, more than cited any other single location consideration (Spooner 1972). Keeble (1976, pp. 83-5) summarises other studies underlining the importance of residential attractiveness for industrialists in the South East, East Anglia and Cornwall. Given a hesitancy on the part of firms to admit to such non-monetary location factors to 'outside' researchers, the strong suspicion must be that these survey results represent some minimum level of importance of psychic income, the true level perhaps being much higher. The importance of attractive living, working and playing environments is also constantly apparent through advertisements encouraging new business investment. Recall too how this same factor also affects the mobile labour that a manufacturer establishing in a desirable area might hope to attract.

Many geographers would argue that satisficer behaviour and psychic income have become increasingly important as locational forces since 1918. Overall, incomes and standards of living have increased during a period when many geographical cost differentials have narrowed. Psychic income may not pay the rent and the wages, but as overall incomes continue to rise so the drive for yet more monetary advance becomes less and less significant. Perhaps hungry industrialists, like hungry heavyweights, are a thing of the past.

Quantity of information

Fig. 3.1f shows a different model. Here the manufacturer may want to locate optimally, but has incomplete information on which to base his location decision. However optimal his 'ends' may be, his 'means' let him down. In practice, we all know more about some areas than about others. Our own geographical backgrounds and those of our family, friends and contacts mean we receive more first-hand information about some areas, while for others we are thrown back upon impersonal, media sources.

As far as manufacturers are concerned, an important contributant to this information surface is the cost in time and money of seeking space for alternative locations. This is but one particular instance of the general problem explored by the behavioural approach to business decision-making, and neatly summarised by its founding father, Herbert Simon (1957):

'The capacity of the human mind for formulating and solving complex problems is very small compared with the size of the problems whose solution is required for objectively rational behaviour in the real world—or even for a reasonable approximation to such objective rationality.'

A common response is to simplify the problem in some way, and to solve it as well as possible within these limits—the so-called 'bounded rationality' approach. Two popular simplifications in the industrial location case are of time ('we'll give ourselves 6 months to look round, then decide') and space ('let's look at the sites within 20 miles first'). Thus in Townroe's (1971) survey of 59 migrant factories, 35 took their decision on a new location within one year of starting to look, 30 looked at no more than 4 alternatives (and 17 at only one). Less than half (23) even wrote down the attributes they were looking for in a new location and 17 settled on the first one they came across that they considered 'possible'. Another 23 picked the first one to which they gave the presumably rather higher accolade of 'satisfactory'! These two factors mean that the resultant area about which firms could claim to have a working knowledge, their 'mean information field', will widen only slowly.

Certainly, there is a general unwillingness on the part of firms to undertake extensive inter-locational cost comparisons before making their 'where' decision. Of a sample of 62 factories opening up in a new (to them) region studied by Northcott (1977) in 1973-6, for instance, only 6 had attempted fully to cost the alternatives open to them, and only 2 of these used this as the basis for their eventual decision. This is nothing new. Twenty-five years before, Luttrell's painstaking survey of 98 new branch plant locations in Britain produced the then startling comment that:

'We should like to have given an example of a classic case in location choice in which operating-cost estimates were made for 2 or more possible places, all imponderables or non-cost factors assessed and then a way found for comparing the good and bad points of one place with those of the other. Unfortunately, we have not been able to find such a case' (Luttrell 1962, p. 79).

One reason for this may be the general unease felt by manufacturers in matters financial. Thus the study used for Table 3.1 also showed how firms were much happier dealing with technical than financial issues (Table 3.2), a finding perhaps related in turn to the lack of adequate opportunities for entrepreneurial training in Britain.

Whatever its fundamental causes, the effects of imperfect geographical knowledge are to dissuade firms from locational strategies seen as 'risky'.

Table 3.2 Management strengths and weaknesses: 'Did the firm regard itself as being particularly strong (weak) in any area of its operations?' *Source:* Centre for Inter-Firm Comparison (1977).

	Strong	Weak
Production efficiency	20	5
Technical or product or service superiority	32	1
Marketing and selling	10	12
Financial skills	10	29
Manpower expertise	18	1
Industrial relations	1	4
Innovation, research and development	2	3

Other things being equal, growth by expansion *in situ*, or by short-distance migration represent low-risk growth channels. When longer-distance moves are in prospect, personal contacts in potential new areas reduce the risks: in Northcott's survey prior business or personal contacts easily headed the list of factors of 'overriding' importance in the choice of a new location, being mentioned by 21% of all respondents. Manufacturers embarking on long-distance moves to the Government's Assisted Areas certainly have a more accurate picture of their geographical boundaries and the regional planning incentives available there than a 'control' sample of non-migrants outside these areas (Green 1977), but quite what is the 'cause' and what the 'effect' here is not easy to tell. A related ploy in the promotional literature, to reduce the 'riskiness' of untried location, is to publicise the 'big name' companies already operating there successfully: 'if they can succeed, so can you' is the message.

Data quality

'Nobody likes a bad reputation, particularly when it's unjustified. Staffordshire today is trying to shrug off a public image which dismisses the county as a flat, boring place connecting the horror of the Black Country with the squalor of the Potteries. The trouble is that, seen from the motorway or the London–Manchester railway—the most common outsider's view—there is little to dispel the image' (*The Guardian*, 15 November 1974).

Just as the amount of information we have about places varies spatially, so does the accuracy of that information, often bearing little relation to the underlying, 'true', data surface (Fig. 3.1g). The lack of 'objective' cost analysis of alternative locations, already noted, opens the door for our 'subjective' images to play their part. The experience of industrial firms after setting up in new locations illustrates how widely image and reality can diverge. In some cases staff previously reluctant to move to a 'poor image' area have become very contented and almost more local than the locals, while in others the pre-move image of readily available labour has become a post-move mirage as 'relative' local unemployment statistics are seen in their true, 'absolute', light.

Strictly speaking, none of us, manufacturers or otherwise, respond to the world as it is, but to what we think that it is. As the sensory impulses we receive from this 'real world' become filtered and distorted in our minds the perceptual images which are so created and to which we do respond will differ from the original stimuli we receive. Because we all have individual filtering and distorting mechanisms, so a family of different images can be built up from the same initial 'real world' impulse. While accepting this, we can still posit certain generalities about the perceptual geography of Britain. First, as the distance of places from our point of observation increases, so the images we are likely to have of them change in strength and in favourability. 'Strength' is a function of data quantity, while 'favourability' partly depends on the type of information we receive (Fig. 3.3a). As distance increases, so the relative importance of 'media' sources in our geographical data store increases. Media news tends to be bad news: in the phrase popularised by a recent Prime Minister, 'a lie is half-way round the world before the truth has got its boots on'. The worse the news the further and faster it travels. The net

Fig. 3.3 Strength and 'niceness' of images of places. The interplay of the source of information, of distance, and of a regional (anti-Northern) element help form the images we have in our minds about places.

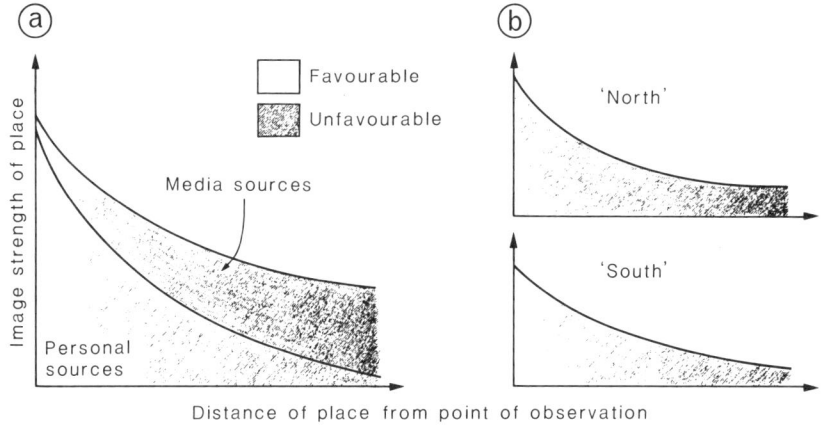

Fig. 3.4 Regional caricature. One of a series of Punch cartoons under the heading 'The South Strikes Back', poking fun at various supposed aspects of life in the 'North'. The northern version of 3 weeks earlier ('Flat Caps Came to Town') looked at life in London through the eyes of Liverpool and Birmingham cartoonists. *Source: Punch*, 9 April, 1969.

"*You'll have to speak your lines a lot louder—Batley folk like to hear every word, loud and clear.*"

effect is that we think worse of places further away than of those close to us—they have a poorer image. The ignorance of, and lampooning of, the 'North' by the 'South' is just one manifestation of this, in Britain (Fig. 3.4). While this caricaturing is not all one way, the 'North' (whatever we mean by that) has a worse public image than the 'South' (Fig. 3.3b). Largely based on the inherited human and physical landscapes thrown up by the Industrial Revolution, contemporary press accounts perpetuate the 'grime, cobble-and-dole-queue' Northern image in the public imagination.

In contrast, favourable images of local areas and of the South emerged from a well-known study of British school-leavers, which asked them to rank the counties of Great Britain in terms of their residential appeal (Fig. 3.5) (Gould and White 1968). Local 'peaks' of residential preference were particularly strong among northern school-leavers. When viewed nationally, though, these peaks tended to be self-cancelling, and the overall surface that resulted favoured southern Britain. A recent study has

Fig. 3.5 Residential desirability among British school-leavers in 1967 based on the aggregate rank-order scores of 92 counties in mainland Britain in terms of their 'niceness' as areas to live in. Generally the south comes out best, although London is a 'nasty' inlier and there are a few 'nice' outliers further north. The similarity with the then-contemporary pattern of Assisted Areas is striking. *Source:* based on Gould and White (1968).

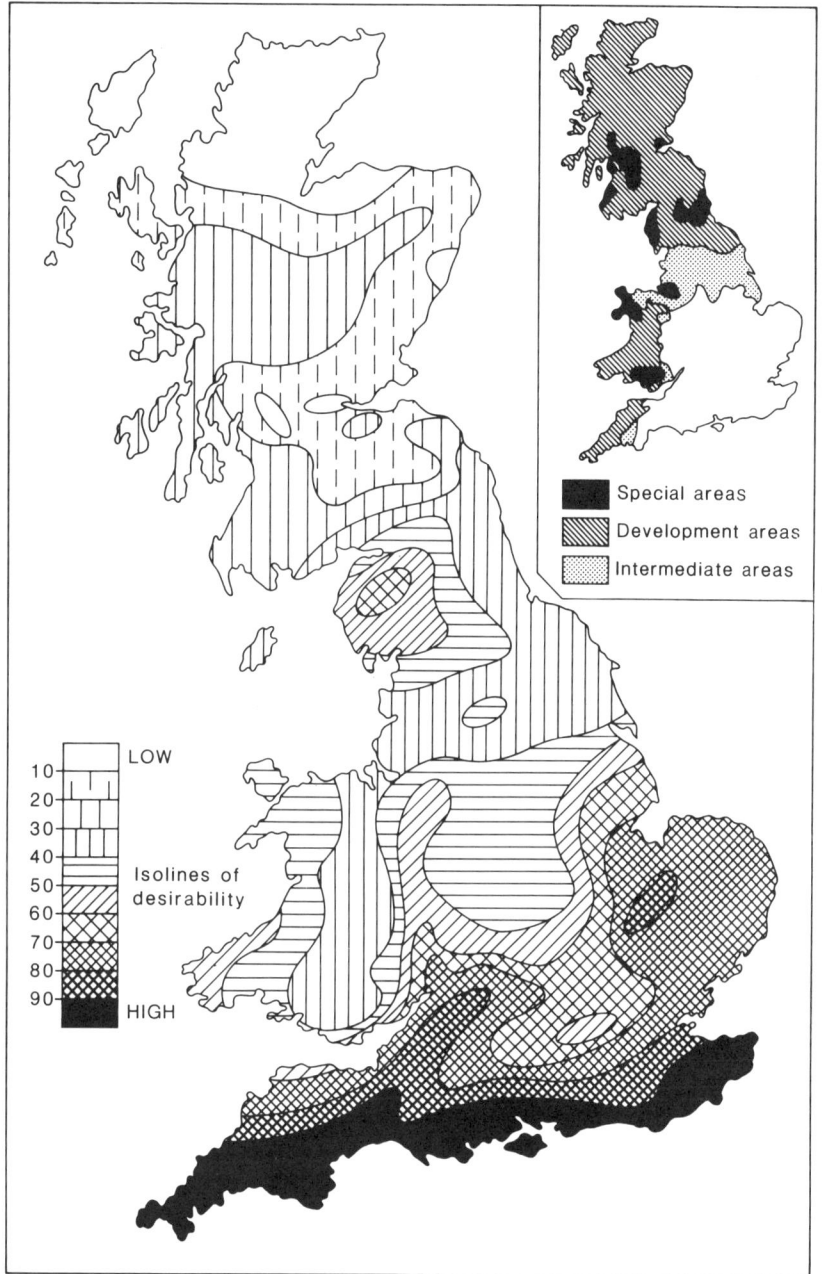

shown an interesting positive correlation between these same data and spatial patterns of manufacturing change from 1959 to 1971 (Keeble 1976). While we must be cautious about extrapolating from sixth-formers to industrialists, confirmation of a similar pro-Southern residential bias comes from studies of college students (Bale 1976) and from industrialists themselves (Pocock and Hudson 1978). One recent television report on the industrial problems of the North went so far as to conclude:

'The biggest obstacle to the North's development is the image that outsiders have of it'

The report cited education, executive housing, landscape and strike record as the particular handicaps. This view seems also to hold sway in the corridors of power, as shown by a press report in 1980 on the Prime Minister's visit to Sunderland:

'[Mrs Thatcher] said she was thrilled to see the way local businessmen were tackling the disadvantages of being in the North-east. Sunderland's trouble, she said, was that it was out of the way, but through quality and word of mouth the area could overcome such a disadvantage' (*The Times*, 24 May 1980).

Little wonder, then, that towns and regions worry about their images, and try to 'correct' them, through their advertising campaigns, focusing on a range of positive perceptual ingredients (Burgess 1982).

Organisational constraints

Chapter 1 emphasised how commercial and political organisations have increasingly affected the course of British manufacturing since 1918. At the same time we must consider the role of social organisations, although their role is in a minor key, at least as far as the geography of industry is concerned.

Commercial organisations

The growth of large public companies tends of itself to undermine any view of the British economy as composed of industrialists restlessly pursuing higher and higher profits. As companies grow, their internal structures become more sophisticated, and ownership (the shareholders) becomes divorced from decision-making (the management). The two retain some mutual interdependence, as at annual general meetings, but the actions taken by management to increase company profits will not automatically be to their own financial benefit. Pursuit of profits for distribution to others is less attractive than pursuit of profits for self.

There is an important spatial aspect to company growth too. We saw how large companies have come to dominate the manufacturing sector, and the importance of the 'numbers of plants' method of growth (Chapter 1). To understand how commercial organisation matters to the industrial geographer we should realise that the units of the multi-plant company operate in two different types of 'space': the first is a conventional 'geographical' space relevant to all companies and based on distance in some form or another, and the second is an 'organisational' space where what matters is position within the overall company structure (Fig. 3.6). Organisational space may show little regard for its geographical counterpart, but can often be the more important to the multi-plant unit, affecting profoundly the way it locates and behaves in geographical space. Of 44 operating subsidiaries of larger organisations surveyed by the Centre for Inter-Firm Comparison in 1977, for example, 29 reported that major decisions were made by 'the organisation' rather than themselves, while 25 were not directly represented on the senior organisation decision-making body. Decision-making hierarchies of this sort impinge on both geographical location and behaviour.

Fig. 3.6 Organisational space and geographical space. These two aspects of the multi-plant company's environment are closely interrelated. Thus locational requirements in geographical space can be determined by a plant's position in organisational space and this can also affect its multiplier and pollution impacts on the surrounding geographical environment.

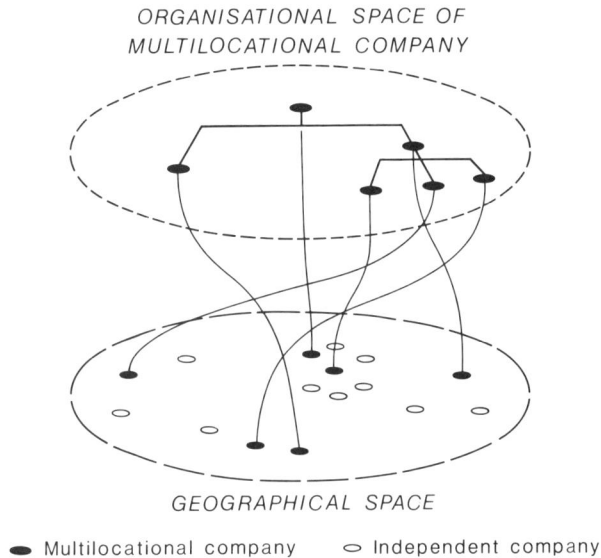

ORGANISATIONAL SPACE OF
MULTILOCATIONAL COMPANY

GEOGRAPHICAL SPACE

● Multilocational company   ○ Independent company

(a) Organisational space and location   A multi-plant unit's location may differ from that of its single-plant counterpart in a number of respects. First, it forms part of some wider corporate locational strategy where, as in chess, the locational value of each piece can be understood only in the context of all the rest, both those of the same side (organisation) and those of the opposition. In 1980, for example, General Motors headquarters in Detroit announced a new factory for Belfast, but as part of some broader European investment programme involving 5 separate new plants. In 1979 the Singer Company of New York decided to close its Clydebank factory, not because Glaswegians in particular were buying fewer sewing machines but in response to a need to trim the corporate sails (and sales) following a fall in world demand.

Secondly, the locational requirements of corporate plants will depend on their place in organisational space. Multi-plant companies seek sites with an eye to the need for inter-plant communication. As location decisions are taken by the headquarters board its own convenience may take precedence. One manufacturer near Heathrow told the writer 'the Airport is a major headache as far as staff here are concerned, but it's convenient for our American masters to get to, and that's all that matters in this firm'.

The large multi-plant corporation also has a bargaining strength at its disposal when looking for a new location. Against any potential restrictions and prohibitions threatened by local or central governments it has the counter-threat of transferring its 'basic' investment elsewhere, with a substantial loss of economic benefit to the community/country concerned. The greater the locational flexibility of the company, the more real the threat. Thus a large multinational with a short list of possible sites reading 'London, Geneva, Milan, Amsterdam' is well able to shrug off pressures by the British government to send it to Newcastle, or by the Italians to send it to Naples. In Holland's words (1976), multinationals 'stride the world in 7 league boots'. Such is their 'locational muscle' that compromise between conflicting corporation and governmental locational preferences is sometimes achieved only in Downing Street.

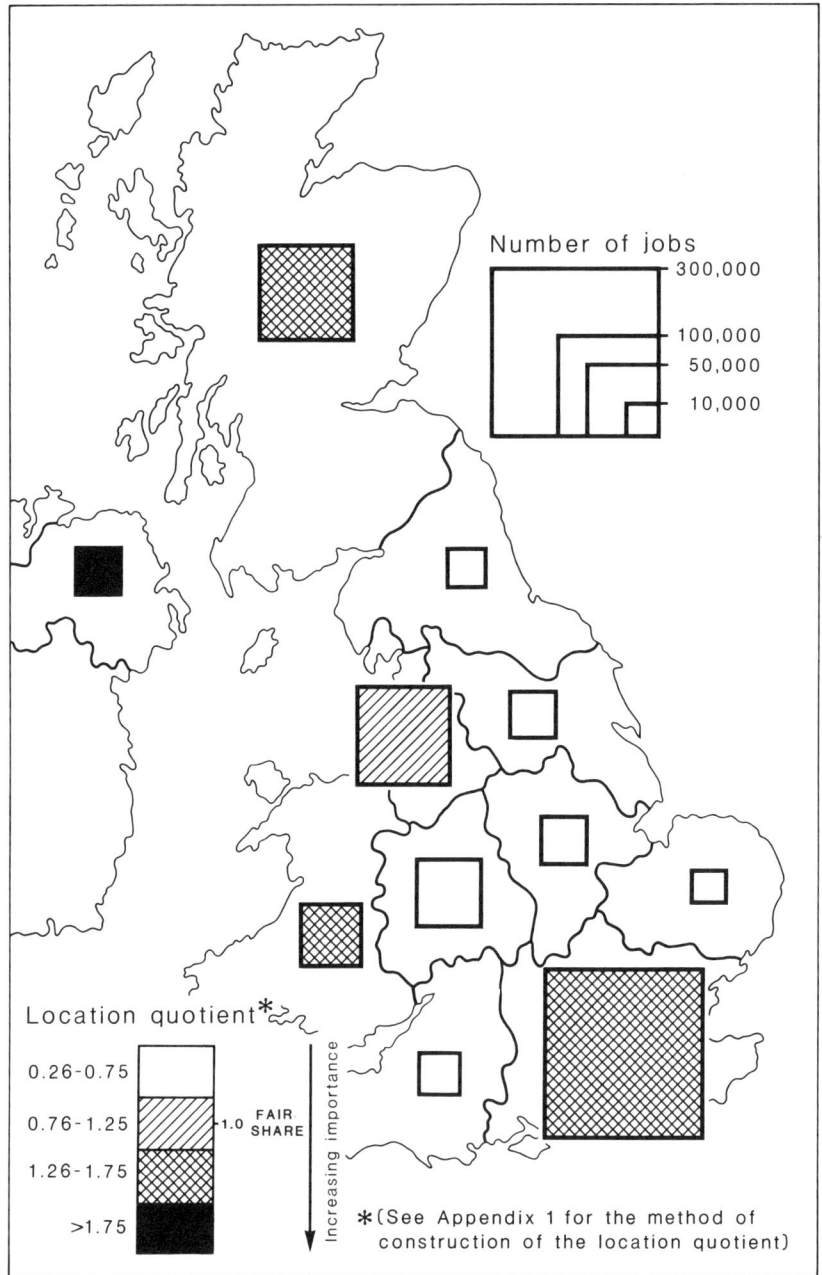

Fig. 3.7 Regional concentration of United States-owned companies in 1971. American investment is relatively more important in the South East and in the peripheries, with a belt of underrepresentation in middle England. *Source:* based on Watts (1979) Large firms, multinationals and regional development. *Environ. and Plann. A* **11**, 71-81.

Large firms may also have different locational standards from those of small ones. Old, inefficient factories in poor environments may well be tolerated by single-plant firms (as the only alternative is a complete move, or to cease business) but not by more demanding and geographically flexible multi-plant firms. Again, the multinational makes international comparisons of, say, operating cost and environmental acceptability. Thus while a firm based entirely in Britain may view London as a bad economic bet in operating cost terms the multinational may see it very differently: a survey of 15 western European capitals in 1980 found only 4 cheaper than London in the costs of employing a senior executive (*Sunday Times*, 6 April 1980).

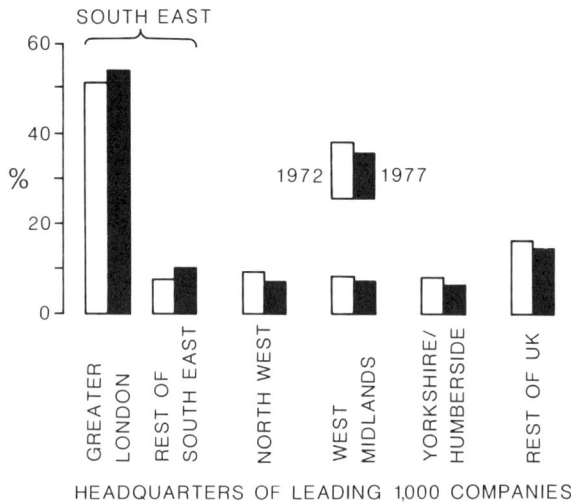

Fig. 3.8 Headquarters locations of the United Kingdom's leading 1,000 companies in 1972 and 1977. The South East (and London especially) has increased its already impressive hold on corporate headquarters over the 5-year period. The data are derived from the 'Times 1,000' annual publication, which covers manufacturing and non-manufacturing firms. *Source:* based on Goddard and Smith (1978).

Finally, large and small companies may have different attitudes towards location. The multi-plant firm is sometimes accused of a callous indifference to the feelings and fortunes of communities dependent upon its branches, especially when it seems to lop them off with impunity (as at the Singer Corporation's Clydebank works): single-plant firms are depicted as more 'involved' in the local community and its well-being. Multinationals' perception of distance is also very different from that of single-nationality firms. A British firm in London may be more reluctant to establish a branch in 'remote' Glasgow than the London staff of a United States-owned company, for whom the London–Glasgow journey is 'merely' that from Dallas to Houston, or San Francisco to Los Angeles.

These various locational characteristics of large firms may pull in different directions. Thus American manufacturing investment in Britain shows a twofold pattern, partly emphasising the London/South-East region, and partly also the extreme peripheries (Fig. 3.7). The first could reflect 'strength' and 'requirements', the second 'attitudes', while 'standards' could play a part in both.

(b) Organisational space and behaviour   Organisational space affects what firms do, as well as where they do it. One very important aspect of industrial behaviour has been for large firms to concentrate their senior, decision-making staff in the 'central', South-Eastern region and their day-to-day manufacturing operations elsewhere. While much research remains to be done in this area, evidence to date suggests that this dominance of the South East in 'control' units has become greater in the recent past (Fig. 3.8). This carries 'multiplier' implications, since these should increase commensurately with the concentration of high-income and decision-making staff in a region.

As well as engaging in this form of geographical sorting, multi-plant companies also have the option of specialising in particular products at particular plants. This may be specialisation in a consumer product or in products used elsewhere in the company and thus exchanged among the different plants (see Fig. 6.1). Either way, the company exploits economies of scale resulting from such specialisation at the individual plant level.

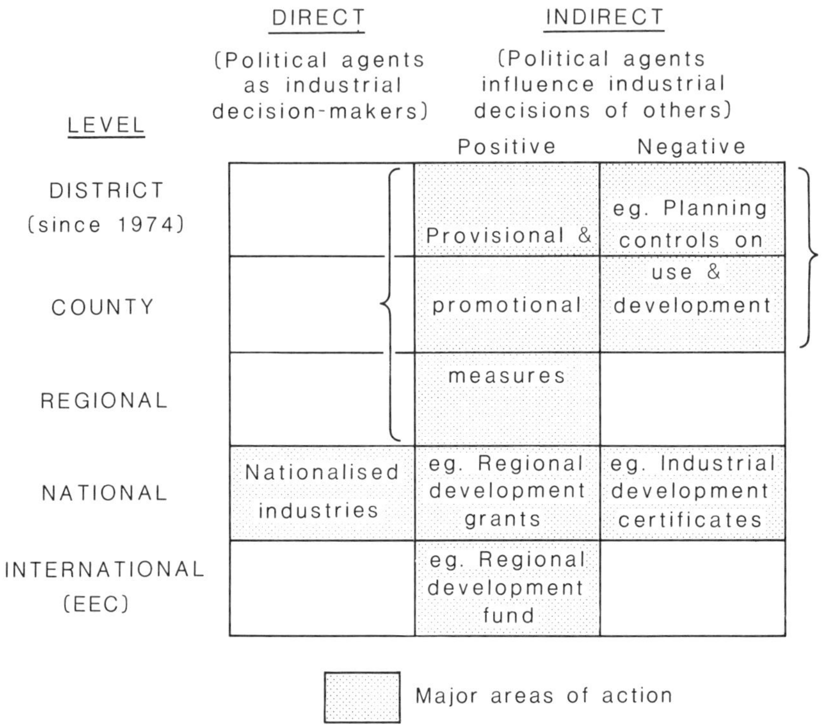

Fig. 3.9 A classification of types of political action relevant to industrial geography. Such influences are most important at the national (Westminster) level where the hand of government can be seen in each of the 3 types of action (columns) shown. After 1974 the 'District' level of local government replaced the previous amalgam of Urban Districts, Rural Districts, Municipal Boroughs and County Boroughs.

LEVEL	DIRECT (Political agents as industrial decision-makers)	INDIRECT (Political agents influence industrial decisions of others)	
		Positive	Negative
DISTRICT (since 1974)		Provisional & promotional measures	eg. Planning controls on use & development
COUNTY			
REGIONAL			
NATIONAL	Nationalised industries	eg. Regional development grants	eg. Industrial development certificates
INTERNATIONAL (EEC)		eg. Regional development fund	

☐ Major areas of action

Finally, the large firm can undertake a range of its own production and service requirements beyond the capacity of the small one. Thus if the optimum level of output of, say, an electro-plating unit is 1,000 units a month, then a large engineering firm with this quantity of throughput may install its own, while a 100-unit-a-month rival may have to subcontract such work to outsiders. If large firms 'internalise' their production requirements in this way the chances of their generating multiplier linkages with other firms is obviously reduced. While this is also a complex research area (Marshall 1979), there is general evidence in Britain of significant levels of inter-plant, intra-firm interdependence both for inputs and outputs among large firms.

Political influences

Political forces constrain Britain's industrial geography in many ways. As Fig. 3.9 shows, we can identify at least five separate geographical levels at which political agencies are important. Only at the national level does 'direct' action apply in the sense of politically appointed bodies being the manufacturing decision-makers, as in the nationalised industries. More common are the 'indirect' influences whereby manufacturers are enticed into certain geographical actions, or persuaded away from others.

(a) Local government Although they represent two different levels of local government in Britain, the effect of District and County authorities is usefully considered together. Their importance has had a chequered history, being quite significant before 1938, very much less so after 1939 until about 1960, after which it has again increased (Camina 1974). Successive local government acts at Westminster have defined and gradually extended the powers of local government in this area. The

Table 3.3 Local government: industrial stimulation measures. *Source:* Camina (1974).

| | % Active | | |
| | Upper tier | | Lower-tier authorities |
	County Councils	County Boroughs	
Items of provision			
Any l.a.-owned land for lease	46	80	26
Land immediately available		72	48
Key worker housing		61	57
Site on l.a. estate	32	58	26
Any l.a.-owned land for sale	47	52	30
Reduced rents (land)	14	40	5
Any l.a. factory for lease	24	35	5
Other Council services		35	15
Loans, grants, etc.	41	34	12
Incentives for office development		20	7
Reduced rents (buildings)		10	1
Any l.a. factory for sale	22	9	5
New factory premises	11	6	6
Items of promotion			
Advice following planning refusal		66	43
Industrial Development Officer	59	62	34
Co-operation	58	56	22
Advertising expenditure	55	47	21
Publicity to workers		33	12
Industrial Development Committee	42	28	23
Professional advertising	20	17	4
County Council professional help		5	24
County Council financial help			5

Notes: 1 l.a. = local authority

2 Lower-tier authorities predate 1974 reorganisation.

extent to which these enabling powers have been adopted varies among authorities, and some have successfully promoted private bills through the House of Commons to widen them in their own particular cases. Thus the Tyne and Wear Act (1976) enhanced that county's capacity to allocate monetary loans and grants to industrial activity (Rogers and Smith 1977), while Bristol Corporation's 1971 West Docks Bill paved the way for that city's mixed blessing of the Royal Portbury Dock.

The overall result is something of a hotchpotch. From her study in 1971/2 Camina concluded that 80% of county boroughs and some two-thirds of lower-tier authorities had a declared policy of trying to attract industry, but in 30% of cases this was not backed up by effective action. Table 3.3 shows the types of 'indirect' attractions offered by the authorities sampled, underlining the variety available. Differences of emphasis arise among the authority types shown but the most important provisions relate to the availability of 'land' (with or without buildings) and housing for key workers. Direct financial support, as provided by Tyne and Wear, is less common, mainly because of other calls on local authority funds, and the overlapping role of central government in this field.

On the negative side of Fig. 3.9, certain authorities have an avowed policy of restricting industrial development, lest the character of their areas be impaired. Mindful of their tourist and educational roles, both Oxford and Cambridge City Councils have taken this view since 1945. The extensive land-use planning controls bestowed on local government by the 1947 Town and Country Planning Act and its successors give Districts and Counties considerable powers in this respect. By limiting the amount of land zoned for industry and by resisting planning applications from new and existing manufacturing firms, local authorities can deliberately restrict development, while insensitive redevelopment of run-down, inner-city areas can do the same unknowingly, by depleting the stock of workshop premises required by newly emergent firms (Chapter 5).

The direct effect of local government action on industrial growth is modest. Camina estimates that most councils so minded attract about one firm (representing at most 150 jobs) each year, yet their very broad planning powers give local government authorities some influence in many things that happen, or fail to happen, in the industrial sector.

(b) Regional The types of administrative authorities operating at the larger, 'regional', level in Britain since 1918 have been very diverse. First, their 'patches' have varied greatly in size, from the 'national' responsibilities of the Scottish Council (established in 1946) and the Development Corporation of Wales (1959) to the much smaller ones of the Tayside Development Authority and South West Scotland Development Authority (both of 1971). Secondly, some have substantial independence of action (like the Highlands and Islands Development Board), some are closely tied to their corresponding local authorities (the North West Industrial Development Association), while others represent the arm of central government 'writ small' at the regional level (as with the Scottish and Welsh Development Agencies). Third, their activities extend from promotion and publicity and the sanctioning of grants to the full suite of 'central' regional planning measures, as outlined in the next section. When these 'regional' endeavours are considered alongside the rarely coordinated industrial attractions offered by 'local' government it is hardly surprising that many manufacturing firms have complained that Britain suffers from promotional overkill!

(c) Central This is the most important political layer, by far. In geographical coverage, in the level of financial backing available and in legislative capacity, central governments in Britain have an immense potential to influence the spatial affairs of an industrial nation either deliberately, or as an incidental effect of policies directed elsewhere. Here we consider the four most obvious of these effects.

(i) The wartime economy As well as altering the overall structure of the nation's manufacturing, the 1939-45 war affected its geography. The Blitz gave many private firms their first incentive to move from the city centres. Whether the move was to the suburbs or beyond, their experience has encouraged further decentralisation in the subsequent peace. Earlier, government rearmament from 1934 onwards stimulated war industry production in factories lying away from those 'unsafe zones' within bombing range of Europe, while also giving a manpower boost to the high-unemployment 'problem regions' of the 1930s depression. Through the later conversion of war-stimulated premises to other uses, the continued existence of some war-based manufacturers after 1945, and the post-war acceleration of industrial decentralisation, the 1939-45 war had a

subtle if largely uncharted effect on Britain's modern industrial geography (Moyes 1975).

(ii) Nationalised industries   The increase in governmental control has been less pronounced in the manufacturing sector than in primary and tertiary activities. Nevertheless, in addition to the steel industry (Chapter 6), other major firms are underpinned by the National Enterprise Board (NEB) (e.g. Rolls Royce, Ferranti, Upper Clyde Shipbuilders and Alfred Herbert), while the shipbuilding, cotton, aircraft, computer and aluminium industries have received substantial support from central government through subsidies, legislation or orders for work. The precise role government itself plays in the locational aspects of such firms and industries is less easy to disentangle. In the steel and NEB cases, decisions are made by boards of directors and corporation members appointed by and answerable to government, constrained by its financial control but free within these limits to pursue normal commercial objectives. Certainly, in some cases the overt hand of government in locational matters does show through. The lucrative subsidies negotiated in 1967 between the Wilson Government and the aluminium industry not only resulted in three major smelters being established in Britain but also strongly influenced their detailed location in the Assisted Areas (heading (iv) below), at Invergordon, Holyhead and Lynemouth (Watts 1970). Elsewhere, government intervention has been stimulated by the weakness of industries or firms, so locational effects are more to preserve the locational *status quo* or coordinate its contraction. In such cases it is particularly difficult to tell what would have happened without such 'intervention'.

(iii) Infrastructure   Much of the infrastructure used by modern industry is a direct consequence of government policy. The most obvious example is transport: here the 'Whether?', 'When?', 'Where?' and 'How much?' of investment are strongly tied to political purse-strings and ministerial or cabinet approval. Such spatial-selective investments may have a stimulant effect upon industrial growth, although this may be tantalisingly hard to measure. Central government has been conscious of this potential, yet not always consistently so. In 1968 the then super-ministry of the Department of Economic Affairs stated, in a pamphlet entitled 'Economic Planning in the Regions':

'Expenditure on such large-scale developments as motorways, ports and airports not only provides widespread national benefits, but also has extremely important effects upon the level of economic activity in individual regions.'

Yet in the very same year the government's terms of reference to the Roskill Commission on the Third London Airport in effect limited its search for a new site to the South East of England, ignoring the same 'transport stimulates industry' arguments of economic representatives from the provinces (Fordham 1970)!

(iv) Regional policy   Here the geographical dimension of central policy is strongest. 'Regional policy' is the umbrella term applied to steps initiated by Whitehall, legislative or otherwise, designed to assist some 'regions'

Fig. 3.10 The geography of regional policy in Britain, 1934-82. The boundaries of areas positively assisted under regional policy (and known, collectively, as the 'Assisted Areas') have changed appreciably since 1934, with a steady increase in the proportion of the country so delimited, until 1979 at least. Northern Ireland (not shown) was covered by its own legislation and incentives throughout this period.

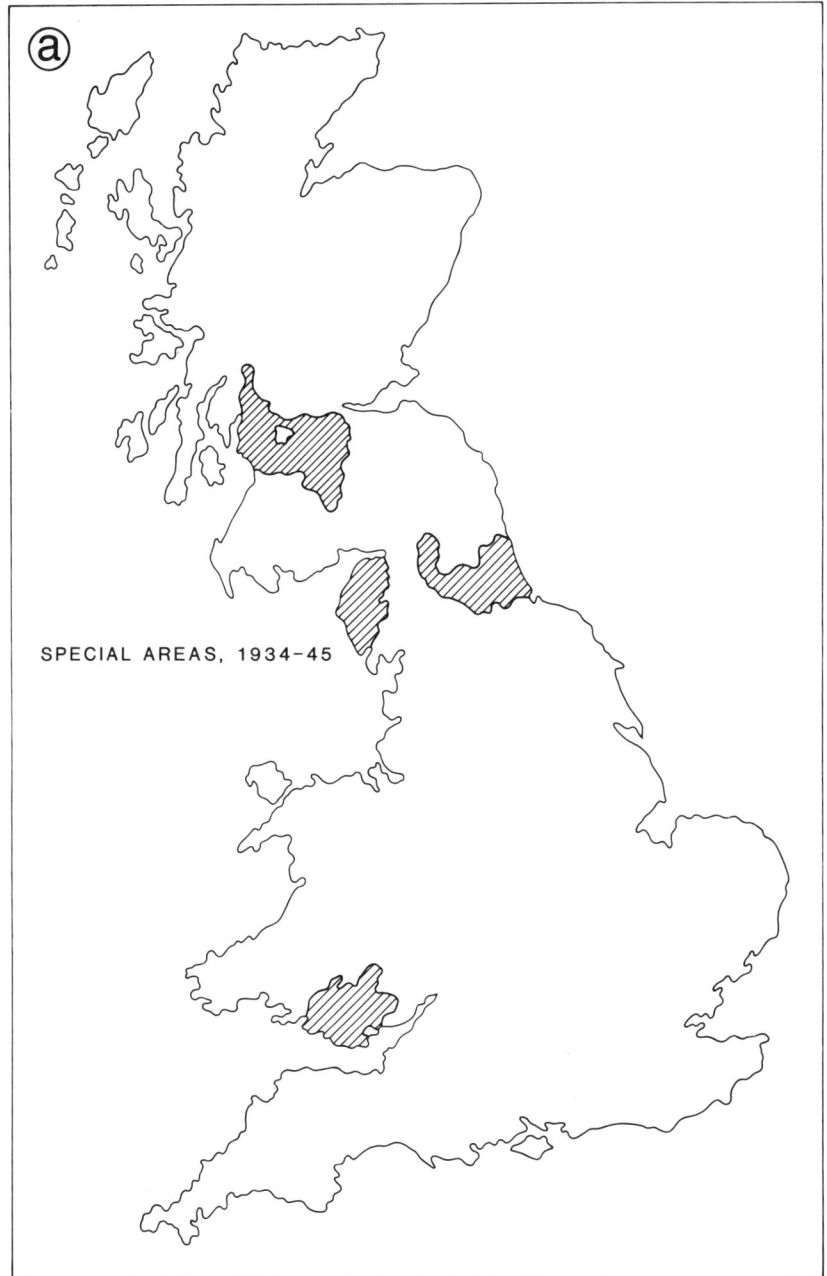

SPECIAL AREAS, 1934–45

economically and socially at the expense of others. Some of these actions concern non-manufacturing, but the main emphasis of British regional policy has fallen upon the manufacturing sector. This is partly because regional problems are often diagnosed as the result of the selective 'free-market' fortunes of manufacturing in different regions in the first place, partly because of the locational flexibility inherent in manufacturing activity and partly because of the further multiplier effects that the redistribution of basic manufacturing activity should bring.

The policy package thus produced is a very comprehensive one. The main 'carrots' offered are the regional development grants towards initial fixed cost outlays, and the provision of advance factories (built by the government-backed English Industrial Estates Corporation and similar

(b)

DEVELOPMENT AREAS
1945–60

organisations in the rest of Britain), although a wide range of other
financial and labour-oriented measures also apply. Many of these
incentives are available on a sliding spatial scale, with the most generous
terms going to the most needy Special Development Areas, and the least
to the comparatively prosperous Intermediate Areas.

From 1947 until December 1981, when the government announced its
intention to abolish them, Industrial Development Certificates (IDCs)
were the main 'stick' directing industrialists' attention towards the
Assisted Areas. By specifying a threshold floorspace size for new and
extended manufacturing premises above which an IDC was obligatory
and by granting certificates more readily in some regions than others
central government had in its hands a very powerful device to direct the

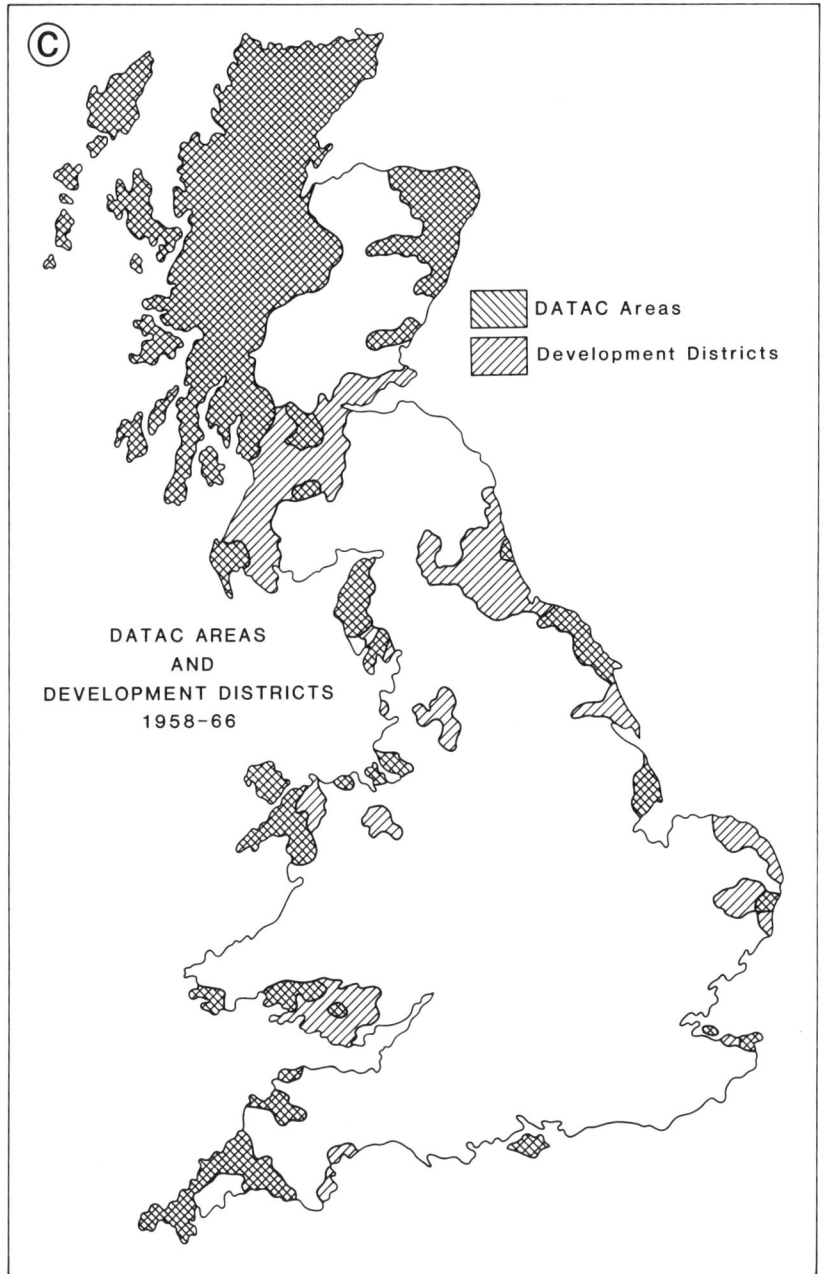

© DATAC Areas

Development Districts

DATAC AREAS
AND
DEVELOPMENT DISTRICTS
1958-66

geography of new manufacturing activity. Moving to a site already covered by an IDC provided one loophole for companies unwilling to consider the Assisted Areas, as it did for IBM at Havant (Hampshire) when looking for a factory site needing to be close to their existing laboratories near Winchester.

The present package represents only the latest phase in the constantly changing form of regional policy since 1934. Fig. 3.10 draws together the major ways in which regional policy has affected different parts of Britain at different periods, while Appendix 2 summarises the main changes of policy over this time. More detailed treatment of British regional policy will be found in McCrone (1969) and McCallum (1979).

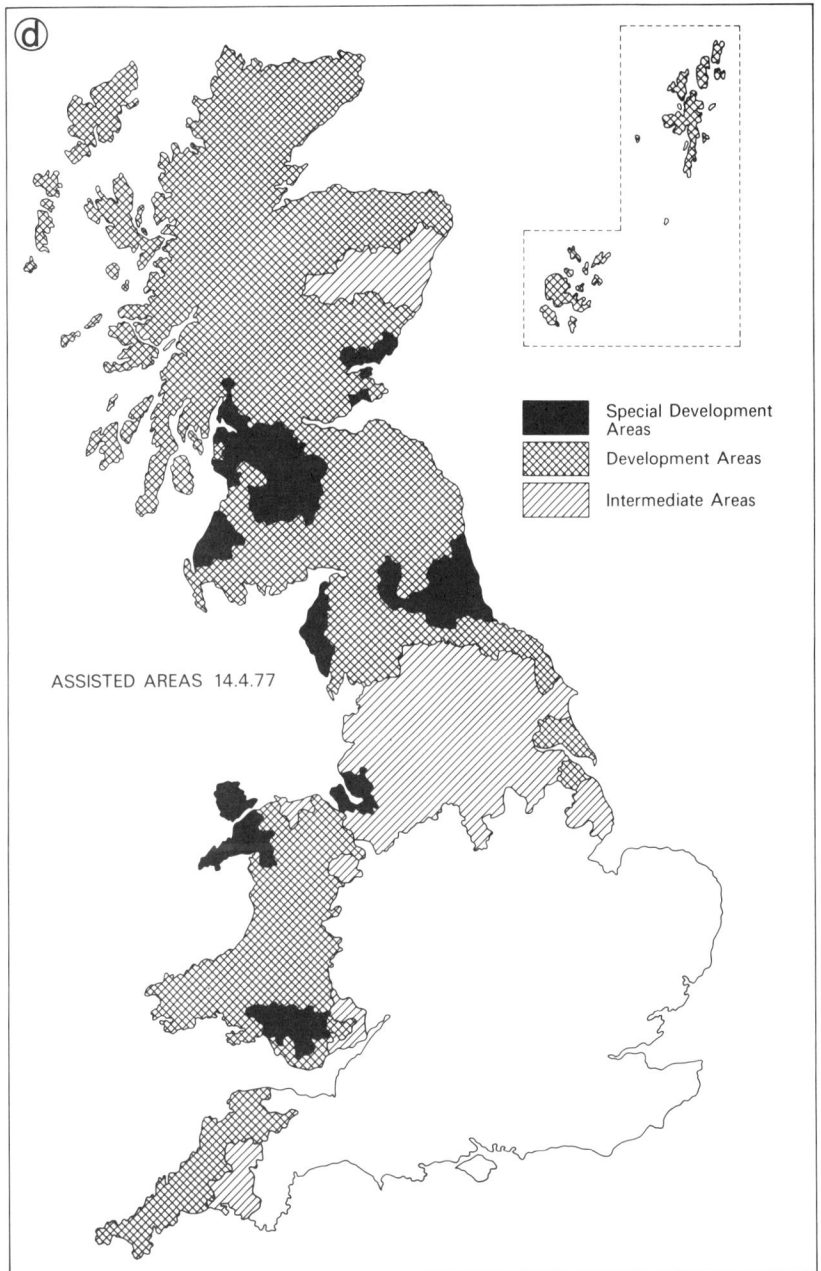

(d) Special Development Areas

Development Areas

Intermediate Areas

ASSISTED AREAS 14.4.77

The level of support enjoyed from successive central governments has also fluctuated over time. One estimate puts the annual regional assistance to industry at about £20m. in 1960, rising to over £300m. in 1969 (all at 1970 prices). What has been constant, however, has been regional policy's concern with assisting the 'peripheral' parts of Britain compared with the prosperous 'central' regions, and its emphasis on unemployment as the major, though not the only, justification. Thus support for regional policy has fluctuated broadly in accord with levels of regional (and national) unemployment, while unemployment levels have been the main criterion upon which the Assisted Areas have been delimited at any particular time.

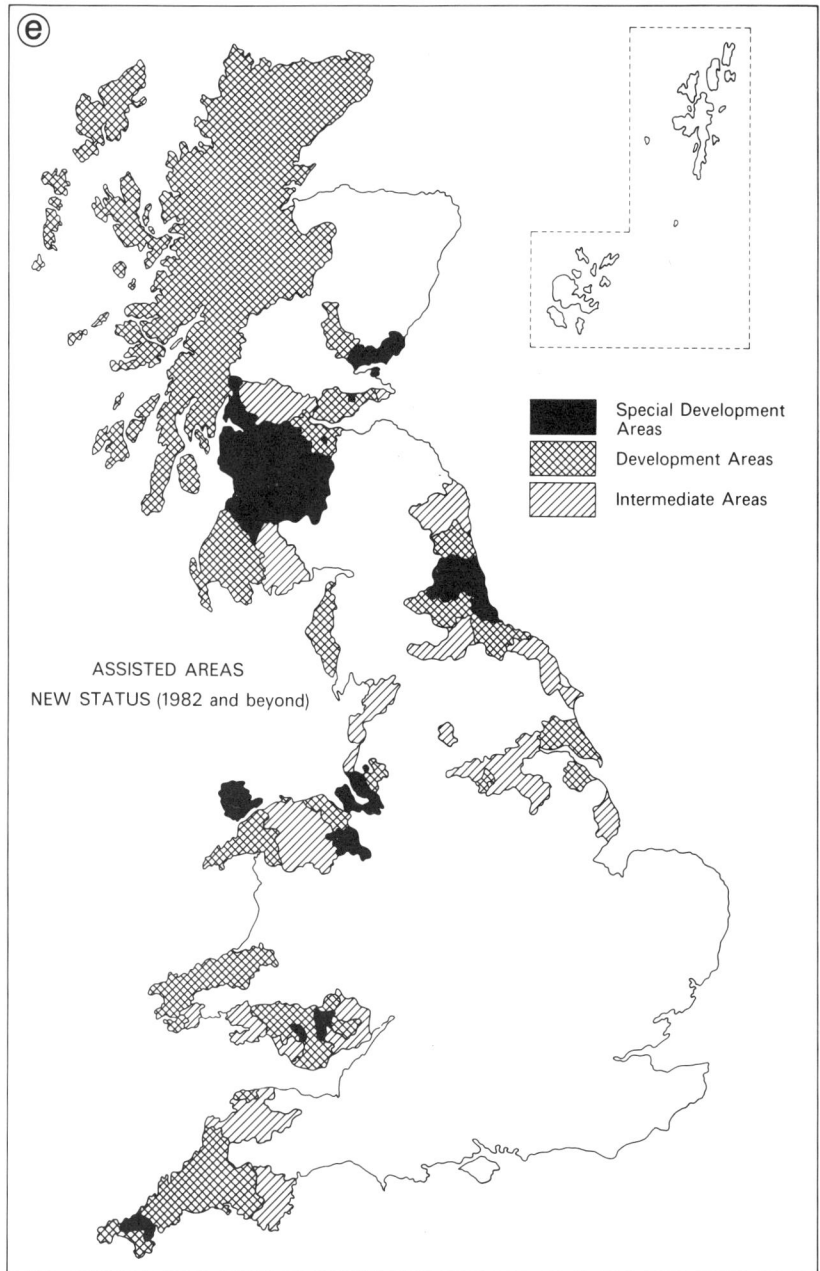

ASSISTED AREAS
NEW STATUS (1982 and beyond)

Legend:
- Special Development Areas
- Development Areas
- Intermediate Areas

Britain can boast a continuous history of regional policy longer than that of any other country. This, coupled with the substantial sums of public money committed to it, raises the question of how significant has been its effect. But the question is a very difficult one to answer precisely, for a number of reasons (Frost 1977). As a result, academics argue over the amount of regional employment directly or indirectly attributable to regional policy and over the effectiveness of the different elements in the regional policy package. This question is taken up again in later chapters, but it is fair to say that most commentators consider that regional policy has had a substantial effect upon the country's industrial geography. The crux of the debate is more over *how* substantial, and whether this has been to the overall advantage of the national economy.

Table 3.4 Allocations from
EEC Regional Development
Fund, 1973-7, by UK region.
Source: Armstrong (1978).

	Industrial and service	Infrastructure	Hill farming
Total (£m.)	64.051	88.122	3.629
Regions			
South West	0.8%	1.7%	
West Midlands	—	0.02%	
East Midlands	0.3%	0.7%	
Yorkshire/Humberside	2.7%	4.4%	
North West	9.6%	10.5%	
Northern	31.8%	28.2%	
Wales	9.3%	17.9%	
Scotland	26.3%	23.4%	87.5%
Northern Ireland	19.2%	13.1%	12.5%

(v) European Economic Community Britain's entry into the EEC in 1973 precipitated a major reorganisation of the Community's hitherto hesitant steps in regional policy. After much haggling, a revised and much upgraded European regional policy was derived, from which Britain was to be the second major beneficiary. The Regional Development Fund (RDF) so created stood at £540m. for 1975-7, and of this Britain eventually received a £150m. (28%) share (Armstrong 1978). Additionally, projects with a definite regional impact can be assisted by three further EEC sources, the European Investment Bank, the Social Fund and the European Coal and Steel Community. Such funds are intended to supplement the national regional programmes of Britain and other members on an 'as well as' rather than an 'instead of' basis. In practice, Brussels' regional policy has had only minor effects on the national version, and none upon the geography of the Assisted Areas, which remains a matter of Whitehall control. The regional distribution of EEC funds within Britain predictably accords closely with these Assisted Areas (Table 3.4), but the overall levels of aid so received are modest compared with Britain's own regional programme: in 1977, for example, Britain's RDF trawl was less than 9% of her own expenditure on regional planning policy.

Social organisations

At first glance, the hard-headed businessman seems unlikely to be swayed in his actions by any feelings of social responsibility. Big business, in particular, is often depicted as riding roughshod over the finer feelings of its workers, and dependent communities.

Nevertheless, social constraints upon manufacturing geography in Britain cannot be so lightly dismissed. As we have seen already, the social ties of decision-makers and their families can strengthen the pull of the locational *status quo*, and the social consequences of regional variations in unemployment have been the main driving force behind the central government's regional policy in Britain. To illustrate some of the other ways in which social influences impinge geographically on manufacturing industry three examples must suffice.

First, consumer tastes for manufactured items may show a regional variation (see also Chapter 2), suggestive of some underlying geography of social attitudes. Allen's (1968) fascinating compendium of regional buying habits records the importance in the West of England of cream, not merely to eat (bought and home-made), but also in colouring for household goods, including bedroom walls. Could this be indicative, he wonders, of the same region's concern with cleanliness (whiteness), as underlined by the apparent fact that the same region places more stress on marital purity than any other region in Britain?

Secondly, the feeling of belonging not just to the 'group', but to the place where that group lives may explain spatial interaction patterns, as in Belfast (Boal 1969). Here, the strong sense of working-class 'territoriality' along 'religious' lines affects journey-to-work patterns of workers and the resultant labour catchments of manufacturing plants. Few residents from the 'Catholic West' travel across 'hostile territory' to jobs in North Belfast. Proportionately more from the same area travel to work in the mixed South of the city than venture into the 'Protestant West' and the Eastern sub-region for work (NIHE n.d.). The East is one of the two major employment districts in the city, but is also a strongly Protestant one.

Thirdly, social conscience pricked by the hardship and stigma of unemployment can encourage individuals and non-government organisations to set up industrial enterprises in unemployment black-spots. One example comes from Torrington (Devon) where the Dartington Glass Works, now employing over 200 workers, was founded by the Dartington Trust in 1965 as a social experiment in an area of limited employment opportunities, high unemployment and high rate of outmigration.

Time constraints

Time is not just a finite constraint on human activities, but also a dimension through which landscapes evolve. In both the physical and human worlds environments change through time, but in both, too, the response is not instantaneous. Rather there is a 'lag', so relics of former landscapes persist to the present. As Mounfield (1977) argues in the specific context of economic geography:

'Our present-day patterns of production and consumption carry the weight of a heavy historical impress. They consist of a fabric of fixed capital investment and attitudes which exist today as a very substantial residual from past decision-making.'

To illustrate his point, Mounfield quotes the example of Kettering (Northamptonshire) where the detailed clustering of boot and shoe factories in the north and east of the town today reflects the sequence in which land previously held under restrictive copyhold tenure and hence unattractive to industrial investors, became progressively released to the market from 1850 as 'no strings' freehold land offering more potential for manufacturing development. Plenty of examples could be found in all parts of Britain of present-day firms established long ago under very different economic conditions from those now prevailing.

This applies particularly to manufacturing. Chapter 1 underlined that industrial 'where' decisions are long-term, and that many present-day manufacturing firms and factories have been around for a long time. To take a few West Country examples, Clark's shoe factory at Street (Somerset) began some 150 years ago making slippers from locally produced and cured sheep-skins, but its annual output of 15 million pairs of shoes is now almost entirely based on imported cattle skins, partly because British cows scratch themselves on hedgerows, which makes their hides unsuitable for shoe manufacture. The 300-year-old Royal Wilton carpet factory (Wilton, Wiltshire) was also based originally on local Downland supplies of wool. Today, though, it is owned by an Irish-based company from whose works at Youghal (Co. Cork) it receives all its woollen yarn. Finally, the Harris meat products factory owes its origins in Calne (Wiltshire) to the enterprise of Sarah Harris, whose butchery used the pick of Irish pigs being driven from Bristol to London. Since 1962 part of the larger FMC group of companies, the Calne factory now receives all its carcases from the nearby Chippenham works of the same parent, which in turn draws on farms throughout southern England for its supplies. (See also p. 4.)

Clearly, in such examples present-day industrial geography can be understood only in terms of the past, when the enterprise was set in motion, and of those forces that have sustained it since. These 'initial factors' should be no different in principle from those discussed earlier in this chapter and the last, even though their specific form will obviously be determined by the relevant historical context. What, though, of those sustaining properties that help these geographical locations to survive to the present?

These can be divided into those of 'inertia' and of 'momentum', although in practice it is often impossible to disentangle the one from the other. Inertia is a negative concept: survival is due more to luck than judgement, more to inaction than to positive response to change. No conscious effort is made to 'keep up with the times', but firms manage to carve out a niche for themselves in the evolving economy that enables them to chug along. Inert firms may be run on old 'what was good enough for grandfather...' lines, by management whose pioneering fire and zest has long since burned out, in old and inefficient premises with out-dated techniques and equipment. Management policy will strongly follow 'satisficer' lines, with relatively low satisfaction levels.

Most manufacturers would object strongly were this caricature to be applied to them, yet some supporting evidence can be found. The refusal by the National Enterprise Board to inject any more public money into the Alfred Herbert machine tool company came in July 1980, but

'most observers... believe the seeds of Herbert's collapse were sown 30 years ago. It is said that the company's conservatism and unwillingness to innovate led to inevitable decline' (*The Times*, 1 July 1980).

Here inertia presages disaster, but this is not always so. A report on the Yorkshire woollen industry in 1969 argued that antique equipment and satisficer behaviour helped the survival of many firms.

'A host of small companies with obsolete and written-off machinery are, by their undercutting, making it hard for the better companies to earn profits that will allow them to finance investment in new plant... The consultants have assembled some eye-opening data showing how small the output of a small mill can be for it still to be commercially viable, once its heritage of old plant has been fully written off. Taking yarn production as an example, a company that has only its operating costs to worry about can survive on a production of 100 lb an hour. One that has invested in the best new machinery needs an output 15 times this size to cover its higher overheads. During a recession, the price-cutting hits the progressive, modernised plant with its overheads relatively harder than the weaker brethren. And there is a sociological factor at work, too: many mill owners are satisfied with a low level of profit—just enough, as one Bradford wag put it, to run a Rover and send their kids to Oundle' (*The Economist*, 14 June 1969).

Momentum is the brighter, positive, side of survival. First, it can arise through the conscious effort to adapt to change. Dundee jute manufacturers, realising the challenge to jute-tufted carpet backing from synthetics switched to polypropylene production to maintain their market position (a 'what' adaption—Chapter 1), while the West Country firms mentioned earlier have adapted the 'how' of existing lines to accommodate changes in the geography of material supply. Such changes in behaviour facilitate stability in geographical location.

Secondly, momentum can arise as new supports sustain an industry once its initial locational justifications have been whittled away. In theory, many of the controls and constraints identified in Chapters 2 and 3 could fill this 'propping-up' role, but in practice some are more likely so to do than others.

(a) Material linkages   A complex of inter-linked and inter-dependent suppliers and customers is more likely to have developed in a long-established industrial area than a new one, other things being equal.

(b) Information linkages   These are evident in the expertise accumulated in local technical colleges, polytechnics and universities or other research institutions. In Britain, for example, a close association exists between the location of industrially specific research centres and the traditional manufacturing homes of those same industries (for instance, shipbuilding research in Wallsend and linen research near Belfast) (Buswell and Lewis 1970).

(c) Labour supply   While ideas of 'inherited skills', once held to explain industrial momentum, are now played down, an area with a tradition of family work in a particular industry and firm, or local apprentice training centres, is more likely to be able to sustain a supply of suitable workers down the generations.

(d) Reputation   Certain firms benefit from their place of manufacture being readily associated in the public mind with excellence in an appropriate type of product. The manufacture of, say, pottery mugs still shows an amazing concentration in Stoke-on-Trent as does cutlery in Sheffield, though whether concentration causes reputation or reputation causes concentration is not easy to decide.

In a sense, of course, all existing locations have an element of inertia/momentum attached to them. What differentiates them is 'how much'. Furthermore, these same notions of survival apply not just to our main focus so far—on firms—but also to manufacturing premises, manufacturing industries, and manufacturing regions, which we turn to in Chapter 4.

4 Manufacturing industry since 1918: general geographies and explanations

Chapters 2 and 3 introduced the variety of forces that control both the industrial location and behaviour of modern manufacturing in Britain, but it said little about the patterns these form 'on the ground'. Chapters 4-6 redress the balance, examining the geographical patterns and trends of manufacturing industry as a whole (Chapter 4) and of selected regions and industries (Chapters 5 and 6).

Industrial geography since 1918

Britain's manufacturing sector has changed in some significant ways since 1918. Has this led to equally pronounced geographical changes? Using, as elsewhere in this Chapter, data collected by Lee (1979), the Gini coefficients (see Appendix 1) in Table 4.1 quantify the changing distribution of manufacturing jobs both among regions and counties. Overall, the shifts are very slight, both between adjacent years and over the entire half century. (With the Gini coefficient, 0 represents perfect similarity between distributions, and 100 maximum dissimilarity.) Bearing in mind the longevity of manufacturing industry and its adaptive abilities in the face of environmental change, this stability is perhaps not surprising. Profound changes may have occurred in the fortunes of particular industries, firms and communities: seen in aggregate, though, the geography of manufacturing industry in Britain has not been rewritten every decade—merely edited.

Regions and counties: manufacturing contributions

Against this background of stability, what has been the manufacturing contribution of different regions? Dominating Fig. 4.1 is the South East's rise to unchallenged primacy, with convergence among the 'also rans'. Geographers sometimes refer to the group of regions comprising the South East, East Anglia and East and West Midlands as the 'centre' and the remaining, more remote ones, as the 'periphery'. In these terms the centre pulled away strongly before the war, containing 50.3% of all manufacturing jobs in 1951 compared to 42% 30 years earlier. Since then,

Table 4.1 Gini coefficients: manufacturing employment change.

	Regional*	County†
1921–31	5.6	2.9
1931–51	5.4	2.4
1951–61	2.9	2.1
1961–71	3.1	3.6
1921–71	13.4	4.7

*As defined in Fig. 4.1

† As defined in Fig. 4.3

Annsborough Industrial ▶
Estate, Craigavon New Town
One of five industrial estates
incorporated in the New
Town plan for Craigavon
(County Armagh), (see
Chapter 5), designed both the
attract new industry to a
'problem region' as a whole,
and also to demagnetise its
dominant economic
agglomeration (Belfast). The
part of the estate shown
makes extensive use of basic
'building block' advance
factory units of some 8000
sq.ft., built originally by the
New Town authority, some of
which are subdivided and
others amalgamated, making
a total of 29 separate sites.
Good road access for freight
and employees is important
to the estate's internal layout
and to its wider regional
context — Belfast is only
some 35 kms away along the
province's M1 motorway (in
the top of the photo). The
estate's agricultural setting
both avoids environmental
problems resulting when
factories and homes are
cheek-by-jowl, and also
allows scope for later
expansion. The present (1982)
tenants include firms in
electronics, shirts, meat
products, baking, printing,
car accessories,
construction, and medical
disposables, exemplifying the
broad industrial base of
modern industrial estates.

Kindly supplied by the
Department of the
Environment for Northern
Ireland.

Ravenscraig steelworks ▶
Begun in the semi-rural
outskirts of Motherwell by
the Colville company in 1954,
this is now one of the British
Steel Corporation's five
integrated steel mills, using
the modern continuous
casting techniques preferred
by major steel users to make
high quality strip and plate
steel. In December 1981, the
plant was home to 245 coke
ovens, 2 sinter plants, 3 blast
furnaces, and 3 oxygen steel
converters (see Figure 6.6)
but, despite its technological
sophistication, its genesis
and survival have been

matters of political
controversy as much as steel
economics (see Chapter 6).
Its continued existence came
under very severe strain in
1982, when BSC, losing £1m
per day in a deeply recessed
national and world steel
market, had apparently
targetted for its closure, with
a loss of 5,000 jobs directly

and perhaps three times this
number through the
local/regional multiplier. A
highly efficient Scottish
lobby of all sectors of the
community and shades of
political opinion (including
the government's Scottish
Office) persuaded the
Cabinet to save the
landlocked plant for the

immediate future at least.

Kindly supplied by the British
Steel Corporation.

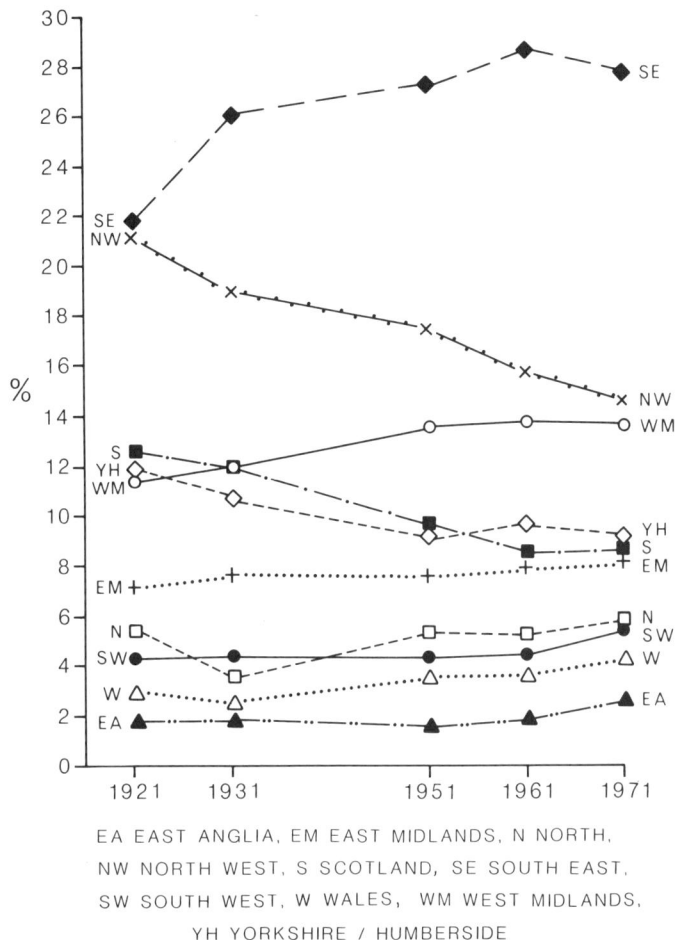

Fig. 4.1 Regional contributions to manufacturing employment in Great Britain, 1921-71. Most regions show a fairly consistent trend across the half-century, although the North, the South East and Yorkshire/Humberside change direction at one date or another. South-East England has pulled well clear of the rest of the field, which has become more bunched over time. *Source:* calculated from Lee (1979).

EA EAST ANGLIA, EM EAST MIDLANDS, N NORTH,
NW NORTH WEST, S SCOTLAND, SE SOUTH EAST,
SW SOUTH WEST, W WALES, WM WEST MIDLANDS,
YH YORKSHIRE / HUMBERSIDE

however, the periphery has fought back, restricting the 'central' share in 1971 to only 52.4%. Some peripheral regions showed increased individual contributions. Other analyses, drawing on different data, confirm that the centre–periphery gap is widening less rapidly than before (Keeble 1976).

At the finer, county, scale the trend is towards a wider dispersal of manufacturing employment (Fig. 4.2) (as it is among employment as a whole), whichever 'n' value is adopted. Dispersal was more rapid before 1931 than in the subsequent two decades, but has quickened again since 1951. Fig. 4.3 shows which countries are growing or contracting in absolute terms and those with an increasing or declining share of national manufacturing. Thus against a 'pre-war' average national manufacturing increase of some 120%, 12 counties grew absolutely but also declined relatively, while the near-stability of national manufacturing employment 'post-war' totals means county relative and absolute trends are almost always in the same direction.

Two new features stand out from these maps. First, a pre-war concentration of leading manufacturing growth counties in the immediate vicinity of London becomes increasingly diffused post-war throughout southern England. Here, then, we can help reconcile the increased regional prominence of the South East (Fig. 4.1) with the post-1951 county trends towards dispersal (Fig. 4.2). Second, and less obvious, is the decline of manufacturing employment in the major conurbations.

Fig. 4.2 Concentrations of Great Britain's manufacturing employment at the county level. Manufacturing employment is consistently more clustered geographically than total employment, and both display a steady decline in concentration over the 50 years. As would be expected, membership of the top 5...20 countries is fairly consistent from year to year, and is usually the same for manufacturing and total employment for any one year.
Source: as for Fig. 4.1

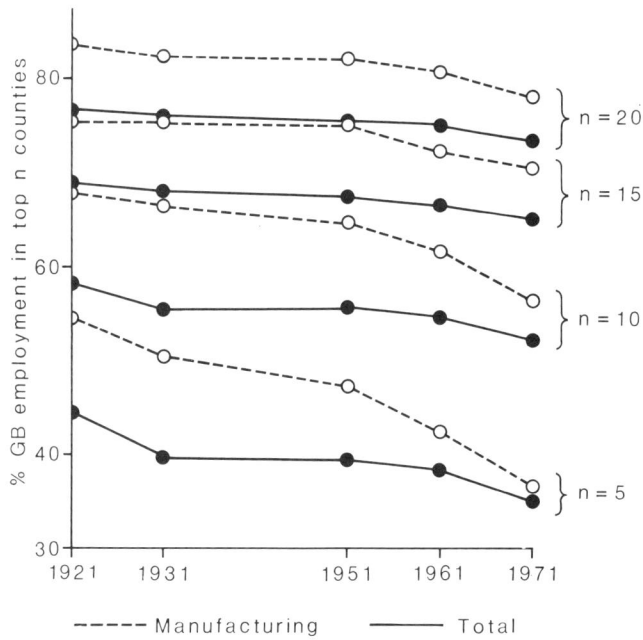

Fig. 4.3 Percentage changes in manufacturing jobs by county, pre-war and post-war. A general diffusion of 'high growth' counties from the London area stands out after 1951, as does the rise of manufacturing jobs in several peripheral counties, notably in the North and Scotland.
Source: as for Fig. 4.1.

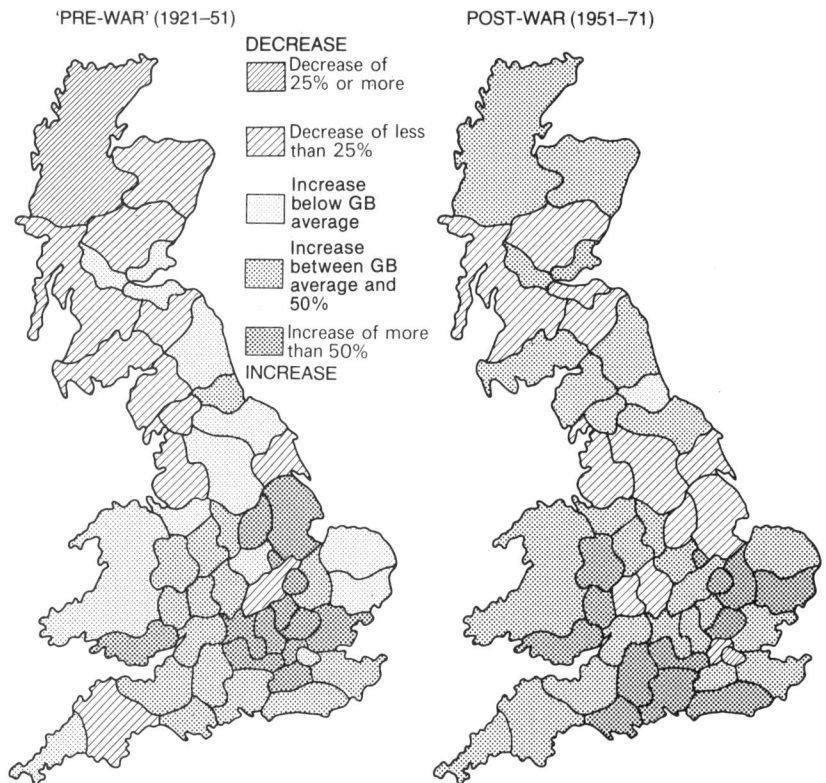

County boundary alignments prevent our doing full justice to this important aspect of Britain's manufacturing geography here (see Chapter 5), but for London and Birmingham (part of Warwickshire) Fig. 4.3 shows post-war declines contrasting with prosperity in surrounding counties. London's decline is particularly dramatic, and spills over into Middlesex, the county it absorbed administratively in 1965: a pre-war

Fig. 4.4 Manufacturing as a proportion of total regional employment levels in Great Britain, 1921-71. Although the rank order of the 10 regions is broadly unchanged (hence very few 'cross-overs' among the lines) regional convergence is very clear. Six regions decline from 1921 to 1971, the East Midlands is much the same, and only three increase. This is what the stage model (Fig. 4.9) would lead us to expect in advanced regional economies. For key, see Fig. 4.1. *Source:* as for Fig. 4.1.

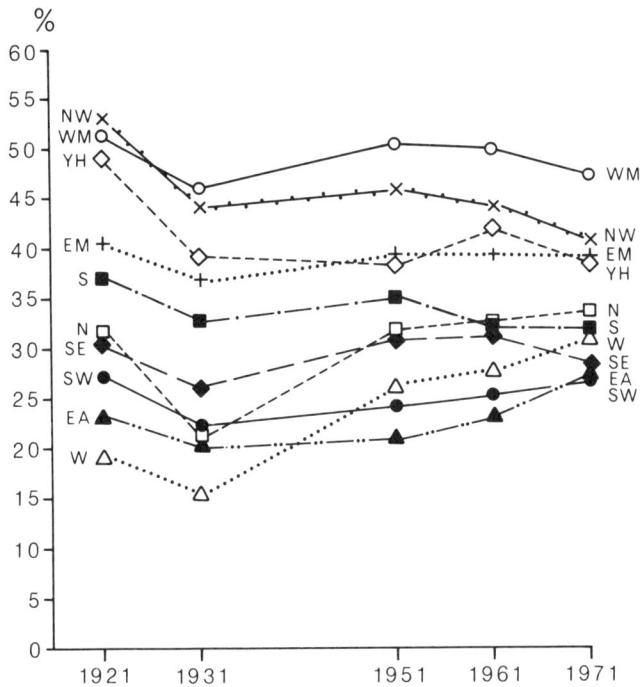

manufacturing employment growth of 21% turned into a massive post-war decline of 51%, while London's share of national manufacturing dropped slightly from 12.2% (1921) to 11.8% (1951), but then plummetted to 5.7% in 1971.

Regions and counties: manufacturing dependence

Fig. 4.4 shows trends since 1921 in manufacturing's share of regional employment. Apart from the universal dip in the graphs in 1931 the dominant feature is of convergence. In 1921 the 10 regions ranged over 33 percentage points, but by 1971 this was marginally under 20. In some traditional industrial regions the manufacturing share has been declining from weakness in the regional manufacturing base (the North West, Scotland, Yorkshire/Humberside). In other regions the influx of new manufacturing activity has shifted the emphasis from primary employment. In Wales, for example, the 10.1% of the 1921 employed workforce in 'mining and quarrying' (largely coalmining) had fallen to 4.5% by 1971, in the North the corresponding fall was from 22.5% to 4.7%, while the comparable figures for 'agriculture, fisheries and forestry' for East Anglia fell from 27.9% to 8.0%, and for the South West from 15.5% to 5.5%. The economically strong central regions of the South East and West Midlands show a different trend again. Here, while the 1971 share of national manufacturing exceeds that for 1921, the role of manufacturing in both regional economies falls over the same period. The explanation lies in the rise of tertiary employment, whose share increased from 64% to 68% (South East) and 48% to 55% (West Midlands) over this period.

County-scale analysis shows features that have been met before (Fig. 4.5). First, a pre-war pattern of manufacturing increase in the inner South East diffuses more widely after 1951. Secondly, a clear centre–periphery

Fig. 4.5 Pre-war and post-war changes in manufacturing's share of employment at the county level. The figures mapped here are the percentage-point differences at the proportion of jobs in manufacturing between the start and end years (thus in Cornwall it changed from 15.6% (1921) to 12.6% (1951) to 15.3% (1971)). The very varied performance of different parts of Scotland since 1951 is a nice example of how the equivalent regional-level changes (Fig. 4.4) can conceal much interesting geographical detail. *Source:* as for Fig. 4.1.

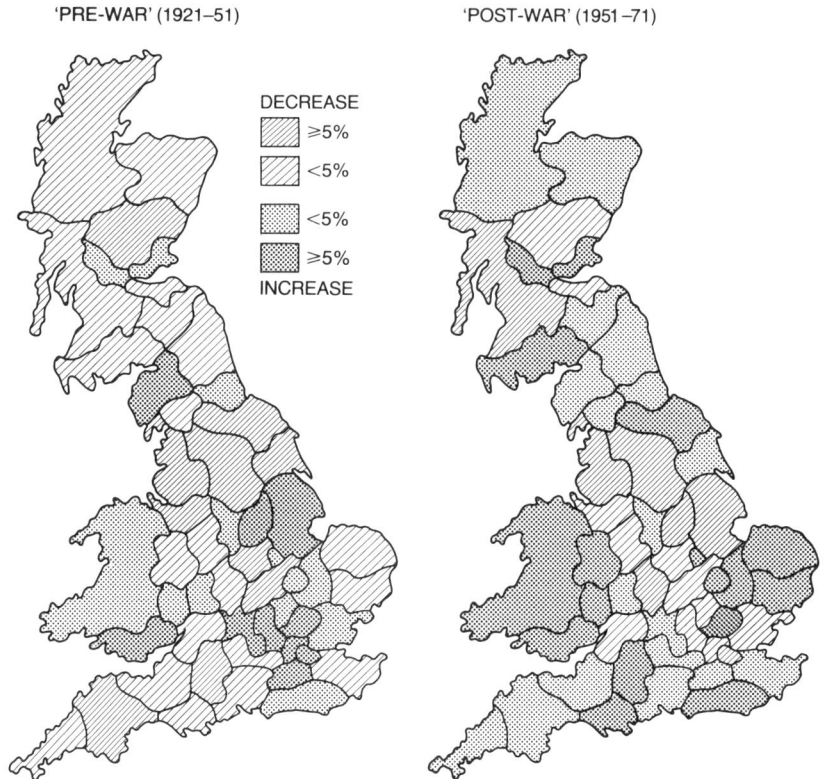

'PRE-WAR' (1921–51)   'POST-WAR' (1951–71)

DECREASE
≥5%
<5%
<5%
≥5%
INCREASE

Table 4.2 Share of manufacturing in county employment.

	Number of counties			
	1921–51		1951–71	
	Increasing	Decreasing	Increasing	Decreasing
Central regions	17	10	16	11
Peripheral regions	5	20	18	7

Note: 1 Counties as defined in Fig. 4.3.

2 Central regions = South East, East Anglia, East Midlands (including Lincolnshire), West Midlands; peripheral regions = remainder.

division pre-war goes into reverse post-war (Table 4.2): almost half (25) of the counties 'change direction' from increase to decrease or vice versa after 1951. Thirdly, post-war decline again appears in London and Birmingham.

Regional industrial structure

Changes in the industrial structure of particular regions, and in the geography of particular industries, can be examined for 1921-71 in ways explained in Appendix 1. All regions show a declining 'index of distinctiveness' as all move closer to the national industrial structure. The North West replaces Scotland as the least distinctive region, but the West Midlands remains the most distinctive (Fig. 4.6a). The 'index of diversity' (Fig. 4.6b) also falls, testifying to a greater spread of regional employment over all manufacturing sectors. All regions are less narrowly based in manufacturing terms in 1971 than 50 years earlier, except for the West Midlands where dependence on a few sectors, and a few firms in those sectors, remains high (Chapter 6). Its present phase of economic

Fig. 4.6 The industrial profiles of Britain's regions, 1921-71. Two indices (explained in Appendix 1) show how the manufacturing profiles of most regions have moved away from heavy dependency on a few sectors towards the national norm (a) and to a more even spread over all possible manufacturing categories (b). The West Midlands is somewhat out of line in (a) and very much so in (b). For key see Fig. 4.1. *Source:* as for Fig. 4.1.

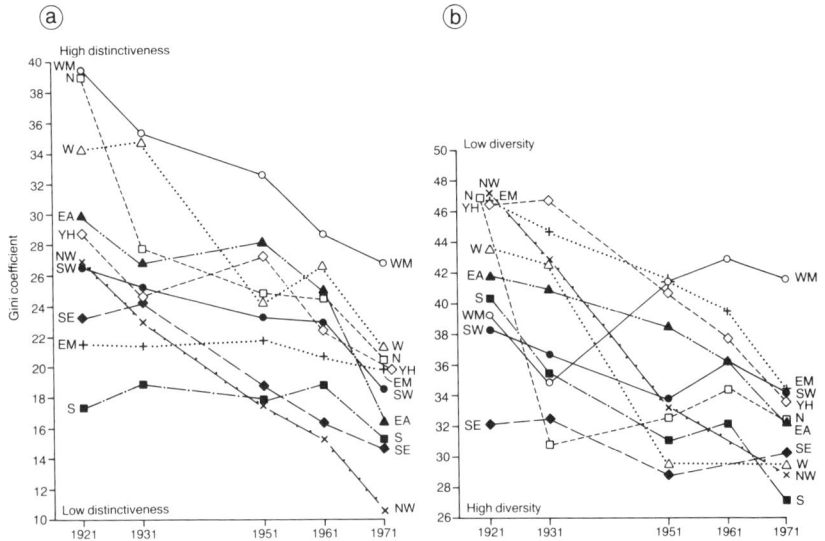

decline suggests it may now be paying for its eccentric behaviour on these two indices.

These various aspects of economic change over 50 years can be summarised in a fourfold classification of regions. In group I are two mature regions, South East and East Midlands, where manufacturing employment has risen in absolute terms and as a proportion of national manufacturing, but service jobs have risen even faster. In the 'declining regions' group II (North West, Yorkshire/Humberside and Scotland) manufacturing is falling in all three respects. In the 'up and coming' group III (East Anglia, South West, North and Wales), manufacturing increases in all three ways, while the West Midlands stands alone in the 'vulnerable' group IV, with its perverse and unique decrease in diversity, while otherwise sharing the characteristics of group I.

Industrial location patterns

The reverse side of the coin, the indices of industrial 'distinctiveness' and 'dispersal' (not illustrated, but see Appendix 1) show almost universal decline. Of 17 industries analysed only the chemicals industry is more distinctive in 1971 than 1921 (perhaps because of the high scale economies of capitally-intensive chemical manufacture), and only the very small 'coal and petroleum products' industry becomes less widely spread over time. After 1921, it seems, industries have been emerging from their formal regional strongholds, and regions have been throwing off the shackles of their former specialisms.

Location quotient analysis

The 'location quotient' (see Appendix 1) can be used to examine industrial and regional trends together. Fig. 4.7 suggests some decline of 'major' clusters (LQ > 2.0), with an increase in 'minor' ones (1.0 < LQ < 2.0). This, of course, reinforces the convergent trend among regional economies already noted. Well established industrial concentrations like vehicles and bricks/pottery/glass in the West Midlands, and textiles in the North West, weakened after 1951. However, we should not overlook the very first comment of this section—on

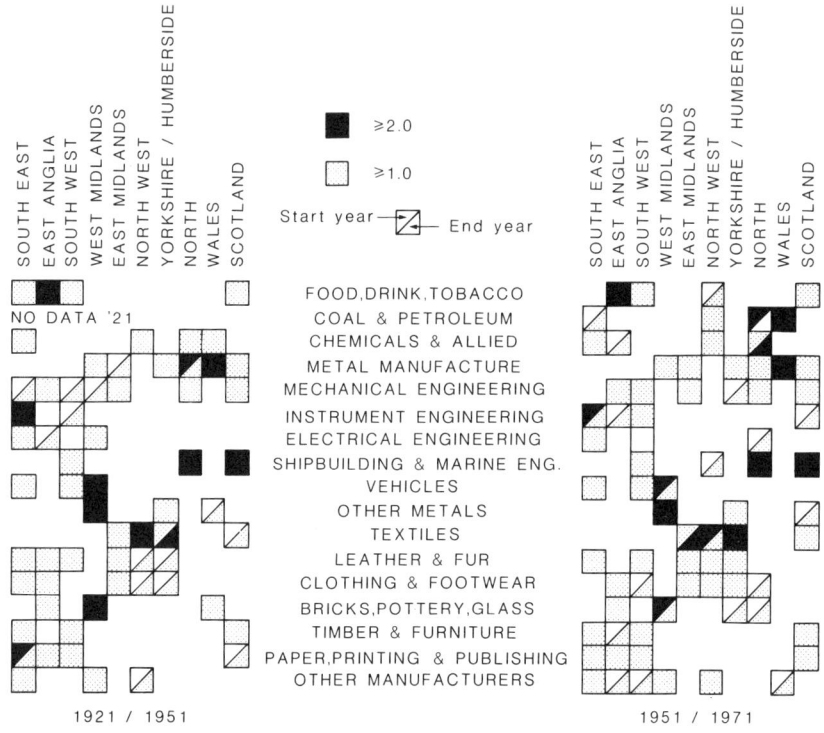

Fig. 4.7 Regional industrial specialisation in Great Britain, 1921-71. Location quotients (see Appendix 1) of 2.0 or more (labelled 'major clusters' in the text) become relatively less common throughout the half-century and 'minor clusters' very much more apparent. Interpreting these clusters is not always straightforward: new ones need not be accompanied by an absolute increase in regional jobs in the relevant industry, nor their disappearance by a fall. *Source:* as for Fig. 4.1.

stability. Thus many 'major' concentrations are constant features of the five decades. Some 41 clusters (major and minor) are common to both 1921 and 1971, representing respectively 69% and 59% of the stock of clusters in those years.

Since 1921, then, the manufacturing contributions of Britain's counties, regional industrial structures and the geography of particular industries, all show convergence. Very similar evidence of industrial and geographical convergence in Britain has been produced by other researchers by different research routes. Keeble (1976, Ch. 3) provides a neat summary of this evidence, and stresses (p. 44) how 'the relationship between location and manufacturing structure appears to be weakening substantially at the present time'.

Explanations

Manufacturing geography and regional economic health

Explaining these trends is less easy than identifying them, yet it is crucially important, given that manufacturing acts as the 'basic' stimulus for economic growth. Look at the geography of regional economic health in Britain (Fig. 4.8). Here is much that we have seen in the manufacturing sector: a prosperous centre and an unhealthy periphery. The sole exception is the South West, which is more 'central' in its prosperity than its location. Comparable analyses of other developed countries, for example Ireland, Italy, France, Sweden, Finland, Norway, have produced similar centre–periphery differences of economic health, and the regional policies instituted by their national governments show similar concentric patterns of regional aid to counteract these 'health' gradients, as also applies in Britain (see Clout 1981).

POPULATION GROWTH 1951–1964
☐ Above UK rate of change
■ Below UK rate of change

NET MIGRATION 1951–1964
☐ Net increase
■ Net decrease

EMPLOYMENT GROWTH 1953–1963
☐ Above UK rate of change
■ Below UK rate of change

AVERAGE UNEMPLOYMENT 1962–1967
☐ Below UK average
■ Above UK average

HOUSING % post-1919 housing
no data
☐ Above UK average
■ Below UK average

SOCIAL CLASS Unskilled as % economically active & retired males 1961
no data
☐ Below UK average
■ Above UK average

INCOME Earned pre-tax income 1966–1965
no data
☐ Above UK average
■ Below UK average

% DERELICT LAND
no data
☐ Below UK average
■ Above UK average

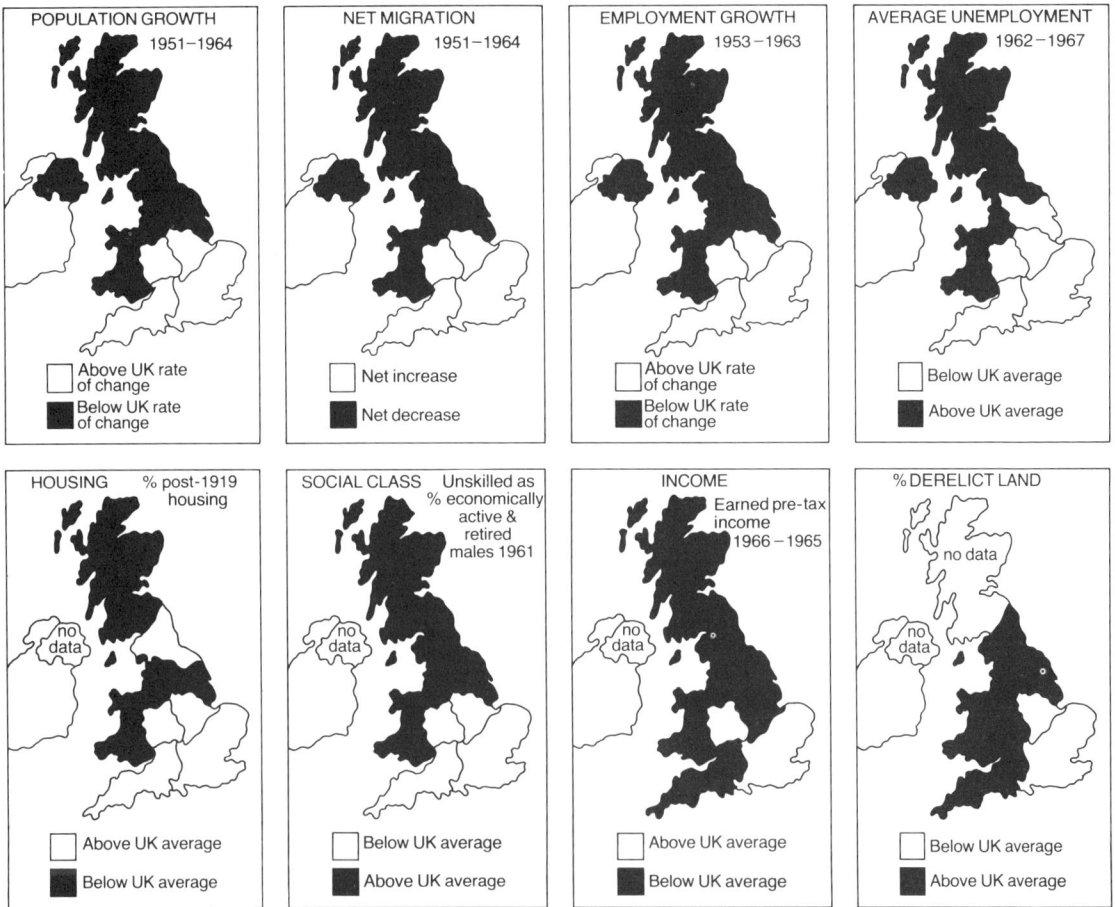

Fig. 4.8 Regional health in Great Britain. Selected indices to show the position in the 1950s and 1960s, from which a clear north-south division usually appears. More official social and economical statistics are published now than then, so it would be easy to update and extend this series of maps for the 1970s and 1980s using the Central Statistical Office's *Abstract of Regional Statistics* (1965-4), *Regional Statistics* (1978-80), and *Regional Trends* (thereafter). *Source:* Hammond, E. (1968) *An analysis of regional economic and social statistics* (Rowntree Research Unit, University of Durham).

Explaining Britain's manufacturing geography is thus more than a mere academic pastime. The catalogue of forces of Chapters 2 and 3 supplies the raw materials of explanation, but no answer as to how they are moulded into broad patterns of manufacturing activity on the ground. Attacks on this problem have come from four different directions: models of regional economic processes; models of the geography of political power; examining the role of industrial structure; and the 'components of change' approach.

Models of regional economic processes

'Regional growth theory' is the umbrella label given to a diverse set of models that try to explain differential regional growth patterns in terms of underlying economic processes.

(a) Stage (sector) models Regional economies are held to pass through a sequence of stages, A → B → C → . . . N. Stage A is the simplest, subsistence, stage while B → N represent progressively greater economic sophistication. Differences among a set of regions will result if either (i) they break out of the subsistence stage at different times and/or (ii) they move through the sequence at different rates.

The best known member of the stage-theory family is the 'Primary → Secondary → Tertiary' model (Fig. 4.9). Here a region's

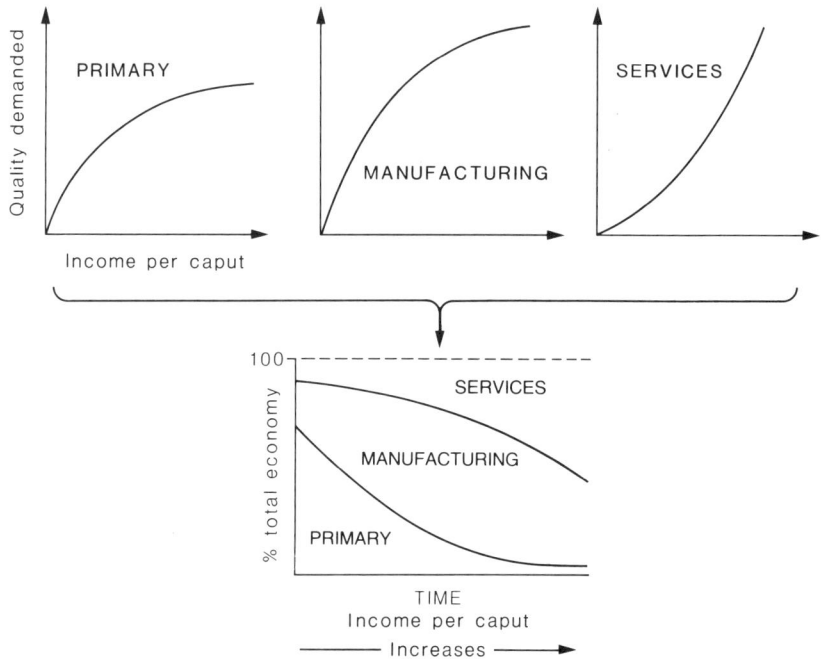

Fig. 4.9 A simple stage model of regional economic growth. With rising incomes, consumers shift their expenditure from primary goods to manufactures and then services, with knock-on effects on employment structures. But by glossing over variations within each sector, this diagram falsifies reality: not all industrial goods have the same income elasticity of demand as that of the 'manufacturing' curve.

employment emphasis progressively moves through the sequence, for two reasons. First, as incomes rise, so consumption moves to progressively more income-elastic items—from food to manufacturers to services—and, secondly, capital (machinery) replaces labour in the same sectoral sequence. We have already found some support for this model in the post-1921 behaviour of Britain's regions concerning manufacturing's share of total regional employment.

Even so, stage theories present little more than a cloak to lay over the history of regional economic development. At best it is coarsely woven, and fits some regions better than others. It fails to explain regional differences in sectoral development (why have the courses of the South East and the North West been different, for example?). Sequences can also be interrupted, reversed and repeated (certainly, the present manufacturing growth phase in the South West and East Anglia is not their first). Finally, where will it all end? Will all regions reach the end-stage (N), or does its attainment by some stymie others? After all, much of the South East's important tertiary sector (insurance, administration, broadcasting, and so on) serves national not regional markets.

(b) Export-base theory   While stage theories are preoccupied with regions serving their own internal markets, export-base theory focuses upon external ('export') demand. Growth follows a sequence summarised in Fig. 4.10, whereby the economy deepens and widens its export involvement, and spin-off sectors emerge and mature along the lines of the 'basic-multiplier' concept. By implication, if regions are faring badly this export sector needs attention.

While originally conceived in a very different geographical environment from that of modern Britain (North 1955), the export-base model still appeals. First, its emphasis on the 'openness' of regional economies (i.e. their involvement in external markets and competition) accords with Britain's deep involvement in intra- and international trade. Secondly,

Fig. 4.10 A five-stage model
to suggest how the export
sector can serve as the initial
trigger to regional economic
advance. The industry (-ies)
constituting the major export
sectors will vary from case to
case, but coal, textiles, ships
and steel would be popular
candidates in nineteenth-
century Britain. Their
replacement with newer
export-oriented industries
(e.g. motor cars, electronics,
man-made fibres) has been a
major thrust of regional
policy.

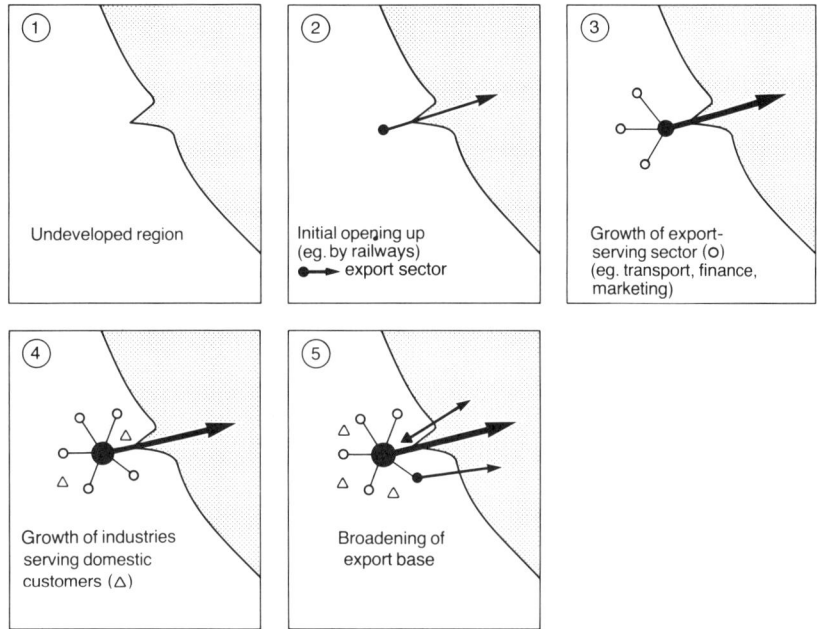

① Undeveloped region

② Initial opening up
(eg. by railways)
●━▶ export sector

③ Growth of export-
serving sector (O)
(eg. transport, finance,
marketing)

④ Growth of industries
serving domestic
customers (△)

⑤ Broadening of
export base

countless economic analyses of Britain's problem regions have highlighted the impoverished state of export staples, such as textiles, steel, ships, coal and, more recently, motor vehicles, in face of overseas competition (Chapter 5). Thirdly, the diversification of regional economies could represent the transition from narrow- to broad-based export sectors (Fig. 4.10). Fourthly, survey data on the geographical origins within Britain of national exports support the 'poor exports leads to poor economic health' argument: in 1964 the value of exports per worker in manufacturing varied inversely with regional assistance.

However, the theory glosses over supply constraints on exporting (such as shortages of capital and out-moded management attitudes), and ignores alternative ways of stimulating regional growth, such as immigration, reduced taxation and government investment (Tiebout 1956). The idea that 'basic leads, and non-basic follows' ignores the fact that attractive non-basic environments (good schools, theatres, pubs) can lure in 'basic' manufacturers. As a predictive device, too, the theory is unconvincing. It dodges the issues of whether regions will converge or diverge (important from the policy intervention viewpoint), and how long-term changes can thrust regional exports into reverse as in 'declining' regions like Northern Ireland (Chapter 5).

(c) Neoclassical models   Here is a group of models based on the free-market movement of resources among regions in search of optimal economic rewards. Consider the most simple case in Fig. 4.11. For some reason capital:labour ratios initially used in manufacturing a product differ between two regions, X and Y. Wages will be lower, and unit returns to capital higher, in Y. Under perfect competition labour will thus move to X and capital to Y, until the marginal rates of return of capital and of labour are equalised. With a great number of simplifying assumptions built in, this model leads to the eventual capital:labour ratio becoming 3:2 in both regions. Here we have a clear prediction towards the convergence of regional economic health. Policy-makers faced with

Time 1   Time 2

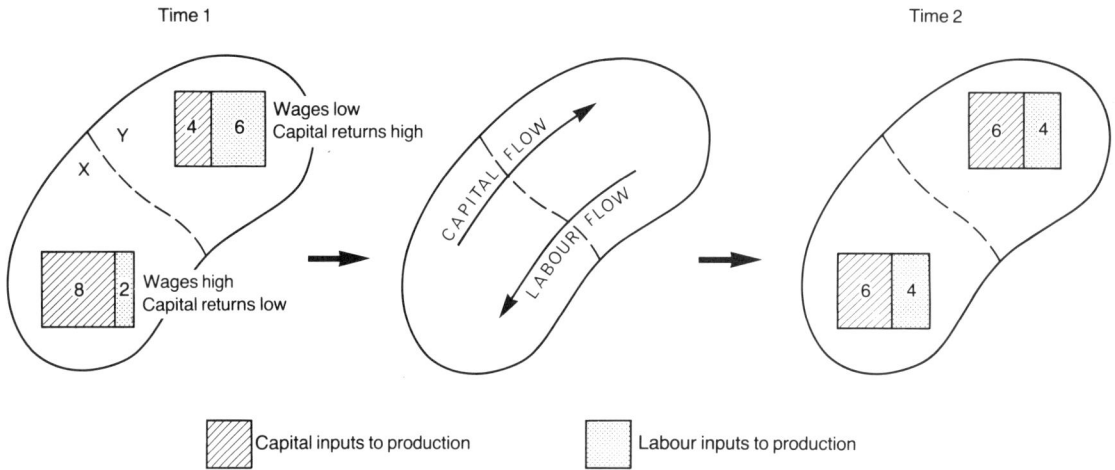

Wages low
Capital returns high

Wages high
Capital returns low

CAPITAL FLOW

LABOUR FLOW

▨ Capital inputs to production   ▢ Labour inputs to production

Fig. 4.11 A neoclassical view
of regional evolution. This
represents the simplest of a
whole family of neoclassical
models, where we assume
that just two resources
(labour and capital) are
equally mobile. The end
result is convergence upon
two identical regional
economies.

persistent inter-regional differences should thus oil the rusty wheels of the
space economy by improving the geographical mobility of resources. But,
unfortunately, this 'naive' neoclassical model excludes many crucial
factors such as economies of scale (and thus factor returns to scale), the
inherently greater mobility of capital than of labour, and the differential
mobility of different types of labour and capital (Armstrong and Taylor
1978). Labour immobility is probably the model's greatest weakness.
Inter-regional movement is a real headache for private householders, and
almost impossible for the one-third of families living in council housing.
Inadequate information also restricts long-distance movement. The
Wrexham Job Centre knows of local vacancies, may know of those in
Liverpool, but will have no idea of opportunities in Glasgow. British
assessments of the neoclassical model have had mixed success
(Richardson 1969, pp. 60-5). No evidence emerged of inter-regional
income convergence over 1949-65, but the directions of labour and capital
movements between regions were predicted rather better than by rival
models.

(d) Centre–periphery models   By chance or design one part of a
geographical area starts developing economically. This 'centre' comes to
dominate the rest of the space economy (Fig. 4.12): here demand rises
rapidly, economies of scale can be exploited and new investment made in
economic infrastructure. The centre becomes the area of political power,
of social progress, and develops a psychology of growth where innovation
flourishes. The periphery, in contrast, becomes a backwater: little
happens there, any development serves the centre's needs, and its
resources decamp to the centre. Regional economic health levels diverge.

After some time, though, relative fortunes may change. Costs spiral in
the centre, noise, pollution and congestion eat away at the environmental
appeal of central living, the centre's standards and innovations diffuse
outwards and governments implement wealth and welfare equalisation
policies across regions. Thus the gap between centre and periphery, if not
actually narrowing, at least stops growing as rapidly.

This model also appeals to geographers through its applicability to a
range of spatial scales: the centre can be the Low Countries/Ruhr in an
EEC context, London in the British one, or Newcastle in a north-eastern
one. We also find no problem in filling in the details of the 'spread' and

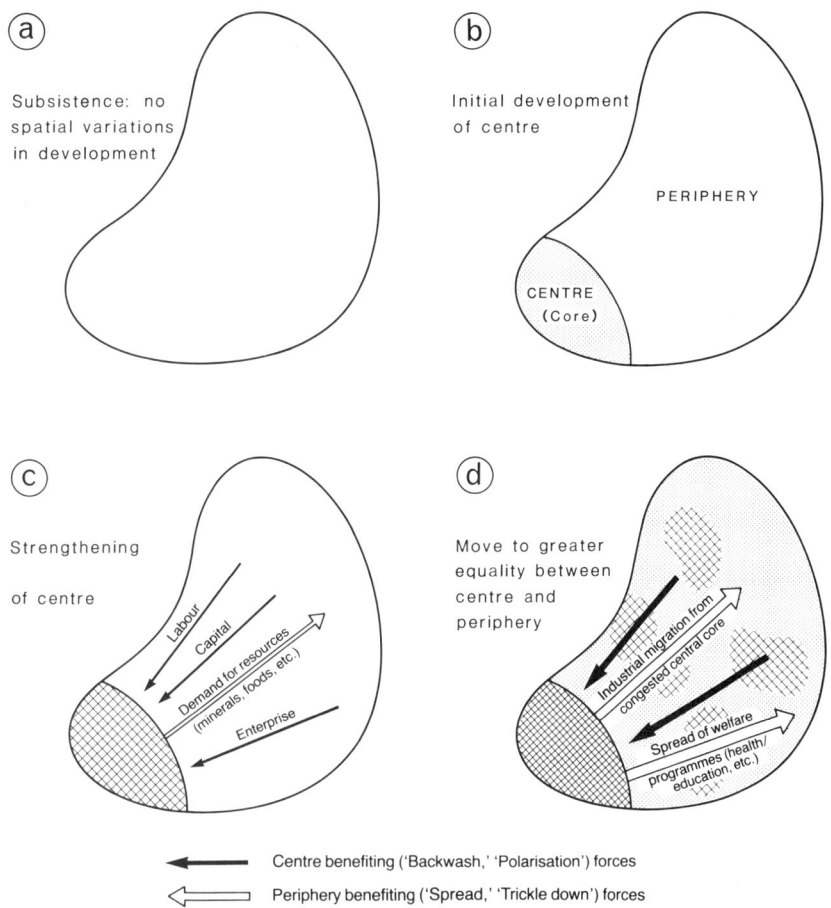

(a) Subsistence: no spatial variations in development

(b) Initial development of centre

PERIPHERY

CENTRE (Core)

(c) Strengthening of centre

Labour
Capital
Demand for resources (minerals, foods, etc.)
Enterprise

(d) Move to greater equality between centre and periphery

Industrial migration from congested central core
Spread of welfare programmes (health/ education, etc.)

⬅ Centre benefiting ('Backwash,' 'Polarisation') forces
⇦ Periphery benefiting ('Spread,' 'Trickle down') forces

'backwash' forces (Myrdal 1957). In the British case, for example, the latter could refer to market potential, transport centrality, access to government and the information environment, skilled labour and an attractive image, while cheaper resources, available land (and labour?) and regional planning lie in the former camp. Regional economic change since 1918 can also be interpreted in centre–periphery terms, in particular the switch from inter-regional divergence to convergence and the added service ingredient to an already prosperous 'centre'.

The problem is, though, that almost any trend can be fitted into some aspect of the centre–periphery sequence. It also becomes very difficult to pin down centre–periphery models to predictions of what will happen where, and when.

Power-based models

Now the emphasis switches from economic processes to political ones.

(a) Government power Two separate aspects can be isolated here:
(i) Buying votes: the 'pork barrel' Political parties and individual politicians, charges Professor Johnston (1979), may attempt to maximise votes to preserve their own geographical power bases. They do so through projects and policies that predispose 'goods' and 'bads' to fall selectively

on different areas. 'Opportunity' comes in the form of the broad geography of party support in Britain, with Conservatives dominating in central regions and Socialists in the periphery. Has Labour's greater emphasis on regional policy, then, reflected the safeguarding of peripheral votes, or socialist ideas of inter-regional equality, or widening inter-regional prosperity differences during their terms of office? Politicians rarely admit that particular actions are taken on political, vote-maximising grounds, although some saw this as behind the awarding of Development Area status to Grimsby in 1967 and approval of the Humber Bridge a year earlier on the eve of crucial by-elections in Humberside. However, such isolated cases scarcely constitute a convincing model of regional economic differentials. In Northern Ireland the 'pork barrel' has received more attention, but with respect to intra-regional differentials (Chapter 5).

(ii) Neglect of the periphery   Equally hard to substantiate is the view that regional problems arise as 'the concern of the capital for its surrounding political space decreases with the square of the distance from it' (Kohr in Glasson 1978, p. 121). No British government would ever admit to this, arguing instead its consistent and deep concern for regional issues. But the sum total of information, advice and criticism that assails politicians must have *some* hint of 'distance decay' from Westminster, hard though it may be to measure.

(b) Politics of the firm   Holland (1976) argues that large capitalist corporations ('meso-economic' agents, he calls them) hold the key to regional development and regional problems. They exert great power over prices and markets, and cluster in the economy's growing industrial sectors. Frequently their geographical behaviour and location run counter to government regional policy. Headquarters are located in central areas, and problem regions receive standardised, 'screwdriver' operations, needing no great skill and creating little regional spin-off. The multi-national's ability to tap very cheap Third World labour, to manipulate where and when profits are earned and taxes paid, and to fix prices, all reduce the allure of Britain's regional incentives. Without a wholesale reassessment of relationships between governments and multi-nationals, says Holland, centre–periphery differences will remain.

British-owned companies can have the same effects. Growth through acquisitions and mergers has seen South East-based companies absorb those in other regions, adding to central control and peripheral dependency (Leigh and North 1978). After acquisition, service linkages and the decision-making parts of the acquired companies are redirected to the home region of the acquirer.

Both multinationals and British companies thus contribute to the branch-plant economy of peripheral regions, whereby control of manufacturing activity is vested elsewhere. Employment may still be supplied in quantity, but its quality causes concern. Branch-plant jobs are seen as low-status, predominantly female, and vulnerable, since in hard times the first company reaction is to cut back at the branches. Recent research suggests things are not as straightforward as this (Watts 1981), although the alleged evils of outside control remain an important public issue.

Shift – share example of regional employment change

South	Cars	TVs	Total
1970	30	65	95
1980	25	260	285
North			
1970	70	15	85
1980	35	40	75
National			
1970	100	80	180
1980	60	300	360

$\therefore$ For *South*

Share
$$= (360/180) - 95$$
$$= +95 \text{ new jobs}$$

Structural shift
$$= \{(30 \times 60/100) - 30\}$$
$$\text{[for cars]}$$
$$+ \{(65 \times 300/80) - 65\}$$
$$\text{[for TVs]}$$
$$- (+95)$$
$$\text{[share]}$$
$$= -12 + 178 \cdot 75 - 95$$
$$= +71 \cdot 75 \text{ new jobs}$$

Locational shift
$$= (285 - 95)$$
$$\text{[1980 – 1970 jobs in south]}$$
$$- (95 + 71 \cdot 75)$$
$$\text{[share + structural shift]}$$
$$= +23 \cdot 25 \text{ new jobs}$$

Results

	South	North
Share	+95	+85
Structural shift	+71·75	−71·75
Locational shift	+23·25	−23·25
Total change, 1970 – 80	+190	−10

Some geographers argue that the movement of branch factories to the peripheral regions shows the success of government regional policy (see later in this chapter). Others who interpret changes in regional economic performance through a Marxist framework, based on class conflict, see it more as the outcome of the crises of declining profits 'inevitable' in the capitalist system. These in turn encourage firms to find operating locations with cheap, non-militant (and hence often female) labour to restore their profitability.

The role of industrial structure: shift and share analysis

While itself a reflection of deeper causes, one major contributing factor in regional distress may be structural weakness. Are problem regions doing badly because of a bias in their industrial structures towards declining sectors and a bias in prosperous regions towards growing ones? If 'yes', solutions may lie in somehow upgrading the industrial structures of the poor regions.

Shift and share analysis, the most popular technique for this type of study, assumes that the economic growth or decline of a region is composed of three elements.

(a) The share This relates to the amount of growth (or decline) of some larger area (usually the nation) of which the region is part. If the nation grows by 10% between 1970 and 1980 the 'share' for each constituent region is a corresponding 10% growth.

(b) The structural shift This is the growth (decline) expected because of the particular industrial structure of the region.

(c) The locational (?) shift This refers to the residual growth (decline) unexplained by (a) and (b). Geographers find it almost irresistible to see in this the spatial position of the region within the nation (hence 'locational'), but this interpretation cannot be proved from the technique alone (hence '?'). It may also reflect, say, regional organisational or occupational structure (along 'branch-plant economy' lines) or, as shift–share's critics argue, problems of the technique, or random 'noise' in the data.

An example will show how shift–share works, taking a hypothetical 2-region 'nation', with just one declining industry (motor cars) and one expanding one (television sets). Once the national share has been allocated (an increase of $360/180 = 2.0$) the South emerges as a region both of good structure (biased towards television sets) and also a positive 'locational' shift. At the other extreme, the North, handicapped by its motor car sector, does even worse than the structural shift suggests. It fails to meet the national growth rate in television production and declines by more than the national rate of decrease for motor car employment. Shift–share, then, can identify important components in the differential growth of a set of regions. While the technique is subject to much criticism (see Richardson 1978, pp. 204-6), Fothergill and Gudgin (1979) have recently supplied a stout defence in the British context. No one would claim it provides all the answers but shift–share's champions see it as a simple and robust technique for a first foray into problems of regional growth.

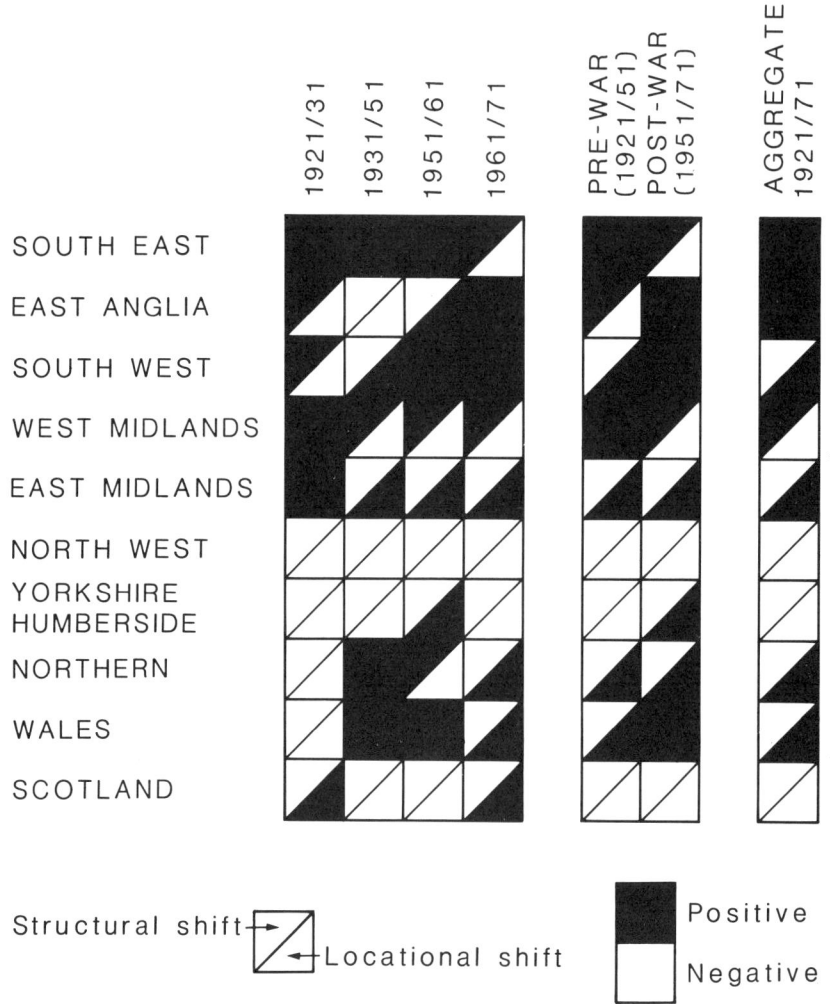

Fig. 4.13 Shift and share performance of Britain's regions, 1921-71. Note how the signs of the two shifts vary for many regions, depending on the time period. The pattern of many of the 'locational' shift results, over time and among the regions, could point to the effectiveness of regional policy. *Source:* calculated from Lee (1979).

Lee's data allow a series of 10 region/17 industry shift–shares to be run for 1921-71 (Fig. 4.13). Structure seems constantly 'good' in the South East and West Midlands, and constantly 'bad' in Scotland, Yorkshire/Humberside, and the North West, while 'location' is persistently good and bad respectively in the East Midlands and North West. Amid the inconsistent remainder the bad recent locational scores of the main central regions are noteworthy. Four of the six peripheral regions have a positive post-1961 locational shift.

Fig. 4.14 shows a different trend, based on the magnitude of the share and two shifts, irrespective of their signs. In (a) we can see how these three ingredients combine to produce the actual employment change observed in one region. Taking all 10 regions together (b), overall trends are consistent with those in the South West (a): structural shift maintains a steady if modest role, the national 'share' dominates the pre-1951 period but declines thereafter, while locational shift has risen dramatically since 1951. Although not illustrated, when the individual regions are examined in detail it is only in Yorkshire/Humberside that the locational shift is not the largest element in 1961-71 and only here, too, does the 1961-71 locational shift contribution fall behind the comparable 1921-31 figure. As regional structures move closer to the national norms, national

Fig. 4.14 Shift and share at the regional level, 1921-71. (a) The South West shows the declining role of national (share) forces since 1931, and the massive rise of the 'locational shift'. Structural forces seem weak throughout. (b) The national picture, averaged over all 10 regions (by giving equal weight to each) also shows how the 'locational' shift has become the major component in regional employment change, be it positive or negative. *Source:* as for Fig. 4.13.

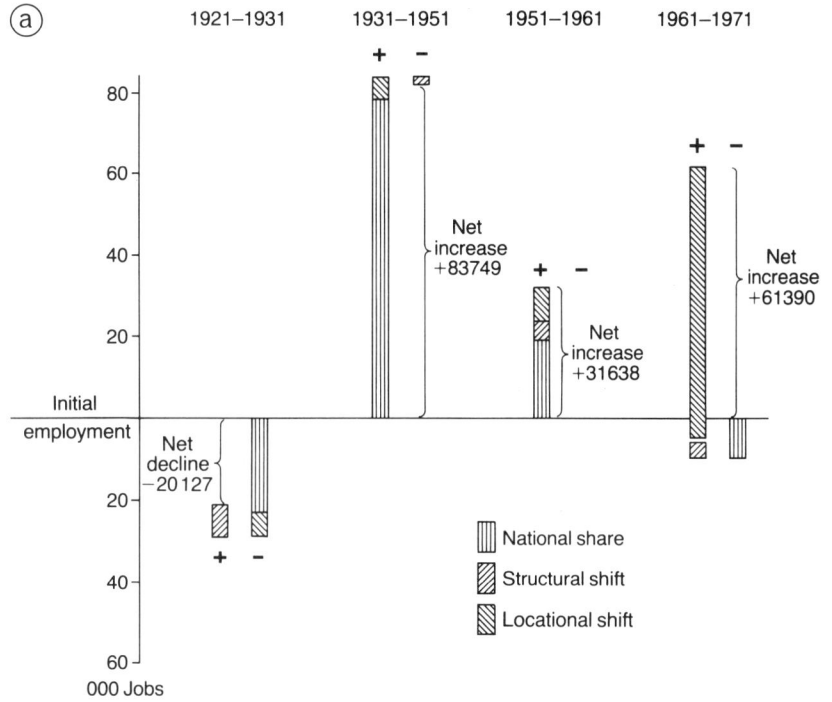

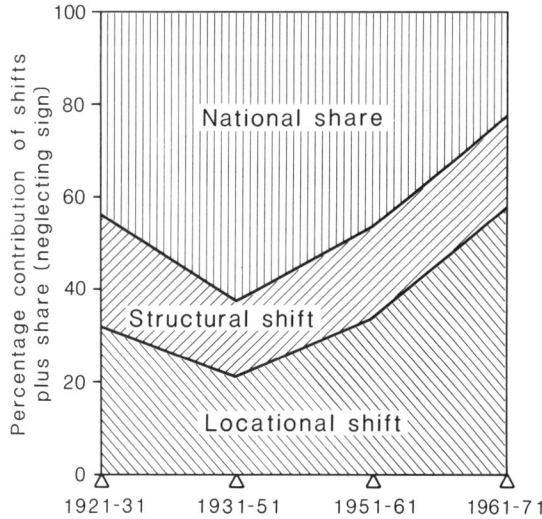

trends have become weaker at 'explaining' differential regional performance and regionally-based (locational) shifts more so. Similar results have emerged from other shift–shares in Britain, using different data bases and time periods (Keeble 1976, Ch. 3).

Why has there been this rise of the 'locational' shift? One reason may be the increasing importance of intra-industry organisational structure in determining where employment expands and contracts. Another may be the greater success of regional policy in the 1960s. Low structural shifts may result from the diversity of modern manufacturing industry so that, say, national 'electrical engineering' trends (used to calculate structural

Fig. 4.15 Net and gross employment change. An example to show how 6 components of change combine to produce the overall, 'net', pattern of regional employment change. In practice, it is very difficult to build up the job accounts of even a small area in this way.

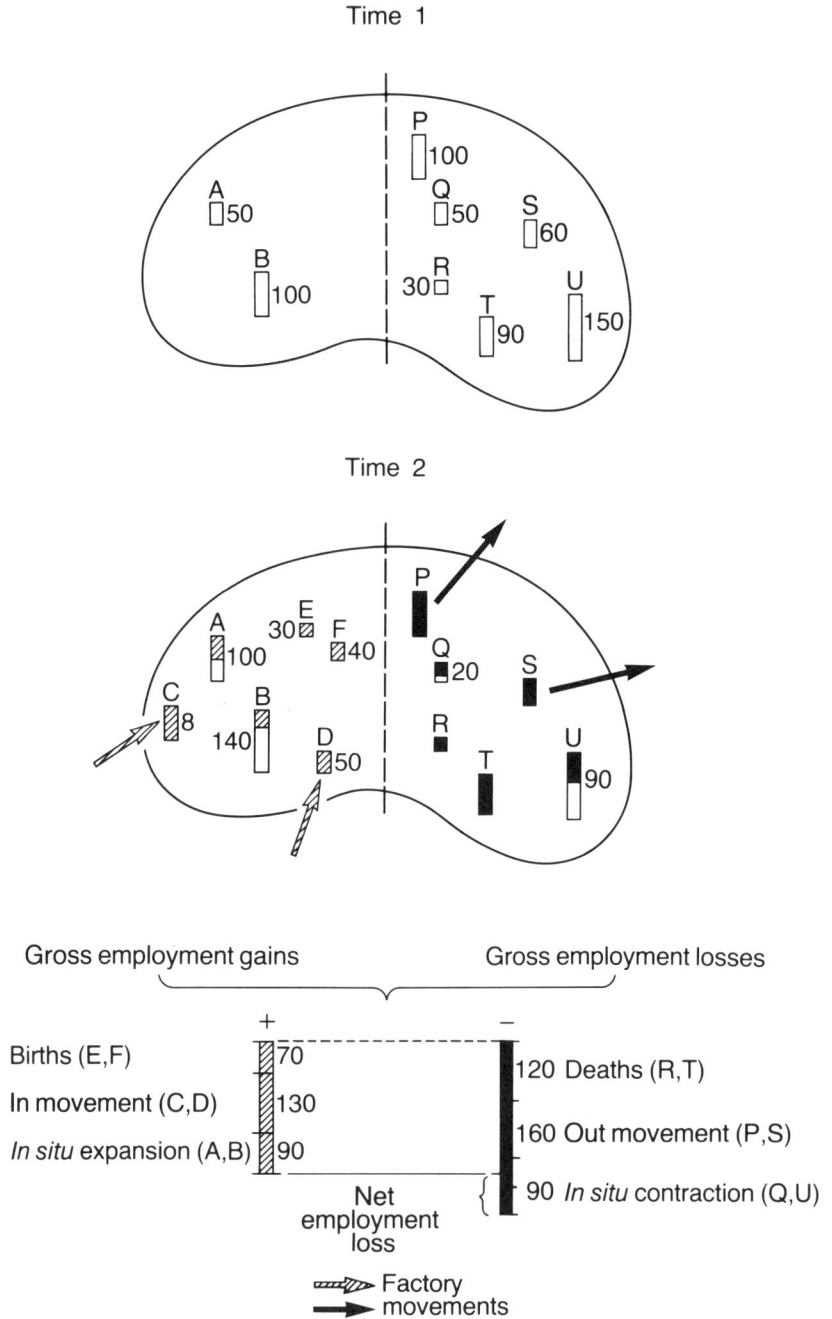

Time 1

Time 2

Gross employment gains — Gross employment losses

	+	−	
Births (E,F)	70	120	Deaths (R,T)
In movement (C,D)	130	160	Out movement (P,S)
In situ expansion (A,B)	90	90	*In situ* contraction (Q,U)

Net employment loss

Factory movements

shifts) are irrelevant to the types of electrical engineering firms found in particular regions. Or, again, as regions become less specialised, so structural shifts become suppressed—if all motorcycles were made in the North and nothing else, all the North's decline would be 'explained' by the share plus structural shift.

Components of change: the 'how' of growth

Most official employment statistics measure only the resultant, or net, change of several processes of change. We know that manufacturing

| | 1945–65 | | | | 1966–75 | | | |
| | Moves | | Jobs (000) | | Moves | | Jobs (000) | |
	In	Balance	In	Balance	In	Balance	In	Balance
Losers								
South East	104	− 628	31.6	− 189.4	199	− 748	11.9	− 90.5
West Midlands	58	− 157	8.7	− 83.4	27	− 160	1.4	− 20.1
Intermediate								
East Midlands	106	− 22	26.9	− 4.1	178	+ 53	13.2	− 1.7
Yorkshire and Humberside	112	− 26	31.3	− 11.7	90	+ 3	8.9	+ 1.6
Gainers								
East Anglia	127	+ 105	16.7	+ 5.9	252	+ 215	16.4	+ 14.1
North West	215	+ 64	104.8	+ 76.6	149	+ 39	20.3	+ 9.0
South West	164	+ 126	36.9	+ 25.9	234	+ 170	19.6	+ 16.6
North	220	+ 203	89.6	+ 84.4	209	+ 182	35.6	+ 33.2
Scotland	259	+ 231	94.7	+ 89.8	215	+ 194	28.0	X
Wales	285	+ 269	93.7	+ 85.2	281	+ 263	32.6	+ 31.7
Northern Ireland	120	+ 120	39.8	+ 39.8	84	+ 67	C	X

Notes: C = Confidential

X = Positive but unquantifiable owing to confidentiality.

Table 4.3 Inter-regional movement. *Sources:* Board of Trade (1968); Department of Industry (1981).

employment in the South West grew by 61,000 in 1961-71, but not whether this represented a gross increase of 61,000 over the decade, with no offsetting job loss, whether 161,000 new jobs partly countered by a 100,000 job loss, or any other such combination. And if the second possibility, where have the 161,000 jobs come from and how have the 100,000 jobs been lost? Net changes give but a partial picture.

We can identify six major 'components' of gross employment change, three responsible for increases and three for losses (Fig. 4.15). These provide an important basis for policy prescriptions. For instance, a region where job losses come from the 'death' of local companies and gains from in-movement may be highly responsive to changes in regional policy and to measures to support indigenous industrial enterprises. What do we know about these different components of change in British manufacturing?

(a) Industrial migration Here we know quite a lot, including the fact that length of move shows a clear but inverse relationship to frequency of move. From this it might seem that industrial migration would have but a small role in the inter-regional patterns of manufacturing jobs discussed so far. Yet two governmental surveys (Board of Trade 1968; Department of Industry 1981) have still recorded substantial factory movement from one region to another. Between 1945 and 1965 some 1,521 such moves occurred and another 1,630 between 1966 and 1975, generating respectively an estimated 439,000 jobs (by 1966) and 168,100 (by 1975).

From the geography of inter-regional movement we can distinguish a clear-cut set of regional winners and losers (Table 4.3). The two dominant losers, the West Midlands and South East, provided 53% of inter-regional migration in the first of the above periods and 59% in the second. Each shows some 'bias' towards neighbouring regions in its pattern of destinations and each also shows a reduction in moves to more distant regions between the two periods, with the increase in South East-based

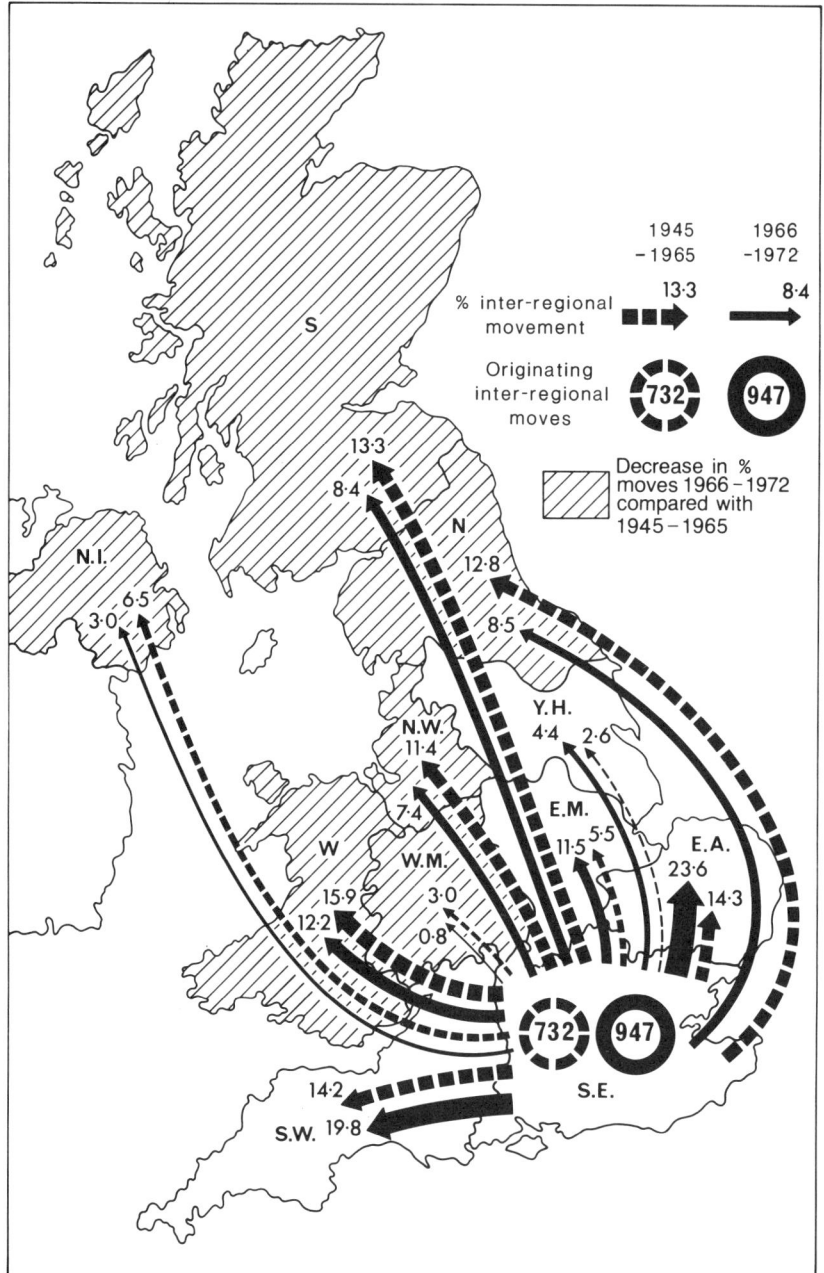

Fig. 4.16 Industrial migration from South East England, 1945-75. Numbers of moves from Britain's major source region of industrial migration were higher in the more recent period, but the proportion of them travelling long-distance to regions of greatest economic and social need was markedly lower. How might we explain this increased popularity of 'neighbouring' destinations? *Sources:* based upon Board of Trade (1968) and Department of Industry (1981).

movement to the South West and East Anglia especially impressive in absolute terms (Fig. 4.16). (Though whether this reflects the extension of regional planning incentives in the South West, the maturing of Expanded Towns in East Anglia (Chapter 5), or 'residential attractiveness' in both we can only speculate.) The earlier survey also details substantial intra-regional movement in some regions. For example, in the North West and Yorkshire/Humberside these are flows from one major industrial sub-region to another, but in the South East and West Midlands they are from the dominant conurbation to the less industrialised fringes.

Turning to impact, in 1945-65 in-migration generated respectively 29% and 21% of 1966 manufacturing employment in Wales and Northern Ireland. Similarly, had the South East not lost migrant jobs its 1966

Table 4.4 Branches and
transfers: contributions to
employment in movement of
destinations in Assisted
Areas. *Sources:* Board of
Trade (1968, p. 23); Nunn
(1980, p. 29).

	1945–65 Movement to Peripheral Areas*			1966–75 Movement to Assisted Areas⊬	
	1945–51	1952–9	1960–5	1966–71	1972–5
Transfers (%)	19.2	9.6	7.2	33.4	40.8
Branches (%)	80.7	90.3	92.8	66.6	59.2

*Northern Ireland, Scotland, Wales, North Merseyside, Devon and Cornwall.
⊬ Northern Ireland, Special Development Areas, Development Areas and Intermediate Areas.

manufacturing workforce would have been 9% greater on this basis alone. Long moves were the most prolific. On average inter-regional moves produced 323 jobs in 1966 while the intra-regional equivalent was not only lower (239) but led to a redistribution of jobs within the region, rather than a regional gain. Against this, long-distance moves were more likely to be of branches than 'lock, stock and barrel' transfers of complete factories (see Fig. 1.10). The 1945-65 survey certainly shows that branches dominate transfers in moves to Assisted Areas (Table 4.4), while the two are in balance elsewhere. The average branch plant eventually provides more jobs than the average transfer (by a ratio of 1.7:1 in the first period and 1.4:1 in the second) but brings less decision-making responsibility with it, threatening to make 'branch-plant economies' of the Assisted Areas. Since 1966 the part played by transfers in this same migration stream has risen (Table 4.4), but the stream itself is much smaller in terms of jobs created.

Important differences are found too in the types of firms that move. They tend to be large, to belong to multi-plant companies, to be oriented to national or international markets, to be concentrated in particular industries (clothing and footwear, engineering, vehicles, chemicals and 'miscellaneous') and to be expanding firms (Keeble 1976). All these characteristics are interrelated, and the last is of particular importance. Time after time surveys of mobile factories have found the dominant reason for moving is the inability to expand *in situ*, due to space and labour shortages, and to planning restrictions on growth (Keeble 1976). Firms only move when they have to, and this brings them within the clutches of regional policy. In so far as some firms forget about expansion if the only 'choice' is an Assisted Area, regional policy's critics argue that national growth is lost.

Finally, timing. We might expect 'peaks' of movement in two circumstances: first, when the economy is growing and secondly when regional policy is pursued most rigorously. To a degree these circumstances are opposites: when firms are expanding the economy is buoyant, output is high, labour is in demand, unemployment is low and regional policy is not strongly enforced. It is probable that 'policy vigour' is the more important factor. Before 1966 industrial movement, particularly inter-regional movement to the problem regions, had been higher in the two 'policy on' periods than the intervening 'boom' (Fig. 4.17). Moore and Rhodes (1976) have calculated the particular impact on movement of different regional policy devices between 1966 and 1971. IDC controls seem especially powerful. Overall, 'policy' produced an estimated 128 moves annually while normal economic pressures for expansion merely 10-15 per annum. Others have questioned the way in which this last element is measured by Moore and Rhodes, but their own estimates, based on slightly different assumptions, confirm the high

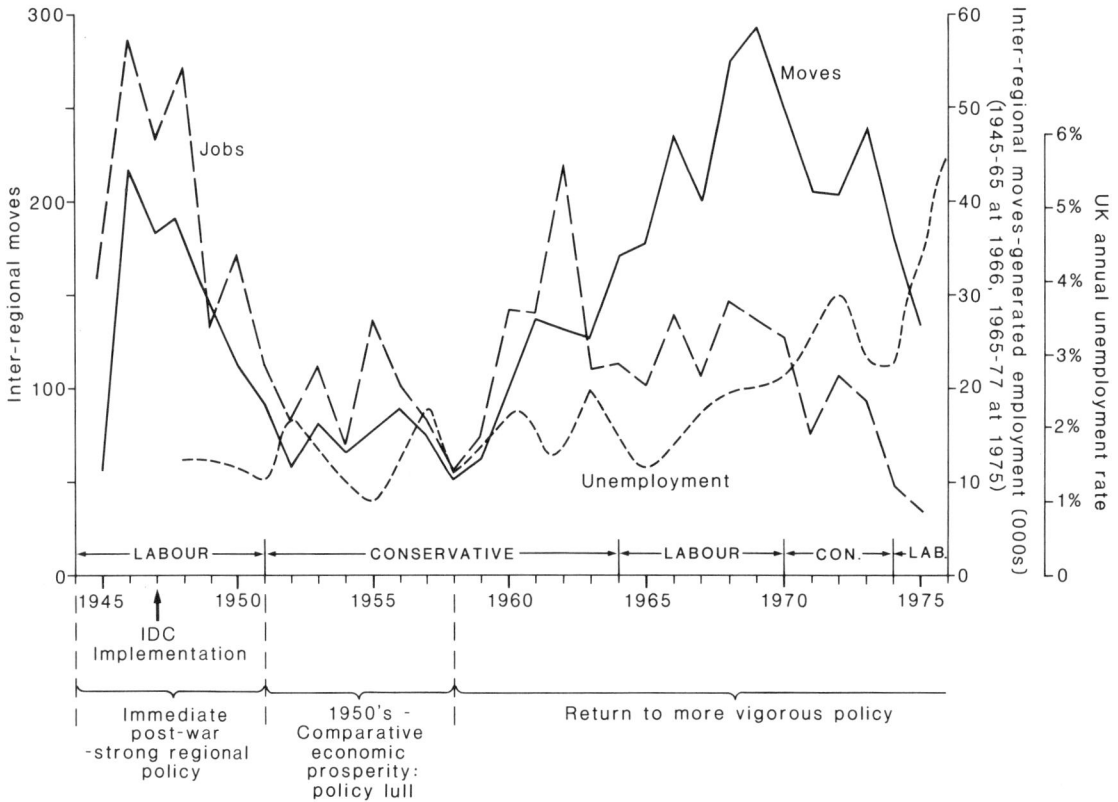

Fig. 4.17 The time-series of inter-regional factory migration from 1945 to 1976. A complex interplay of political control at Westminster, the severity of regional distress and the state of the national economy underlies the remarkably varied pattern of migration as a whole, and the more detailed ratio of jobs to moves. Post-1976 trends will almost certainly witness a further fall in both aspects of movement under Conservative policy and an ever-deepening recession.
Sources: as for Fig. 4.16, with the addition of (a) Department of Employment (various dates) *British Labour Statistics Year Books* (HMSO, London); (b) Department of Employment and Productivity (1971) *British Labour Statistics: historical abstract 1886-1968* (HMSO, London).

importance of regional policy in stimulating inter-regional migration (Ashcroft and Taylor 1979; Mackay 1979).

However, since 1970 the dramatic fall in long-distance migration has been accompanied by no significant reduction in government expenditure on regional policy (Department of Industry 1981, pp. 103, 107). This suggests the national decline in manufacturing has lessened the pressures for expansion which lie behind much industrial migration, while higher unemployment levels mean that such firms as are expanding are less likely to encounter significant labour shortages (another stimulus for movement) in their existing localities.

Even so, the broad temporal and spatial patterns of industrial movement still suggest regional policy is an important factor underlying non-local factory movement, strengthening the belief that regional economic change could be partly interpreted in this same light.

(b) Births The so-called 'incubator' hypothesis sees 'births' (completely new firms) as most likely in urban (especially inner urban) areas, given their range of existing industries, firms, and other external economies (Chapter 2). Unless they are set up by established non-manufacturers their failure rate is high too. The contribution made by survivors to manufacturing growth takes a while to develop: only 7% of the 1963 manufacturing employment of North West London, for example, was supplied by births over the previous 25 years.

(c) Deaths For single-plant companies 'deaths' (closure) means company liquidation. Here closure usually comes from weakness, but the fault may lie more in the general economic climate than with the firm's location as such. With multi-plant companies, though, it may not be 'failure'. One plant may close as part of a wholesale programme of company restructuring—cutting out old inefficient plant on lucrative sites and using the cash, labour and equipment in more profitable sites elsewhere. Closure may involve no loss of jobs to the national economy in the short term, and in the longer term may pave the way for net employment growth. Organisational change also plays a part, as in March 1980 when the Wardle Group announced the closure of its profit-making Caernarvon plastics factory, with production to be transferred 'to reduce costs' to the Colne (Lancashire) works of a subsidiary, acquired in 1978. Caernarvon's Plaid Cwmru MP saw this merely as an attempt to justify the earlier takeover (*The Times*, 1 March 1980).

(d) *In situ* **decline**　This, too, can form part of multi-plant reorganisation, and so result from weakness (a half-way house to total closure, preparing the workers and community for hard times ahead) or from strength. This is a difficult research area, either way, partly because such figures on redundancies and short-time workings as appear in the media are not a consistent, long-term data source from which to build up a reliable geographical picture of this component.

(e) *In situ* **growth**　Expansion on site represents the easiest locational option for the growing company, and its repeated popularity is seen in survey data summarised by Keeble (1976). These identified *in situ* expansion as the major single channel of growth in Britain, both in numbers of 'location' decisions taken and in employment so generated. Lewis's (1971) study of the western Home Counties between 1945 and 1966 estimates that *in situ* growth exceeds closures and decline by a net 47,000 jobs, in turn representing 53% of the corresponding net manufacturing employment increase, while in towns such as Slough and Oxford almost all manufacturing growth came about in this way.

　Finally, we should realise that these components are not seen as mutually exclusive ways of achieving change by the manufacturing firm. Rather they are often used in combination, as when the merger of two former companies into ICL in 1968 was achieved by an amalgam of migration, expansion and death (Massey and Meegan 1979) (Fig. 4.18).

(f) **The regional balance sheet**　The experience of an industrial region is even more certain to show examples of many different components. However, building up a coherent, accurate picture of the components of gross employment change in a region is both laborious and difficult, and only a handful of such studies have been carried out in Britain.

　Gudgin's (1978) analysis of the East Midlands produced a components-of-change balance sheet for 1948 to 1967. Over this period net regional employment grew by 20% or 96,200 jobs, but the gross increase was some 231,000. His estimates of the contributions of growth components show the East Midlands the main source of its own growth. Only 11% of the employment increase in this non-Assisted Area has come through in-migration. The major growth is through *in situ* expansion of local companies; but Gudgin also stresses the importance of births. While being only 11% of the total 1967 manufacturing jobs stock, these nevertheless

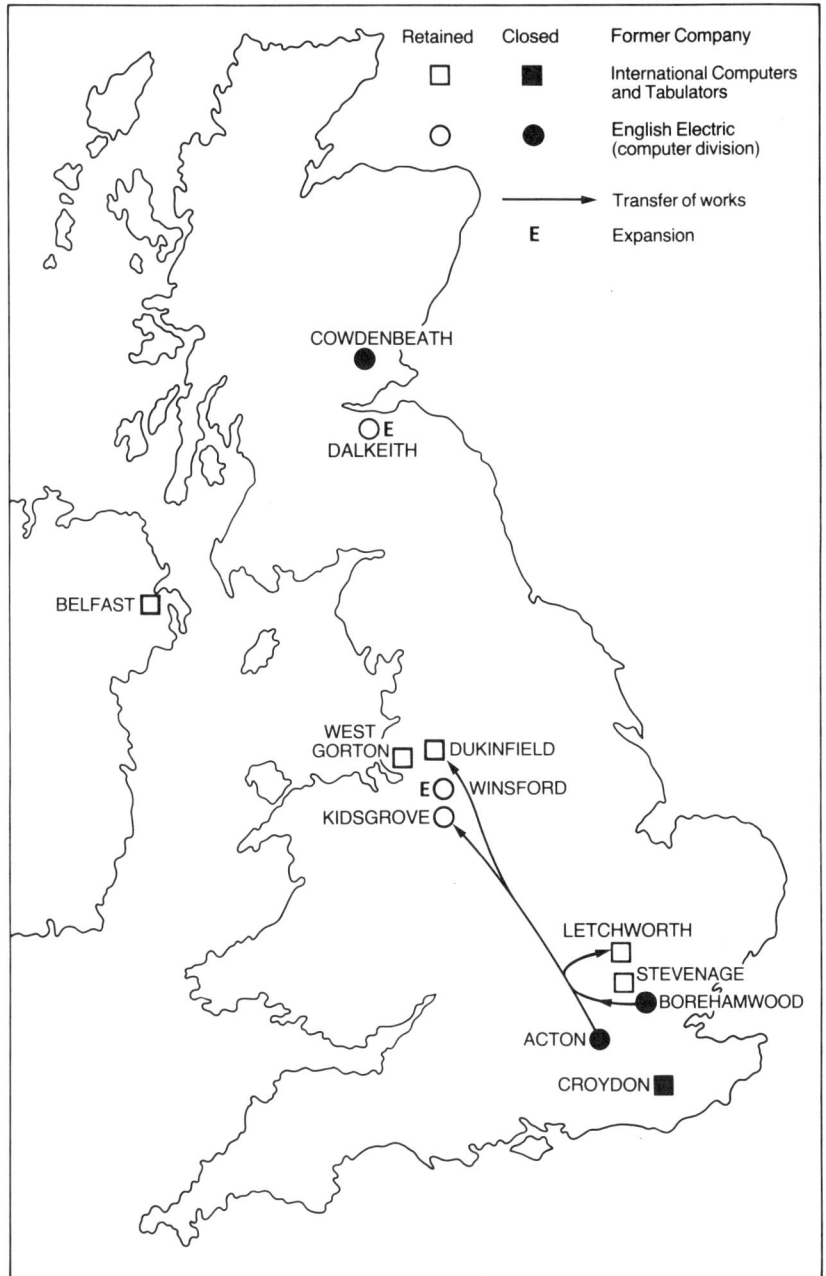

Fig. 4.18 Spatial impacts of corporate reorganisation. International Computers Ltd was established through the efforts of the Industrial Reorganisation Corporation to bolster Britain's position in domestic and international computer markets. The effects 'on the ground' were to the net benefit of the North West over the South East, but several separate components of change are involved in the shifting regional balance of jobs. *Source:* Massey and Meegan (1979).

represent 43% of all 1967 factories, nearly 30% of gross job increase, and two-thirds of the net job increase over the study period.

More detailed analysis (Fig. 4.19) shows how the four growth components vary substantially within the East Midlands. As the subdivisions become smaller this variation becomes more dramatic. But the underlying causes of the different components (the 'why' of the 'how') remain to be unearthed. Industrial size and multi-plant firm structures are all 'possibles', as is the region's spatial position within Britain, but with no comparable studies from other regions these deeper questions remain unresolved.

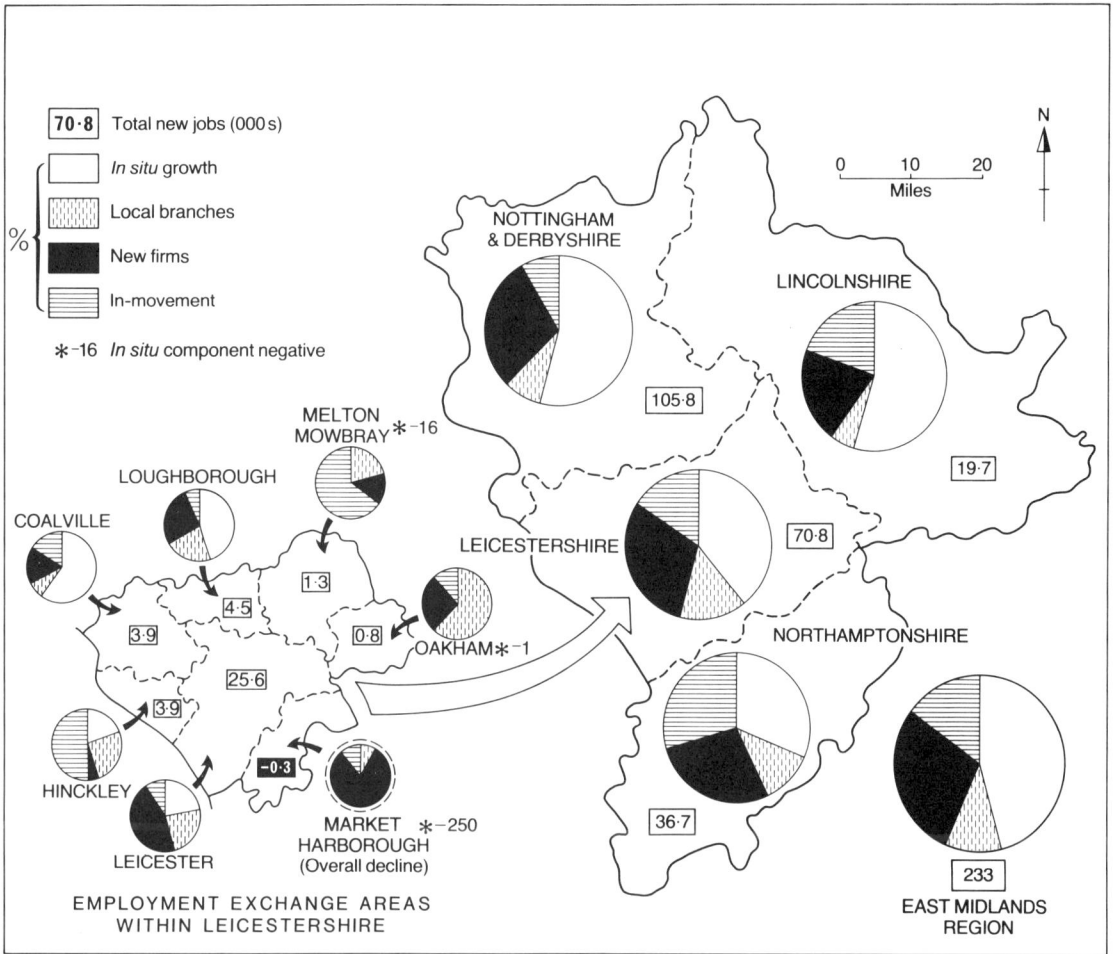

Fig. 4.19 Components of change in the East Midlands, 1948-67. The overall increase of 233,000 manufacturing jobs is unevenly spread through the component parts (one area of Leicestershire even registers a net job loss) and the relative role of the different change components varies substantially too. Some of the smaller districts may bear the imprint of decisions by one or two key firms. *Source:* compiled from Gudgin (1978).

Conclusions

Many important trends can be seen in the manufacturing geography of post-1918 Britain, and these are important in understanding the whole question of regional growth and decline. Several explanations of these have been offered (not all of them reviewed here) but the root causes are still hotly debated. Economic models also disagree among themselves over their predictions, while political models are more tentative and controversial. Perhaps there is no more reason to expect all regions to be suffering from the same illness than all patients in hospital. A wide range of possibilities is available, too, when we consider the 'how' of growth. Here, though, as with the 'why', we are at least in a better position than before to appreciate the complexity of the problems awaiting geographical analysis; and that is a step in the right direction.

5 Some areal examples

This chapter focuses on three case studies, showing how the previous chapter's national-scale account glosses over the finer details of geographical pattern and process in smaller areas.

The South East: a region of plenty

The South East of England is Britain's largest (with about 30% of the national population and 20% of manufacturing jobs in 1981) and most written-about region. Chapter 4 showed its increasing dominance of Britain's manufacturing since 1921 and its steady increase both in manufacturing numbers and in national manufacturing share to 1971. More recent trends, though, reveal a different picture. From the latter end of the 1960s absolute manufacturing levels began to fall. Between 1971 and 1975 the region lost 250,000 manufacturing jobs (net), representing at 12% the greatest relative decline among all UK regions. The most recent statistics, for 1973-8, show this continuing (a net 31,100 jobs being lost) and forming part of an overall regional net loss of 75,000. Despite its prosperous past, then, the region's future seems less certain. Is this a further stage of centre–periphery reversal? If so, what are the implications for Britain's regional policy, closely dependent as it is on industrial movement from the South East? Certainly, for some, the South East is 'the goose that ceased to lay the golden eggs' (Hall 1978).

This may be too alarmist. Almost irrespective of the indicators used, the South East remains Britain's most prosperous region (Table 5.1). 'Basic/multiplier' arguments suggest links between manufacturing growth and current regional prosperity, but this sets aside the question of why the South East's manufacturing should have been so successful in the first place (at least, until 1970). Geographers have advanced four interrelated answers.

Why prosperity?

(a) **Good structure** Since 1921 the South East's manufacturing bias has been towards growing industries. Fig. 5.1 shows how it still has more than its fair share of instrument and electrical engineering and paper-based industries, while being spared a heavy burden in nationally declining ones like clothing, textiles and shipbuilding.

(b) **A good location** Although probably underplayed in the shift–share analyses of Chapter 4, the South East offers a range of excellent locational bases for modern manufacturing, as reviewed in Chapter 2, other than in major industrial raw materials. The nation's dominant metropolis provides a major market and labour source, while an overall regional population density of 618 per sq. mile (UK average = 230) means a high density of customers and workers. Nodal supremacy in

	South-east England		Northern Ireland	
	Index	Rank	Index	Rank
Gross domestic product per caput (1977)	111	1	75	11
% Unemployment (1978 average)	69	1	188	11
Weekly earnings gross per caput (1978)	103	1	89	11
Disposable income per caput (1978)	110	1	81	11
% Households (1978) with:				
Central heating	110	2	66	11
Telephone	118	1	69	11
Dependants per 100 workers 1978 (relative to UK average)	− 15	1	+ 40	1
% School-leavers with no qualifications (1978) (no UK figure given)	12.8%	2	35.5%	11

Note: UK = 100

Table 5.1 Indicators of regional health. *Source:* Regional Statistics, 1980 (CSO).

domestic and international communications, and the fact that the region is an unchallenged legal, financial, political, administrative and professional information centre, contribute to an unrivalled battery of economic 'pulses', to which access to the EEC is an additional bonus. A large, well-structured industrial base and the region's information and capital environments stimulate invention and innovation, so perpetuating the structural bias towards growth. Berry's principle of 'biggest first, earliest most' works well in the South East.

(c) Headquarters base Large corporations bring multiplier effects and the prospect of employment security to the 'base' region. The South East is the dominant headquarters region, and this dominance is still increasing (Fig. 3.8), the cumulative result of three separate processes—acquisitions, *in situ* growth, and the transfer of headquarters operations to the region (Goddard and Smith 1978).

(d) Residential appeal Strongly related to (a), (b) and (c) is the elusive aura of affluent superiority pervading life in the South East, and the feeling that what deserves to be known, heard, seen and done is first and foremost apparent in the South East. As manufacturers become more 'footloose' these considerations loom ever larger in the nation's job geography. Whitehand (1967) has identified one manifestation of this as the 'cocktail belt' of exclusive, low-density, dormitory areas around London, where 'a quite distinct cultural landscape has resulted'. His mapping of its key feature—large detached houses in their own grounds—shows these clustering in the Chilterns and North Downs, in close association with commuter railways 'to Town'. For many, whether cocktail belt residents or not, the composite appeal of fine scenery, major shops, unrivalled entertainment and cultural outlets, and the reflected glory of a house in the 'top region' make workers keen to come and reluctant to leave.

Inside the South East

The 'inner city' excepted (Chapter 5), pockets of relative poverty are harder to find in the South East than in other regions. Rural/urban prosperity differences are kept in check, as few communities lie beyond London's commuter tentacles. Only in the fringes of Thanet (north-east Kent) and the Isle of Wight has the South East been 'assisted' at any time under regional policy, and only in the eastern and southern fringe areas

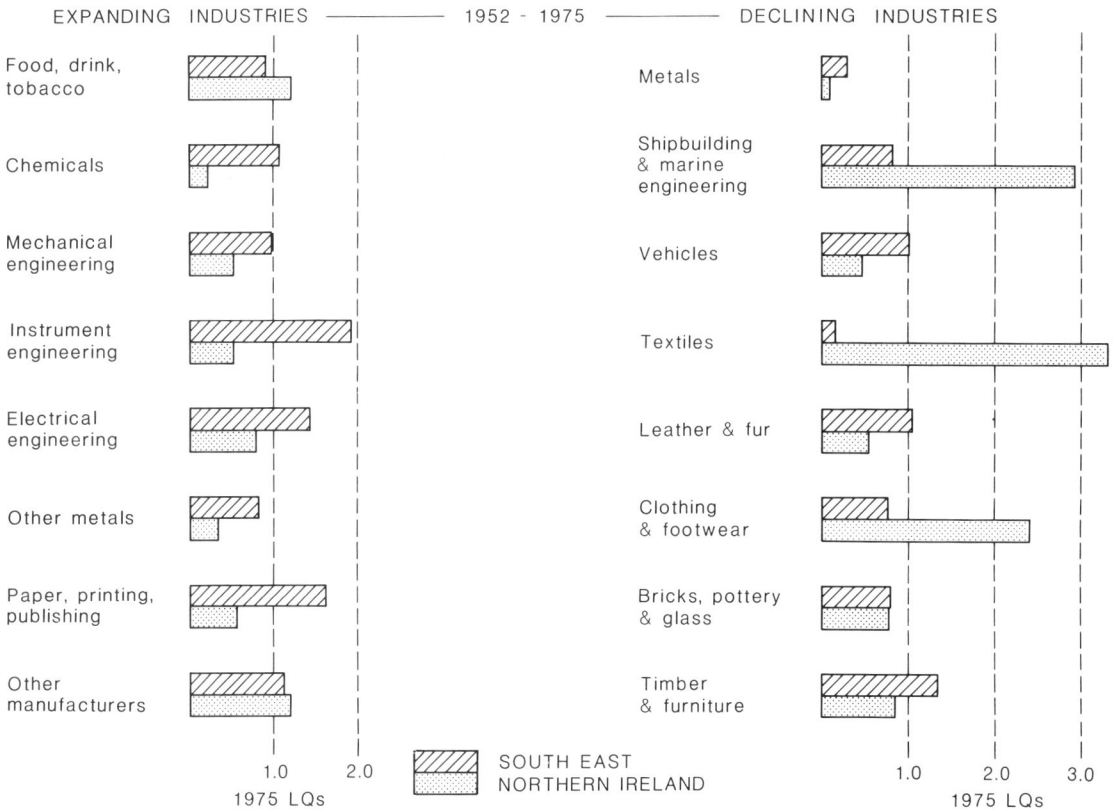

Fig. 5.1 Manufacturing employment profiles in South-East England and Northern Ireland, 1975. The South East has much the healthier industrial structure while Northern Ireland is especially heavily biased towards three nationally declining industries. Note also how the smaller region has a much wider range of LQs while the South East's more even spread of jobs provides greater security against economic decline in particular product areas. *Source:* based on Fothergill, S. and Gudgin, G. (1978) Regional employment statistics on a comparable basis. *Occasional Paper* 5, Centre for Environmental Studies, London.

does local unemployment rise above national levels, and then largely for 'seasonal' reasons.

Geographically, the South East resembles the cross-section of a tree, with concentric rings encasing the (metropolitan) core. This pattern persists through the geological and geomorphological structures and the human geography alike. Road and rail links cut through the gaps in these rings, homing in on London, and bringing in an estimated 1,126,000 commuters to the city centre during the morning rush-hour.

Over time, the dominance of core over rings has weakened as waves of population growth have moved steadily outwards. County employment data show a broadly similar trend since 1921, with all counties outside London and Middlesex expanding both pre- and post-war in aggregate and manufacturing employment (Fig. 5.2). Recent manufacturing trends in jobs and floorspace show that the emphasis has continued shifting outwards from 'London' to the 'Outer Metropolitan Area' to the 'Outer South East'. Superimposed on this is a north–south division. Broadly speaking, manufacturing forms a larger component in employment north of London than south of it. But in 'manufacturing share' terms since 1951 the greatest increases have been south of the capital (especially Sussex and Hampshire) and some northern counties even show a fall. Data at a finer spatial scale highlight these same two trends (Keeble 1976, Ch. 9): when compared with 1960-6, manufacturing job growth between 1966 and 1971 favoured the outer fringes, and in both periods the major expanding areas lay south of London.

In a sense, then, manufacturing has colonised new terrain within the South East, both concentrically and sectorally, rather than concentrating

HERTFORDSHIRE

BUCKINGHAMSHIRE

OXFORDSHIRE

BEDFORDSHIRE

BOUNDARIES:-
GREATER LONDON
OUTER METROPOLITAN AREA
OUTER SOUTH EAST
COUNTIES

MIDDLESEX

ESSEX

LONDON

BERKSHIRE

HAMPSHIRE

KENT

KEY

Manufacturing as % total jobs

County as % South East manufacturing jobs

1921   51 1971

SURREY

SUSSEX

0   20   60 Kms
0   20   40 Miles

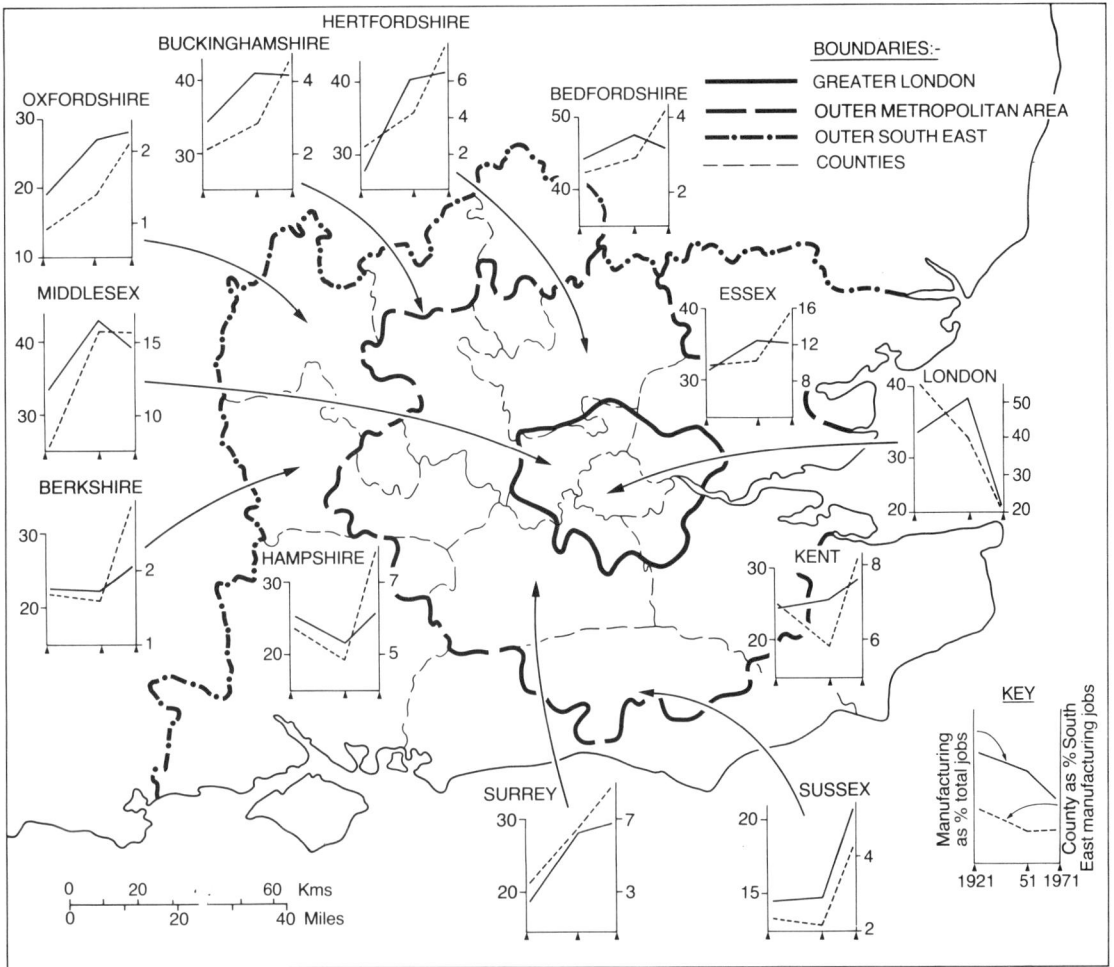

Fig. 5.2 The geography of manufacturing change in the South East at the county level, 1921-71, Manufacturing's share of county jobs has been rising most rapidly south of London, post-war, while the capital's relative industrial decline results in almost all other counties increasing their share of the region's industrial jobs after 1951. Note that the 'y-axis' scales vary from county to county. *Source:* Population Census tables for 1921, 1951, 1971.

on established industrial communities. One well studied component of this change has been factory migration. Within the South East this was already a well-established trend before 1945. Of 630 factories surveyed north of London between 1928 and 1932 (Smith 1933), 313 were dubbed 'in-migrants', of which 243 had relocated from London. Availability of space, the spread of cheap electric power and road transport, lower rents and rates all encouraged this movement, while the continued need to serve London markets restrained it.

Studies of industrial movement from London to other parts of the region in the 1960s underscored 'land' costs and shortages as a key 'push' factor, and the need to retain London links in settling on a new site (Keeble 1976, p. 260). Cheap electricity fades from the scene, and in its place 'managerial convenience' (i.e. where the boss lives) helps fix new locations, and planning pressures undermine old ones. Perhaps the main 'new' movement control, though, is labour, either as a 'push' factor when scarce or as a restraint on movement distance to retain 'key labour' after the move. The detailed geography of intra-regional movement for 1945-68 demonstrates both the radial direction of movement and the dominance of branches over transfers (SEJPT 1971b).

To keep a balance, though, recall that factory movement is not the be-all and end-all of change; in-migration has contributed less than 50% of

99

Fig. 5.3 Major manufacturing centres and specialisations in South-East England, 1966. Within London manufacturing centres favour the north-east, and western sectors, while specialised clusters are noticeably absent in the west compared to the eastern (especially the inner eastern) boroughs. The wider, regional, picture shows all the major manufacturing centres, and the majority of the specialised ones, north of the Thames. *Source:* based on South East Joint Planning Team (1971a).

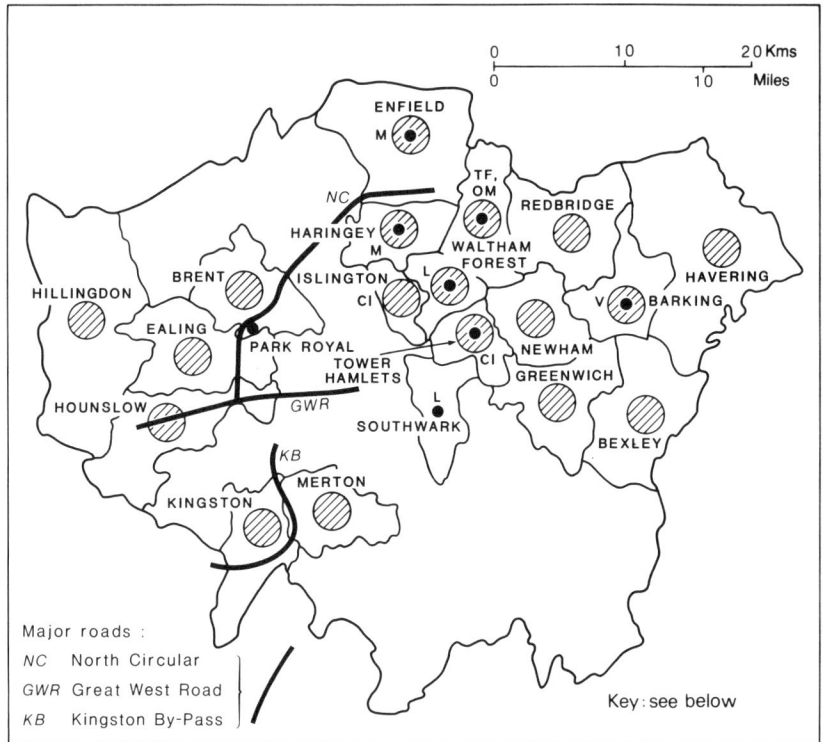

Major roads :
NC   North Circular
GWR   Great West Road
KB   Kingston By-Pass

Key : see below

Centres of 50,000+ employment where manufacturing share exceeds regional average (1966)

———— County Boundaries / London Borough Boundaries

Local Specialisations (LQ > 4.0) 1966 :– **BPG** Bricks, Pottery & Glass **Ch** Chemicals **Cl** Clothing **EE** Electrical Engineering **L** Leather & Fur **M** Metals **OM** Other Manufacturers **P** Paper, Printing & Publishing **S** Shipbuilding & Marine Engineering **TF** Timber & Furniture **Tx** Textiles **V** Vehicles

the net manufacturing job increase of the region's expanding areas
(Department of the Environment 1973, p. 53), so the residue must come
from the relatively neglected '*in situ* expansion' and 'birth' components.

Where are the manufacturing jobs?

The leading manufacturing areas (Fig. 5.3) fall into two groups of three
categories each.

London

(a) City centre   Manufacturing and non-manufacturing firms coexist in
the office clusters of central London. Surveys of central London offices
as a whole (Economist Intelligence Unit 1964; Cowan 1969, p. 106) show
that the main factors binding them there are the need for external contacts
between offices and with other central London institutions, while the
actual business contacts among different office types show that these
resemble the spatial clusters of offices apparent at the same city-centre
scale (Goddard 1975). But it is not a perfect 1:1 relationship, and
advances in telecommunications technology should weaken it further.

(b) Inner London   Industrial areas of small factories and
workshops—clothing, furniture and printing in particular—cluster in the
'Victorian crescent' of inner London. Their origins are usually attributed
to skilled immigrant labour, and their perseverence to a large stock of
cheap, rentable, convertible premises and inter-linked supply–demand
chains among small specialised producers. Despite these areas resistance
to change, though, little recent work has been carried out to test these
ideas 'in the field'.

(c) Arterial roads   Along major suburban roads, like the North Circular,
the Great West Road and the Kingston bypass we find twentieth-century
factories, often on industrial estates (as at Park Royal) and clinging to
transport arteries as to a life-support system. The enterprise of estate
developers (in the pre-planning era before the Second World War) and the
importance of efficient communications to other parts of Britain and
London underlie their growth. Diversity of industrial trades is greater
here than in (b), and local-scale linkage ties seem weaker. Recently, some
gaps have appeared along the spine roads. Firestone, Coty, Rank–Pullen
and Trico–Folberth have all closed on the Great West Road since 1978,
although redevelopment of some of these sites is under way.

Outside London

(d) Thames-side   Bulk-import industries using cheap, water-borne
transport and break-of-bulk sites line the lower Thames basin on both
sides—foodstuffs towards London, oil refining, paper, cement and
vehicles (using imported coal and iron) further downsteam are all
examples.

Fig. 5.4 Major planning initiatives in South East England. The bulk of the planned towns lie north of London (and a few overspill outside the region altogether), with the Expanded Towns further from the capital than the 'first generation' (pre-1950) New Towns, perhaps explaining their relatively slow build-up of jobs. London's Green Belt, while apparently restricting expansion, is under threat of unwarranted piecemeal development in some areas.

(e) New and expanded towns (NETs)   Those planned industrial centres away from the built-up metropolis have attracted a range of modern industry (Fig. 5.4). Since they were selected partly with an eye to intra- and inter-regional communications and access to national markets (only Crawley New Town lies in London's 'shadow' in this respect) and offer modern premises and the pick of mobile labour, it is small wonder that their manufacturing growth has been impressive, with a bias towards growth sectors (especially engineering) (Brown 1966).

(f) Other free-standing towns   Here is a wide variety of industrial experience and specialism. Some are old-established (paper-making at Dartford, furniture at High Wycombe), others are modern (aircraft at Weybridge and Stevenage, computers at Havant), some are relatively diversified, but others are dangerously one-industry/one-firm towns (British Leyland at Oxford, Vauxhall at Luton). Despite the recent growth south of London, northern towns are still more manufacturing-oriented, perhaps reflecting their 'access to national market' advantage. Keeble and Hauser's (1972) statistical analysis of patterns of regional manufacturing growth over 1960-6 outside London identified labour availability as the dominant control, with a diversified manufacturing base also being helpful.

Freedom or fetters?

Some commentators see few constraints upon what manufacturing activity now goes where within the South East. Thus, basing their report on a region-wide field study of factories, Economic Consultants Ltd said in 1971 that:

102

'No single part of the region offers major locational advantages or suffers from any major locational disadvantages in comparison with other parts of the South East. To this extent the future pattern of the location of industry within the South East is unlikely to exert a major influence on its overall operating efficiency' (SEJPT 1971b, p. 11).

A later study of engineering firms in different parts of the South East also found no differences in economic performance attributable to location. Leaving aside 'labour' (which can be 'manipulated', anyway, through housing provision) and certain locationally-constrained industries like cement, this seems to imply that manufacturers could go where they wished.

Such a *carte blanche* view is subject to two qualifications, though. First, even if all parts of the region are suitable for some degree of industrial growth this does not mean that each individual firm can go anywhere. Many firms gain locational advantage through 'closeness' to geographically fixed location factors like docks, airports, R & D establishments and major concentrations of customers or suppliers, even if their ideas on how close they should be are vague and fuzzy. Some fixed factors are more geographically demanding than others, so firms stressing their need to be close to the London Docks or the Stock Exchange really do cluster around them to a degree not found, say, with professional institutions or international airports (Hoare 1973). Secondly, the greater the locational choice enjoyed by manufacturers on economic grounds the greater the scope to 'direct' them on planning ones.

(a) Restrictive planning   This can be subdivided, as follows.

(i) IDC policy   Although this has generally operated against the South East inter-regionally, certain parts of the region have received sympathetic IDC treatment: for example, to reduce Portsmouth's dependence upon its naval dockyard, to cushion railway works closures at Ashford, Brighton and Lancing, and to stimulate the NETs.

(ii) Green belts   Of Britain's many green belts only London's has been formally approved by Whitehall (Fig. 5.4). Here planning applications are allowed only if in keeping with the low-density, open nature of the landscape. New major manufacturing growth would almost certainly be a non-starter.

(b) Planning that is sometimes restrictive, sometimes positive   There are two main categories.

(i) Structure plans   These and their pre-1971 ancestors, Development Plans are statutory documents by which county planners guide future land-use patterns. Once approved by central government, these and many more detailed Local Plans form the yardsticks for deciding planning applications. Structure plans indicate where industrial expansion is favoured (for example, Banbury, Bicester, Didcot, Witney in Oxfordshire, Hungerford and Newbury in Berkshire, and the Medway towns in Kent), and define the planning authority's general attitude towards industrial development—Surrey, for example, takes a restrictive view while Essex and South Hampshire are more encouraging.

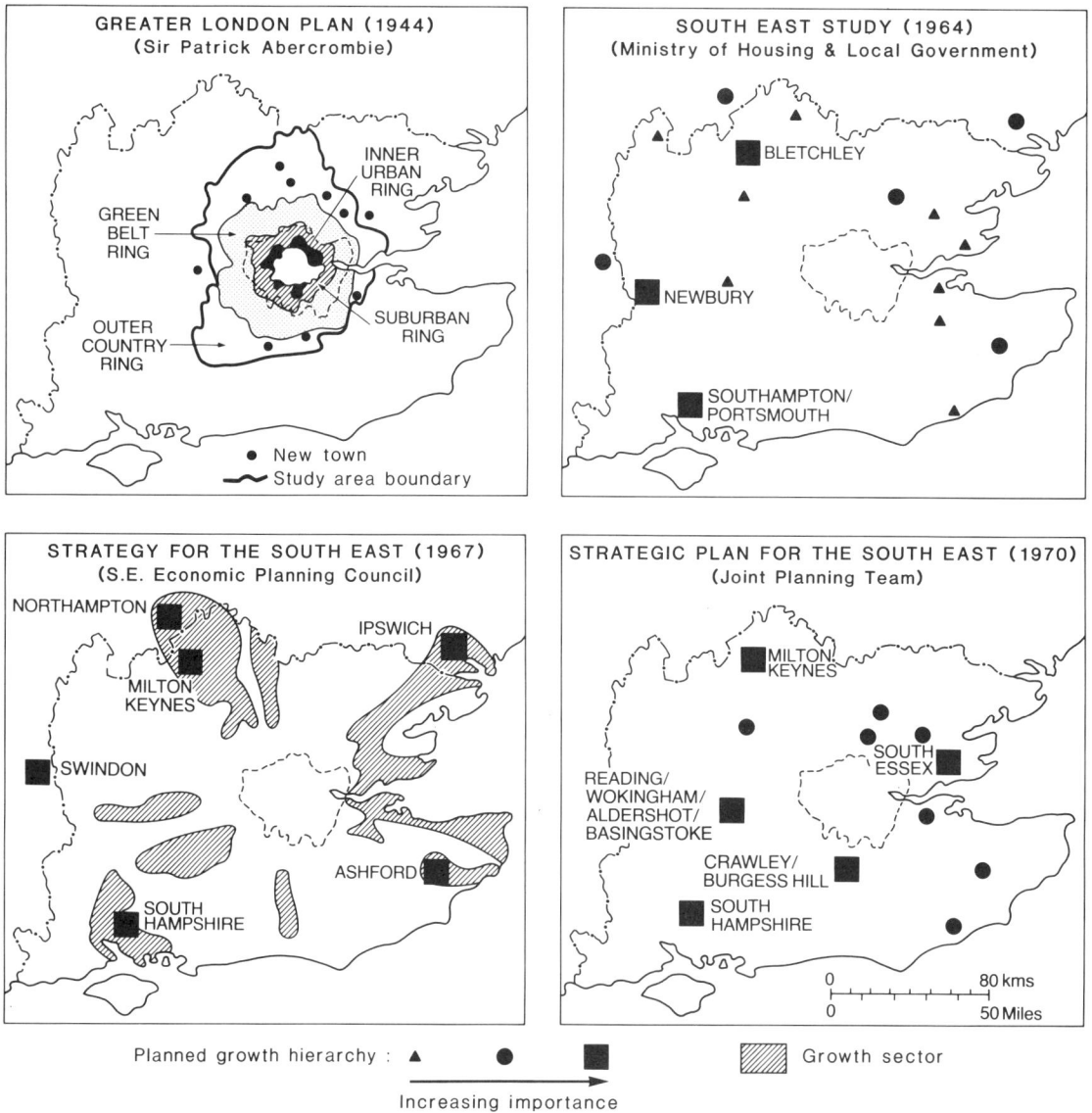

GREATER LONDON PLAN (1944)
(Sir Patrick Abercrombie)

INNER URBAN RING

GREEN BELT RING

SUBURBAN RING

OUTER COUNTRY RING

● New town
〜 Study area boundary

SOUTH EAST STUDY (1964)
(Ministry of Housing & Local Government)

BLETCHLEY

NEWBURY

SOUTHAMPTON/PORTSMOUTH

STRATEGY FOR THE SOUTH EAST (1967)
(S.E. Economic Planning Council)

NORTHAMPTON

IPSWICH

MILTON KEYNES

SWINDON

ASHFORD

SOUTH HAMPSHIRE

STRATEGIC PLAN FOR THE SOUTH EAST (1970)
(Joint Planning Team)

MILTON KEYNES

SOUTH ESSEX

READING/WOKINGHAM/ALDERSHOT/BASINGSTOKE

CRAWLEY/BURGESS HILL

SOUTH HAMPSHIRE

0 ⊢⊢⊢⊢⊢⊢ 80 kms
0 ⊢⊢⊢⊢⊢ 50 Miles

Planned growth hierarchy : ▲　●　■　　▨ Growth sector

Increasing importance →

Fig. 5.5 Four post-war planning strategies for South-East England. Elements of all these strategies have survived through to the present pattern of planned development in the region. The 'planned growth hierarchy' shown is more valid for comparison within rather than between schemes.

(ii) Strategic planning　This supplies a broad framework binding together county plans and other spatially relevant decision-making. Since 1944 the South East has seen four major strategic plans (Fig. 5.5) by a variety of agencies, all of which envisaged population/industrial expansion selectively within the region. Though they are of great apparent significance for industrial location, their actual role is more questionable. Some have been overtaken by events, overturning their assumptions of population and job growth. Some made over-optimistic assumptions about the volume of industrial movement available to feed designated growth centres. Their advisory basis is frowned on by county planners as an intrusion into their less grandiose but statutory planning responsibilities. But on the positive side, major new industrial/population 'countermagnets' like Milton Keynes and South Hampshire are the direct outcome of the region's strategic planning.

Table 5.2 London's New and Expanded Towns: achievements to December 1976. *Source: Town and Country Planning* 45, No. 2 (February 1977).

	Completed dwellings	Industrial occupants	Completed factories (000 sq.ft.)	Industrial employment
New Towns (8 schemes)	141,907	896	31,692	105,489
including:				
Basildon	26,047	238	6,748	22,373
Harlow	24,788	313	6,898	19,300
Expanded Towns				
Current (22 schemes)	49,224	1,222	37,326	
including:				not available
Swindon	7,939	139	9,005	
Basingstoke	4,745	115	3,963	
Completed/terminated (6 schemes)	4,282	Not available	135	

(c) Usually positive   To be included here are the following.

(i) New towns   Popularised by Abercrombie's strategic plan (Fig. 5.5), New Towns became a practical possibility following the New Towns Act of 1946. The first crop of eight designated by parliament between 1946 and 1949 were intended to relieve pressures on London. All were designed to a master plan, through which small existing settlements were greatly expanded into communities of 25,000 to 80,000, balanced both socially and in terms of jobs and homes. Perhaps the jobs emphasis was too heavily biased towards manufacturing, but even so their employment build-up has been impressive, both through in-migration and later expansion (Table 5.2). Most New Town firms originated in London—of Brown's sample (1966) 71% had moved from the capital, with sectoral movement being the rule—factories moving from south London to Crawley, from the east end to Basildon, and so on. After Assisted Areas, New Towns have received the most preferential IDC treatment. The net result has been an industrial population biased towards growing sectors and skilled employment, which in turn has encouraged the selective movement of skilled manual families. In neither jobs nor people, then, can New Towns claim to be representative of their mother city, London.

(ii) Expanded Towns   The same probably goes for these (Fig. 5.4). After a slow start the 1952 Town Development Act spawned package deals between London and other towns in the South East and beyond for the balanced 'export' of jobs and populations. As with New Towns, preferential IDC treatment was enjoyed, but unlike them overall planning remains in the hands of existing local authorities rather than a separate corporation. Average amounts of new employment per settlement are less than in the New Towns, but growth in Swindon and Basingstoke surpasses the best they can offer. The GLC has recently claimed that, overall, the Expanded Town programme has resulted in the greater total factory migration from London.

Increasingly, the region's NETs have come under attack from two quarters. The Assisted Areas claim they soak up mobile firms otherwise destined for them, while London sees them as economic and social blood-suckers. Those opposed to spatial planning on principle argue that, as with the Assisted Areas, such intrusions into normal business decision-making result in lost growth nationally. Such are the conflicts at the heart of spatial planning in Britain.

Northern Ireland: a region of poverty

Northern Ireland presents a very different picture from the South East. A small region (only 1,500,000 population in 1971, or 2.7% of the UK total), its share of UK manufacturing was predictably modest—marginally over 2% over the 1951-71 period. Over these same decades manufacturing fell from 36% to 31% of regional jobs, a 'middle-of-the-pack' performance, although structurally Northern Ireland is the nation's most specialised region, and less 'diversified' than all but the West Midlands in 1971 (Appendix 1 and Chapter 4). Unlike the South East, during 1973-8 overall employment rose (by 19,000), but, as in the South East, manufacturing jobs fell, by 33,000 or 15.6% (the largest relative decline of all regions). This largely accounted for the worst regional recent 'employment shortfall' (i.e. working-aged population change minus job change), with the increase of potential workers over actual jobs being 'absorbed' only by emigration and unemployment.

Northern Ireland is at the foot of the UK league table not just in unemployment, but also in output per caput, incomes, dependants per worker and penetration of household durables (Table 5.1). Were the cost of living correspondingly low these symptoms would be less serious, but regional house prices in the late 1970s were topped only by the South East, while 'shopping basket' surveys consistently show figures of household purchases way above the national average.

Reasons for regional problems

(a) Structure   With its three dominant manufacturing sectors (contributing to its high specialisation) all being in national decline—food, textiles, shipbuilding (Fig. 5.1), shift–share analyses of regional manufacturing performance (Steed 1967; Quigley 1976) are predictably dominated by large negative structural shifts (with small offsetting positive 'locational' ones). As a good structure encourages new enterprise so a bad one suppresses it, especially when, as in shipbuilding and, to a lesser degree, linen, large firms dominate the dominant sectors.

The dismal recent history of both these staples is well known (Northern Ireland Office 1974; Busteed 1974). In shipbuilding, Harland and Wolff (the only firm to matter) employed some 21,000 at its Queen's Island (Belfast) site in 1950, over 10% of regional manufacturing jobs. Although reduced to 7,000 (1980) it remains one of the province's two largest single industrial plants, and still rules the hearts and minds of Ulstermen as do its huge Goliath cranes the landscape of Belfast. It suffered less than other major British yards from war damage and this, combined with its deep-water site, suitable for launching large ships, provided a post-war springboard. But problems without (competition from reconstructed European and Japanese yards aided by government subsidies) and within (the inefficient organisation of labour, the result largely of union restrictions, and the relatively 'sleepy' condition of management) changed all that. Reorganisation and reconstruction followed. The yard reoriented from naval and liner markets to new, less labour-intensive oil and bulk carriers. It diversified into electrical engineering and industrialised housing, reformed its administration, closed branches in mainland Britain and laid off labour in Belfast (Steed 1968). But problems persist: claims of overmanning, of sectarian recruitment, of excessive job demarcation, and the collapse of the oil tanker market following the Yom Kippur war of 1973, mean government subsidies have continued (£250m. since the mid-1960s), each new infusion being warningly described as 'the last'.

Linen textiles and the related clothing industries comprise a mix of large and small firms, processes and products (Steed 1974). Linen is less homogeneous than in its heyday. Flax once grown in the province is now entirely replaced by imports and by synthetic materials, and local ownership has been eroded by 'mainland' takeovers like Courtaulds and Carrington Viyella. As more linkages became intra-company a smaller proportion of output went to markets in the region (51% by value in 1952, 31% in 1972) and the industry as a whole has wasted away (Taylor 1979). Costly and scarce supplies, changing consumer tastes from linens, conservative 'family firm' management, and cheap Third World imports all contribute. Government aid is available for firms wishing to invest and re-equip, but no coordinated programme for change exists – in contrast to Lancashire's cotton industry. Clothing firms have been more successful in retaining labour (losing only 4,000 net jobs between 1951 and 1971, compared with textile's 32,000) but here, too, cheap foreign competition is a serious threat.

(b) A poor location   Northern Ireland suffers from a paucity of manufacturing resources, its small size, and its separation from the British mainland. The adage that 'the only resource is the people' underlines the lack of any major economic supplies of materials or fuels. It has unemployed labour for sure, but even that is a questionable resource. Low population numbers and the second lowest population density in the UK generate correspondingly low labour and market potentials outside Belfast, home of one-third of the population. The time and cost of transport 'across the water' add to the problems of serving the larger mainland market, and to the costs of crucial inputs like fuels. Problems of market access and of transport/communications were far and away the major regional problems mentioned by manufacturers who had moved to Northern Ireland (Law 1964), and by those who considered doing so but then abandoned the idea (DTI 1973, p. 607).

(c) Branch plant economy   Industrial restructuring through regional policy had other consequences. Of a survey of 30 manufacturing plants moving to Northern Ireland between 1965 and 1969 only two were transfers, compared with 22 branches and 6 divisions of non-Ulster companies (Murie *et al.* 1973), while the pattern of ownership of the region's manufacturing firms as of the mid-1970s emphasises the high rates of outside control for large firms (Table 5.3).

Reference to 'branch plant' arguments underlines the potential threat this concept poses. Certainly, the recent recession has seen major closures and redundancies among the units of outside controllers like Heinz, Spillers, Courtaulds, Grundig, Standard Telephones & Cables, Rolls Royce, British Enkalon and ICI, while detailed studies of the engineering and man-made fibres sections emphasise the low regional multiplier effects of externally controlled plants (Hoare 1978; Taylor 1979). As a small consolation, the Tootal company is to concentrate its thread production at Lisnaskea (Co. Fermanagh), selectively closing its Lancashire units.

(d) A bad image   The outside public image of a small, off-shore region must depend more than most on 'public information', and after a decade of civil unrest almost all such information in current circulation is bad. While the 'troubles' have had remarkably little effect on existing manufacturers, most of whom still view the region favourably as a production environment (Schiller 1978), the impact upon outside firms looking for new locations can be dramatic. Despite strenuous official efforts to emphasise the 'true facts' and the financial benefits of an Ulster location the region still captured only 12 of 710 (1.7%) inter-regionally mobile factories in 1971-5, compared with 5.2% in 1966-71 and 6.7% in 1945-65. The later 1970s saw some revival of outside interest but manufacturing growth in Northern Ireland now depends more than ever on the momentum of the existing stock of enterprises.

The role of government

Using their independent industrial development powers under the 1920 Government of Ireland Act, Stormont administrators have played the key role in generating industrial employment by means of a 5-pronged economic programme.

(a) Cost reductions   These have been achieved through loans and grants for investment in buildings and plant, and subsidies to running costs (rates, energy and transport costs, and wage-bills). Overall, types and levels of aid have kept in step with (pre-war) or somewhat ahead (post-war) of those 'over the water': thus labour subsidies survived after the demise of the Regional Employment Premium in Great Britain (see Appendix 2), and in February 1979, the basic rate of industrial grants in Northern Ireland was 30-40%, compared with 22% in Britain's Special Development Areas.

(b) Sites   The government acquires sites for future industrial use, prepares basic services, assists with housing for prospective workers, and builds standard factories in advance of demand or to the specifications of future tenants.

(c) Shortages of modern industrial skills   These have been tackled within the Province through 13 Government Training Centres, with a capacity of 4,000 places both to train labour from scratch and retrain those with outmoded skills, a provision rate some 10 times that in equivalent centres in mainland Britain.

Table 5.3 Control of Northern Ireland industry. *Source:* Quigley Report (1976).

Manufacturing size group	Country of control (%)			
	Northern Ireland	Great Britain	N. America	Rest
≥ 500 employees	22	45	21	12
250–500 employees	22	55	16	7
≥ 20 employees	67	28	2	3

(d) Advertising   Promotion of Northern Ireland as an industrial centre is handled through Ministerial visits, and permanent Department of Commerce offices in London and New York.

(e) Self-help   The Local Enterprise Development Unit (LEDU), dating from 1971, stimulates small indigenous enterprise with financial aid and commercial advice (Busteed 1976). Its success in generating over 9,000 jobs in its first five years and at a cost per job only 20% that of 'traditional' regional policy has generated much interest in 'mainland' regions. Increased state ownership (another means of reducing the 'ownership problem') periodically comes under the microscope, but Ulster's experience with it to date has not been a happy one.

Estimating the impact of this policy involves deciding what would have happened anyway with no regional policy and what the indirect as well as the more obvious direct effects of policy have been (Frost 1977). An official estimate in 1978 puts gross, direct sponsored manufacturing jobs since 1945 at about 64,000, representing some 44% of overall manufacturing employment (Department of Commerce 1978), while direct and indirect employment calculated by a shift–share approach suggests 35,000-40,000 new manufacturing jobs between 1950 and 1970 (Moore *et al.* 1978). As time goes on, so the relative importance of the second-phase expansion of existing sponsored firms has outpaced that in newly sponsored firms—in 1966 the latter provided 65% of sponsored jobs but by 1975 only 15% (Quigley 1976, p. 75).

Structurally, government action has brought a change for the better. While still high, dependence on textiles, clothing and ships declined from 66% of manufacturing jobs (1952) to 44% (1975). The major growth sectors have been engineering (especially electrical), metal-based industries, and man-made fibres (officially classified, like linens, as 'textiles'). Since 1950, when Courtaulds located in Carrickfergus, five more major man-made fibre multinationals invested in Ulster; Courtaulds rayon production is based on natural fibres but the remaining companies' inputs come from the synthetic fibre arm of the chemical industry. With a total regional employment of nearly 10,000 (1971) these represented Britain's (and arguably the world's) largest such regional concentration. But spin-off linkages are low, and dangerously lop-sided employment structures were created in small Ulster towns. Since 1979 plant closures (ICI at Kilroot, DuPont at Londonderry, Courtaulds at Carrickfergus and British Enkalon at Antrim) have dealt massive blows to the regional and local economies. Among the engineering firms, the 1978 arrival of De Lorean Cars is interesting, as the first car assembly plant attracted to Northern Ireland. By some this was seen as a prestige regional catch, especially for the unemployment black spot of west Belfast, but by others as an unjustified high-risk venture and giant rip-off of the taxpayer. When in 1982 the company went into receivership its founder, John De Lorean, admitted he had underestimated the risks involved. But whether the blame for failure lies in the 'what' of an over-priced, under-engineered luxury car failing to meet its American sales targets or the 'where' of a west Belfast location, where alleged 'sniper attacks' on the company made it nigh impossible to retain skilled but highly mobile British management teams, is far from clear.

Fig. 5.6 County-level changes in the manufacturing geography of Northern Ireland, 1926-71. The dominant theme is the shift of jobs from the two major towns to the counties, both relatively and absolutely: in 1926 Londonderry city had nearly twice the jobs of its county and in 1971 about half. Down's limited involvement with planned growth centres means it receives less Belfast overspill than Antrim. *Sources:* Northern Ireland Population Census volumes for 1926, 1951, 1961, 1971.

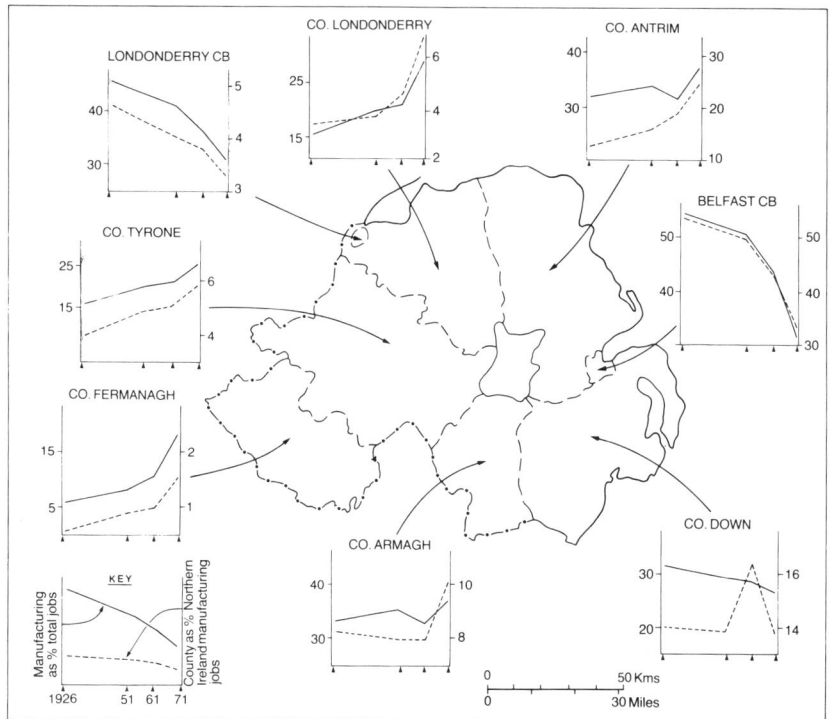

Fig. 5.7 Major manufacturing centres and specialisations in Northern Ireland, 1971. Despite the relative advance of the west (Fig. 5.6), five of the six local authority areas with over 5,000 jobs are in eastern Ulster. Several of the specialised centres reflect the presence of just one firm: some of these have closed since 1971. *Sources:* based on Northern Ireland Census of Population (1971) *Economic Activity Tables.*

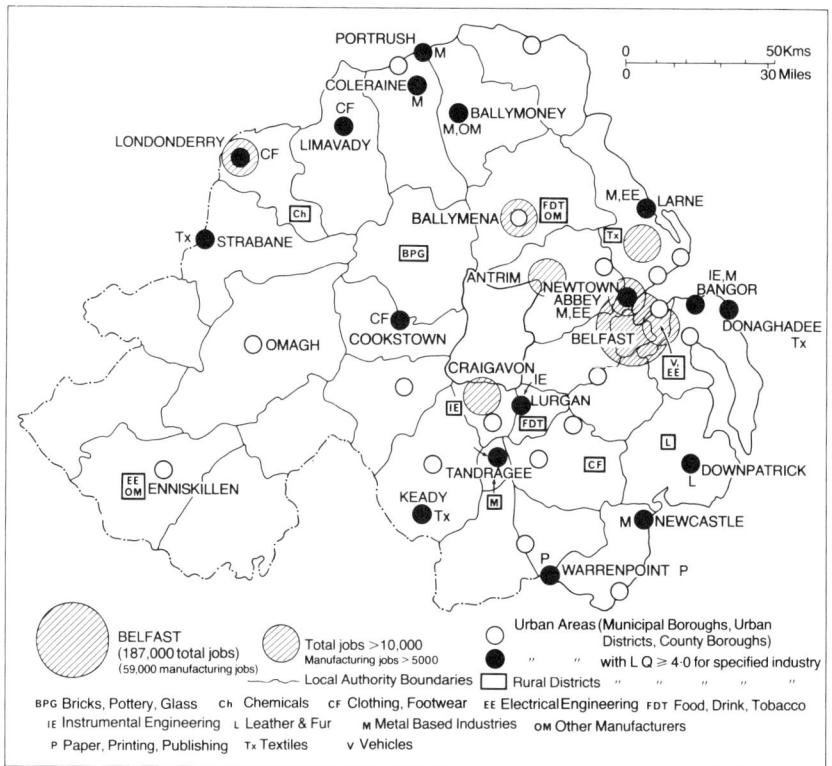

Intra-regional geography

Internally, Northern Ireland and the South East have much in common. The post-1968 period has seen the progressive decline in the dominant centres (Belfast and Londonderry) both in their share of regional manufacturing, and in industry's importance in their local economies, with all other counties (except Down) rising on both counts (Fig. 5.6). But centre–periphery differences remain; in 1971 the three central counties (Belfast, Antrim, Down) still contained 72% of regional manufacturing (and 69% of remaining jobs) (Hoare 1982).

Major specialised employment 'clusters' (LQ ≥ 4.0) appear in Fig. 5.7. In 22 of the 67 local authority areas pre-1972, no single industry even reached the 'fair share' score of 1.0, emphasising the limited relevance of manufacturing in much of the region. The general impression, again, is of dominance by the east, although here and elsewhere high LQs often represent just one firm. Regional health indicators show a similar centre–periphery pattern—percentage unemployment is higher in the west, duration of unemployment longer, unemployment : vacancy ratios greater, and incomes lower (Hoare 1982). Accepting that the centre's concentration of manufacturing contributes to these differences, we have still to explain the dominance of the east in Northern Ireland's manufacturing geography.

Centralising forces

(a) Economic   Belfast and its sub-region seems a natural focus for growth along 'centre–periphery' lines. Historically the point of entry of Huguenot settlers (responsible for the birth of textiles) and the 'planters' of the sixteenth century onwards, the east has developed into the paramount labour pool, the dominant cluster of industrial suppliers, commercial and domestic markets, supporting infrastructure (research, government and legal departments) and the focus of internal and external communications. Psychologically too, it benefits: a recent survey in Ulster suggests that the urban labour force have more positive work attitudes than its rural counterparts (Miller 1978).

(b) Demographic   Northern Ireland's majority Protestant community predominates in the east and its Catholic minority in the west. Larger family sizes may predispose Catholics to higher unemployment, while formal education levels are higher among Protestants in key areas like science and technology. Analysis of these educational differences reveals no additional centre–periphery element at work here, so (b) is not merely a rewriting of (a). The notion of the 'Protestant work ethic' also suggests a demographic difference important to manufacturers. Ulster's Protestants certainly have a more positive attitude towards the role of 'big business', but otherwise the evidence on religious differences in work attitudes specific to Ulster is inconclusive (Hoare 1982).

(c) Political   A highly contentious aspect of manufacturing location is rooted in the basic geographical equations of Northern Ireland:

Periphery (west) = Catholic   = political opposition to Unionist party
Centre (east)   = Protestant = political support for Unionist party

Unionists monopolised the regional parliament (Stormont) from 1929 to 1972 and, say their opponents, directed new manufacturing jobs to the east, ensuring both the support of the Unionist faithful and high emigration rates from the Catholic west. A range of devices was allegedly used to achieve this goal (Hoare 1981), perpetuating a geographical mismatch between industrial growth and social need (chronic unemployment). Certainly, independent assessments of Unionism at work agree that discrimination was practised in other areas (especially housing and local government), but no research exists into the truth of the specific 'industrial location' charge. Unionist politicians retaliated by saying that, first, they did what they could for the west, but, secondly, that they could only persuade manufacturers, not direct them.

Decentralisation forces

(a) Economic   Signs of Belfast's experiencing certain diseconomies of scale come from the Matthew Report (1964) which identified problems of outdated premises, congestion, high rents and rates, car parking, and labour shortages. The Quigley Report (1976), over a decade later, underlined the last of these, as Belfast's ratio of vacancies to unemployment was Northern Ireland's highest. Though less studied than in the South East, some factory movement from the 'centre' can also be identified.

(b) Economic planning   Government-owned sites, factories and training centres have their own geographical patterns, and the regional planning financial support offered to firms also varies spatially: the higher the local unemployment, the higher the grant. Some shift away from Belfast does appear in the geography of assisted firms over time, a trend continued by LEDU activities.

(c) Physical planning   This also has shifted from Belfast. Since 1969, two issues have dominated—the overwhelming concentration of activity in Belfast and the problems of neglect in the west. Four reports focused on these problems have progressively extended both the remit of spatial planning away from the Belfast sub-region and the numbers of growth centres designated (Fig. 5.8). As in the South East, these centres are planned to receive a balance of jobs (largely, manufacturing) and homes. Again, too, the justification offered for the precise centres identified is pretty thin, and the same divorce between economic and physical planning agencies raises question-marks for the successful coordination of the two. Unlike the South East, though, no jealous lower-tier planning authorities muddy the waters (the same Department handles both regional and local physical planning in Northern Ireland), but neither has there been any IDC system to 'encourage' industrial mobility, as from London to the outer South East.

A comprehensive assessment of physical planning impact is not easy to make. Its New Town element (Craigavon, Antrim/Ballymena and Londonderry) had attracted a 35,000 population growth and 18,600 manufacturing jobs between designation and 1976 but the jewel of the planning crown, Matthew's 'New City' at Craigavon, was barely one-third of the way to its target population. Industrial development of some 99 new plants (8,000 jobs), including the Goodyear Tyre plant, has outpaced population growth (despite 'lump sum' financial carrots to

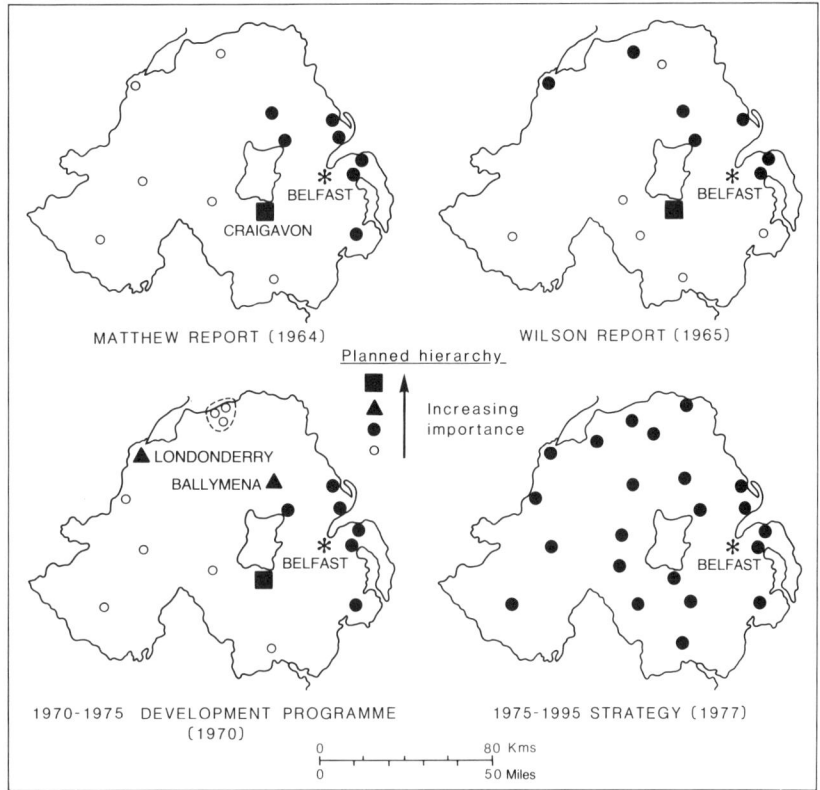

Fig. 5.8 Four regional plans for Northern Ireland, 1964-77. Not all the towns picked out for growth in one plan are designated also in later ones, though the latest (1977) is all-embracing—probably too much so in a small region with little growth to spread around. The 'hierarchies' shown should be seen in an intra-plan rather than an inter-plan sense.

families making the move to Craigavon). This is partly due to its bad name for vandalism, but also to the immobility of residents of Belfast's 'territories' for whom jobs in Craigavon, 35 km away, are within commuting range. The latest strategy has scaled down its 1995 target population to 85,000 (originally, hopes had been for 100,000 by 1981), with 'growth centre' status bestowed on all local government centres beyond the immediate surrounds of Belfast. At best this is a reassessment of previously advocated advantages of concentrated growth to counteract Belfast's magnetism: at worst a bowing to the political rivalries and realities of a divided community in a depressed region. (See also p. 72.)

Inner cities

Problems

While not a 'region' as were the previous examples, the 'inner city', discovered by geographers and planners in the 1970s, is now an arena of spatial planning relevant to manufacturing geography. Serious problems have been identified in the inner parts of major cities in both the prosperous and distressed regions alike.

What are these problems? Their relative importance varies from case to case, but Table 5.4 identifies the most common ones, showing the scope of the inner-city problem, and the 'multiple deprivation' it generates for inner-city residents. This derives partly from the interdependencies among the problems shown, both within and between the columns of Table 5.4, which are such that labels like 'economic' and 'social' can be highly arbitrary in practice.

Economic	Social	Environment	Political
Loss of workshop premises on redevelopment	High unemployment	Derelict land	Loss of rateable value (income)→ low standards of maintenance of services
	Social polarisation	Vandalism	
Low incomes and low purchasing power	Outmigration of most mobile		
Reduced stock of suppliers and customers	Concentration of least powerful elements of society: single-parent families immigrants handicapped and/or unhealthy low-income households		
Unskilled workforce	Absentee landlords		
	Multiple occupancy of dwellings		
	Poor standards of housing		
	Low educational standards		
	High percentage of immigrants		

Table 5.4 Inner cities: symptoms of distress.

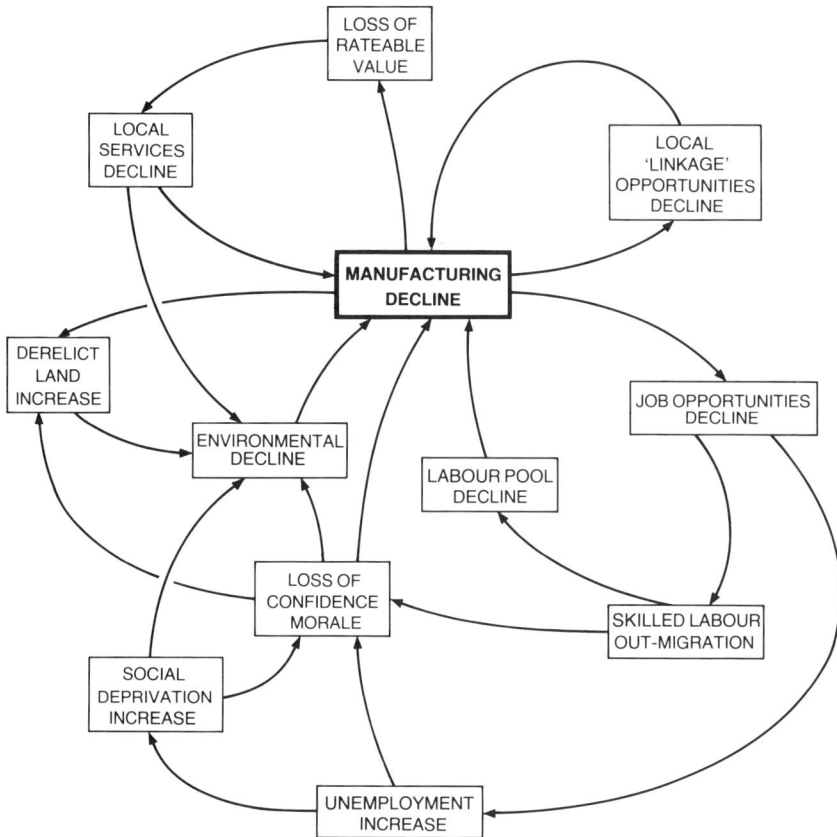

Fig. 5.9 The vicious circle of manufacturing decline in inner cities. In such a complex system of inter-linked events identifying 'causes' and 'consequences' becomes very difficult. But most inner-city gurus, from the political left and right alike, see the loss of 'basic' manufacturing activity as the key starting-point.

As to the specific role of manufacturing, no concensus exists in the literature on the inner city. Suffice it to say that manufacturing changes are seen in many quarters as at least one major generator of inner-city distress. Fig. 5.9 shows how a change (for the worse) in inner-city manufacturing jobs can translated into a downward slide in other inner-city components, as well as showing the effect of some of the reverse,

	1951–61 changes (%)		1961–71 changes (%)	
	Population	Employment	Population	Employment
Urban cores (≃ Inner cities)	+ 1.8	+ 6.7	− 2.7	− 3.1
Metropolitan rings (≃ Outer cities)	+ 13.3	+ 6.6	+ 17.2	+ 15.0
GB total	+ 5.0	+ 4.9	+ 5.1	+ 1.7

Table 5.5 Inner-city employment trends, Great Britain: population and jobs. *Sources:* Drewett *et al.* (1976); Cameron and Evans (1973).

'feedback', flows. Even if isolating the independent role of the manufacturing component is impossible, the complex effects of its decline on the inner city are clearly far-reaching. Equally clearly, the interrelationships shown are cumulative: manufacturing decline stimulates other trends which reinforce rather than dampen down the initial decline.

Some inkling of urban manufacturing decline appeared in Chapter 4, and more detailed evidence from British Population Censuses shows that, in major cities, 'inner' employment as a whole has been in steady relative decline compared with outer areas since 1951 at least. Since 1961 this has become an absolute decline and, within this, manufacturing is the major single ingredient in these job losses (Table 5.5).

Deeply ingrained urban employment changes are at work here. Why, only recently, have these become seen as a 'problem'? While there are no easy answers, one factor is the same mushrooming of research, focusing the public attention on urban issues as never before. Another is the feeling, hard to justify (or refute) that manufacturing decline, while acceptable in moderation, has 'gone too far'. The GLC argues that they (and, by inference, other big cities) are not just losing 'surplus' jobs they do not really need, which do not require a 'big city' location, and which merely clog up the urban works. Rather, the job losses are now sapping the very life-blood of the capital and are leading to firms occupying sub-optimal locations outside the city. To this is added an about-turn in relative movements of people and jobs. Before 1961, broadly speaking, jobs followed people in leaving cities (Table 5.5; Drewett *et al.* 1976; Warnes 1980), but since then job losses have caught up, and in places outpaced population decline.

'Causes'

Until the mid-1970s the causes of this manufacturing decline seemed pretty straightforward. 'Decline' resulted from plant relocation from inner to outer city or beyond. Several studies had highlighted the scale and centrifugal nature of industrial migration (Edge 1973; Keeble 1978), and the reasons for it, especially the search for space and labour. But increasingly sophisticated data bases then allowed inner-city manufacturing to be examined in 'components of change' terms. The results made surprising reading. 'Deaths', not 'out-migration' formed the lion's share both of gross manufacturing job loss and of plant loss (Table 5.6) (Dennis 1978), often exceeding on its own the three growth 'components'. But what happens when inner- and outer-city changes are compared, and when we use the stock of firms in different city areas to calculate rates of change? Where the first is done, deaths still seem more important in inner-city balance sheets than in the outer city although in the one case where rates of change were calculated (Glasgow) inner-city

Table 5.6 Inner-city
manufacturing: components
of change. *Sources:* Thrift
(1979); Lambert (1979).

	Greater London 1966–74	Inner Manchester 1966–72	Inner Bristol 1966–71	Inner Bristol 1971–5
Total employment decline	− 383,400	− 30,387	− 2,148	− 5,165
'Deaths'	− 183,200	− 28,260	− 2,443	− 3,529
Out-moves	− 97,100	− 7,135	− 463	− 411
In situ Change	− 116,000	− 5,984	+ 1,054	− 1,263
'Births'	+ 9,900	+ 6,514	+ 196	+ 372
In-moves	+ 3,000	4,478	+ 56	+ 82

employment decline resulted more from abnormally low birth rates than from high death rates (Thrift 1979).

If the facts of this manufacturing change are well established its causes are less so, although a number of ideas are current.

(a) Permissive factors (allowing job losses to occur)   Here the most important are communications improvements in road, rail, the telephone system, telex and other 'information' channels, reducing the need for check-by-jowl inner-city locations for efficient information flows within and between firms. The spread nationwide of efficient power systems, especially electricity, is another example.

(b) Encouraging factors (stimulating job loss)   Locational explanations argue that inner cities have become less attractive for manufacturing enterprises, leading to factory migration, selective closure or contraction (Keeble 1978).

(i) Space problems   The office boom of the mid-1950s, planned clearance and redevelopment of inner-city districts, coupled with IDC and other zoning constraints reduced the supply of industrial land and increased its cost. Suitable premises for small firms are swept away in bulldozer's rubble, while large technically-sophisticated firms find their ground-space needs cannot be met either. Selling a valuable inner-city site can buy the required space elsewhere (Chapter 6).

(ii) Labour problems   Labour has decentralised, and skilled labour especially so; it has been enticed away, for example, by new local authority housing under NET agreements. Progressive deterioration of inner-city environments reduces their attractiveness for senior staff too, on 'psychic income' grounds.

(iii) Aura of failure   Decentralisation and non-urban manufacturing is now sufficiently established to remove fears that a non-central site is a recipe for industrial disaster. Instead, it is now the inner city that suffers the crisis of confidence.

(iv) Linkage losses   Loss of a few big firms can have negative multiplier effects on their suppliers and subcontractors. Trade declining through London and Liverpool docks similarly affects import-processing firms.

(v) Transport problems   Traffic congestion in inner-city streets increases problems for firms dependent on long-loader road transport, and for a modern, car-oriented labour force.

(c) Structural explanations   These blame the inner city's increasing bias towards old declining industries (for instance textiles in West Yorkshire, ships in Newcastle and Belfast) as growing firms move out. While these arguments are appealing at first glance, shift–share analyses show industrial structures in London and Birmingham to be better than the national average, while that of inner Manchester is similar to the rest of the city.

(d) Size explanations   Here smallness is equated with weakness, and thus tendency to decline. Research does suggest that small firms have been more likely to close than large, and that inner cities have more than their fair share of small firms. Small firms may be impotent in the face of planning proposals for inner-city redevelopment, and be easy meat for take-overs and subsequent rationalisation and closure by large corporations.

(e) Organisational explanations   These, in apparent contradiction to (d), place the blame on the inner-city manufacturing dominance of big corporations! Certainly, in some big-city economies like Glasgow the control exercised by multi-plant firms is above that of their surrounding regions, and big corporations have been seen as a major factor in inner-city employment change (Thrift 1979). Stripped of usable equipment and translated into cash on the land market, inner-city sites make a valuable contribution to multi-plant reorganisation. Elsewhere, though, the evidence is inconclusive—in Liverpool and Manchester single-plant firms are at least as likely to close as multi-plant units, although those suffering recent organisation change seem also especially prone to decline or closure (Dicken and Lloyd 1978).

   None of these explanations is wholly adequate on its own, nor are they mutually exclusive (multi-plant companies may be better able to see the locational drawbacks of inner-city locations, for example). And as cross-city studies reveal differences in the make-up and nature of change in inner-city manufacturing there is no reason to assume the causes for change will be any more constant over space.

Solutions?

With such a variety of interpretations of just one aspect of inner-city problems, answers to the question 'What should be done?' are equally diverse (Kirby 1978).

(a) *Laissez-faire*   Decentralisation being so well-established, perhaps there is little that should or could be done. British cities are undergoing change, and planners should plan with this rather than against it. In Warnes' words:

'The driving forces behind the dispersal of population and employment are so intimately bound up with the modernisation of a city's physical facilities and with improvements or changes in its inhabitants' lifestyles and they have been so durable, that it is surely the folly of Canute's advisers in present economic circumstances to attempt to reverse or even resist them' (Warnes 1980, p. 43).

(b) Improved mobility   Here two courses are possible: first, raise the skill level of unemployed or misplaced workers (occupational mobility) and secondly, improve housing finance, inter-authority co-operation in housing allocation, and the willingness of NETs to take the unskilled (geographical mobility). Inner Area Studies (Department of Environment 1977), especially the Lambeth one, underlined the latter, but central and local government seem lukewarm, while the former approach offers little short-term palliative to inner-city unemployment.

(c) Planned decentralisation to a better life   Champions of the NETs argue continued adherence to phased, balanced dispersal to high-grade environments. At least this is arguing with the tide in a general decentralist sense. Against it, though, planned migration does nothing for those who cannot or will not move, and so increases inner city polarisation, while the surprisingly small proportion of urban population and job loss accounted for by NET movement suggests this may be irrelevant to the main issue.

(d) Radical   Solutions derived from the political left see the inner city as one further facet of the general issue of ownership of industrial capital and the growth of big corporations. Greater state ownership, public accountability of large corporations and worker influence in locational (and other) decisions become advocated remedies. Community Development Project teams, set up by the Home Office to examine localised problem areas (many of them inner cities like the Canning Town case study, below) were leading advocates of this line. However, their steady move leftwards weaned and then orphaned them from their Establishment parents. Whatever their justification otherwise, such solutions are currently beyond the pale politically.

(e) Inner-city employment generation   What has actually been done has been perhaps the most obvious course—to boost inner-city employment by a series of 'fire-fighting' measures (Fig. 5.10 and Table 5.7). Critics see this as a cosmetic, piecemeal programme from a government which feels it must do something (almost anything), while it fails to realise the strengths of urban decentralisation, where root causes lie not in the inner city but in wider social and economic forces. The way inner-city initiatives accord with continued regional policy commitments is also unclear, and the whole justification of helping deprived people by areally-based policies (be they inner-city or regional) is in question when the 'deprived' living outside these assisted areas are ignored.

Canning Town: a case study

One inner-city area that has been studied in some detail is Canning Town (Fig. 5.11) (Canning Town Community Development Project 1975). This part of inner London depended on manufacturing for 47% of local jobs in 1966, compared with only 30% for Greater London as a whole. Comparatively few residents travelled outside the parent borough (Newham) for work, so local prosperity was closely involved with local jobs, and these jobs in turn depended heavily on the London docks. About 5,500 of the 23,600 manufacturing jobs were thus in ship-repairing

Fig. 5.10 Recent central government inner-city initiatives. Those shown all date from 1970 or later. The range is superficially impressive although not all are strictly 'inner-city'. Table 5.7 details what is involved with the 'post-January-1981' crop while Thrift (1979, pp. 197-8) discusses more initiatives than are shown here.

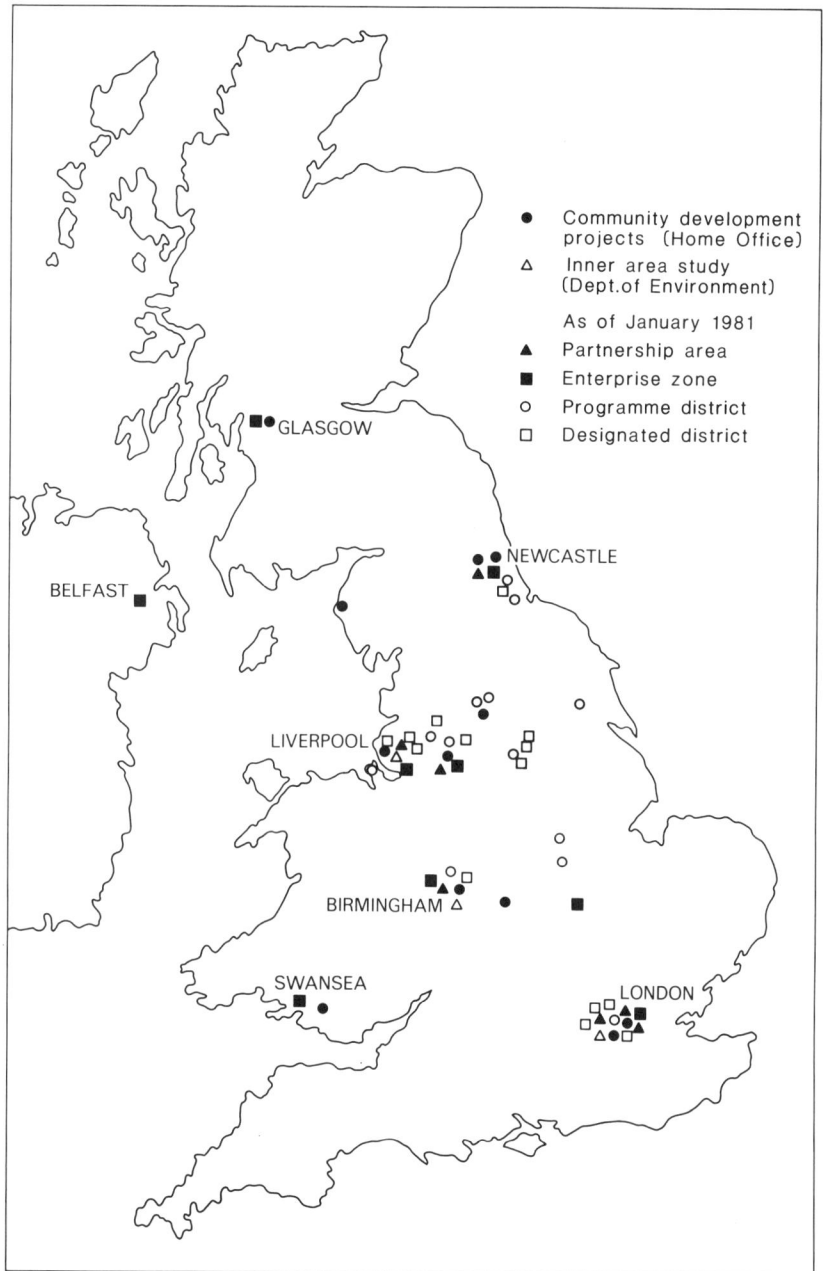

and marine engineering and another 13,000 in traditional port trades like food processing, chemicals and timber. Furthermore, 10 firms, all controlled from outside the area, supplied 63% of the manufacturing jobs. In short, the economy was dependent upon very precarious supports. The experience subsequently, in the 1966-72 period, is summarised in Table 5.8. Despite a net influx of firms the employment they generated was insignificant compared with that lost through the 'deaths' and 'in situ contraction' components of change. Considering total employment, some 6 firms, all based elsewhere, were responsible for 75% of all jobs lost, with Tate and Lyle (2,400 losses, in closures and contraction), Unilever and Harland and Wolff (respectively 1,500 and 1,460 losses due to closures) the main manufacturing contributors.

1 Operational under Inner Urban Areas Act (1978)

(a) Partnership areas (between central and local government). 75% central grants on a wide range of approved commercial/industrial projects submitted by local authorities, including 90% loans for land purchase, installation of services, advance factories, improvement of buildings, and supplying loans and grants to industrial concerns in approved Industrial Improvement Areas.

Annual budgets (1980/1) per scheme range between £7m. and £25m.

(b) Programme Districts. As (a) except annual budgets range between c. £2m. and 3.5m. (1980/1).

(c) Designated Districts. As (a) except:
(i) grants confined to industrial/commercial uses
(ii) block grant for all Designated Districts is set at £4m. (1980/1).

2 Enterprise Zones (announced in Budget of 1979)

Sites of about 500 acres or less in areas of severe physical and economic distress.

Range of assistance over 10 years for new and existing firms, including:
(i) exemption from development land tax
(ii) 100% capital allowances on industrial buildings
(iii) exemption from rates on industrial buildings
(iv) simplified planning procedures.

Fig. 5.11 Canning Town: an inner-city problem area. London's one representative in the Home Office's Community Development Projects (1970) described by a then-Cabinet Minister as '...blackspots... where social crisis and tension are at their highest' (Richard Crossman, The Diaries of a Cabinet Minister Vol.3, p.125). Canning Town displays several features common to Britain's inner cities, although its abutting London's declining dock system provides an additional, distinctive, element in its problems. *Source:* Canning Town C.D.P. (1975).

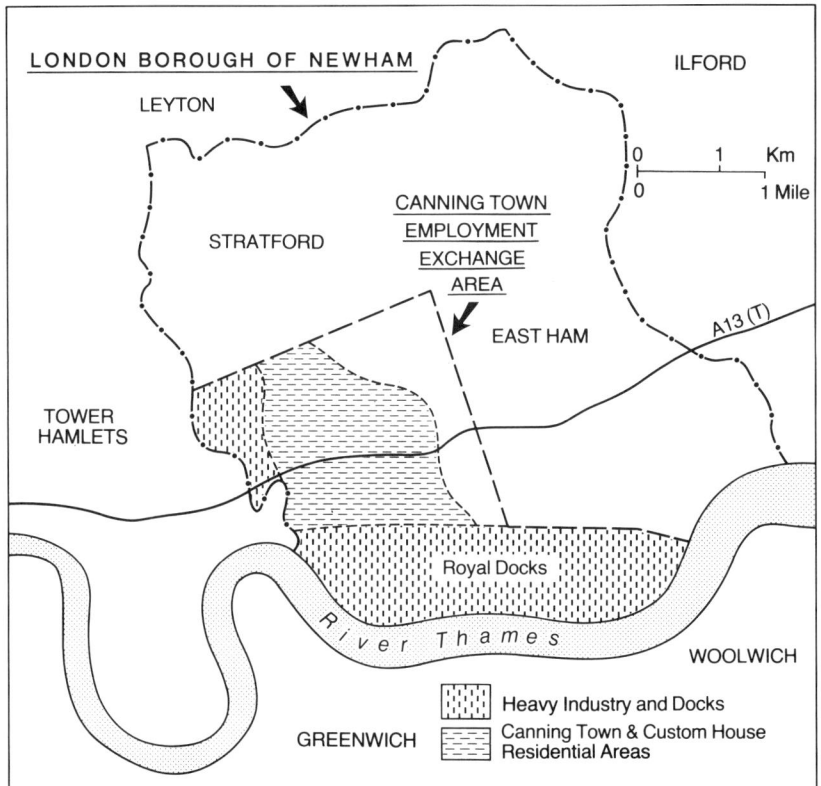

	1966	1972
Jobs	40,000	28,500
Firms	193[1]	273[2]

[1]Of these, 76 were no longer present in 1972.
[2]Of these, 117 had not been present in 1966.

Note: data relate to: manufacturing industry plus
        construction, public utilities, docks, warehousing,
        postal sorting, road transport and distribution.

As population decline occurred at only about half this job-loss rate the results was inevitably an increase of local unemployment. Local residents had essentially filled the poorly paid jobs: in 1966, for example, only 30% of locally-employed employers and managers lived in Newham, compared to 70% of equivalent semi- and unskilled workers, while 80% of Canning Town's male workers were 'manual', compared to only 52% in Greater London. Once unemployed, local ex-workers therefore lacked the money and work skills to enable them to move to new jobs in growing industries, and to new homes outside the inner city.

The reasons are many, but the decline of the port of London as trade moved down the Thames or away from it completely, the lack of opportunity to expand in old, congested and inefficient nineteenth-century premises, and the opportunity to realise the land value of inner-city sites to finance 'greenfield' expansion elsewhere were potent factors.

6 Some industrial case studies

The manufacturing geography of each industry shows some unique features and some more commonplace ones. Of the four examples discussed in this chapter one (brewing) has been labelled 'market-oriented', one (cars) as 'footloose', and one (iron and steel) as 'multi-locational' by Riley (1976). At best, though, such labels are but half-truths.

Motor cars

By the Great War the motor car in Britain was still a plaything of the rich, and the experimental side-line of several small engineering workshops. After 1918, though, the industry 'took off' into large-scale production with private car output soaring from 71,000 in 1923, through 305,000 in 1939 to 1,868,000 in 1964 (Allen 1957, pp. 160-3). In the same period the characteristics of the modern industry were forged, and with them its geography.

Characteristics

(a) **An assembly industry**   Car manufacturers assemble other manufacturers' outputs, rather than making vehicles from scratch. Wood (1976, p. 156) estimates that 60%-70% of the value of car components came from 'outside' suppliers, although such reliance on other companies varies with company policy and the monopoly position of suppliers (Turner 1963). Triplex supplies almost all car glass and Lucas the electrical inputs, while car bodies are often made 'in house'. Ford originally sought maximum self-sufficiency, importing parts from the American parent plant, and taking over British suppliers, like body-makers Scott Brothers. However by 1970 it was buying-in 60% of its components, and the same year saw a new 'spreading risks' policy which had moved away from single-source suppliers. BL, in contrast, switched from buying batteries from Chloride and Lucas on a 50:50 basis in 1982 as part of its drive to obtain more competitive prices through a 'single-sourcing' policy, threatening thereby redundancies at the loser, Chloride's Dagenham factory (*The Times*, 27 March 1982).

Outside dependence in general reflects the complexity of the modern car and its requiring a myriad of parts far beyond the scope of even the largest producer: Vauxhall uses 25,000 different 'manufactured' components, while the Triumph Herald depended on inputs from 1,500 supplier companies. As car manufacture expanded, suppliers shifted to cars from earlier product lines—Lucas from oil lamps, Smiths from clocks, for example—so furthering the growth of car production. As one geographical consequence manufacturers prefer 'minimum risk' locations near supplier concentrations, where regular deliveries are assured (reducing the size of stocks held) and input costs minimised. Another is the rapid spread of strike damage through such a closely-knit linkage network: in July 1970 a 3-week strike of 650 at Lucas laid off 24,000 throughout the industry, while 3 months earlier a strike at Crosby Springs was the 108th to affect Ford's suppliers that year!

(b) Market access With extensive penetration of the national market (57% of British households ran a car in 1979) access to major market concentrations has replaced sales to the adventurous few in the minds of producers. Location on the spine of Britain's market potential surface (Fig. 2.8) minimises delivery costs and maximises customer service, the more so since increased scale economies (see below) reduce the number of production sites from which this market can economically be served.

(c) Economies of scale Mass production of a limited model range goes hand-in-hand with scale economies at both the plant and firm level. In 1913 Ford produced 6,000 cars when based in Manchester. Now, at Dagenham, its annual output is 500,000, while the average size of car plants is three times the British manufacturing average. By 1968 four firms supplied 95% of British-made cars. Absorption of suppliers and rivals by the successful few, and high death rates among the remainder contributed to a massive organisational restructuring of the industry, now dominated by Ford, Talbot (formerly Chrysler, formerly Rootes), General Motors (Vauxhall) and the only indigenous element, BL.

Four important consequences result:

1 Some companies have inherited too many plants, notably BL's 1976 crop of 48. Its plans for streamlining, like the 'Edwardes Plan' of 1978, trimming a 180,000 workforce by 12,500 with possible plant closures, run the gauntlet between union opposition, and vital government funding, in the new car market where BL's share fell from 32% (1973) to 24% in 1977.

2 Combining plant and firm scale economies through plant specialisation results in regular inter-plant transfers of parts and components (Fig. 6.1). Ford became the first exclusive user of a freightliner service (between Halewood and Harwich) in 1968 and now claims to be British Rail's biggest customer.

3 Large multi-national car giants have the locational power to direct new investment overseas, rather than to Britain.

4 Increased mechanisation has raised the importance of the quantity rather than the quality of labour, as a locational directive.

(d) Political importance 'Probably the country's most important manufacturing activity' (Keeble 1976, p. 181), it supplies 10% by value of national exports, provides 500,000 jobs directly, consumes 20% of British sheet steel output, and is a bell-wether of the whole national economy. Whitehall partly controls its fortunes via macro-economic management (interest rates, petrol taxation, import quotas and so on) and direct infusions of cash, such as saved Chrysler UK in 1975 and such as BL have received through its 'owners', the NEB. Locationally, too, car plants, with their large numbers of employees, have been a corner-stone of regional policy.

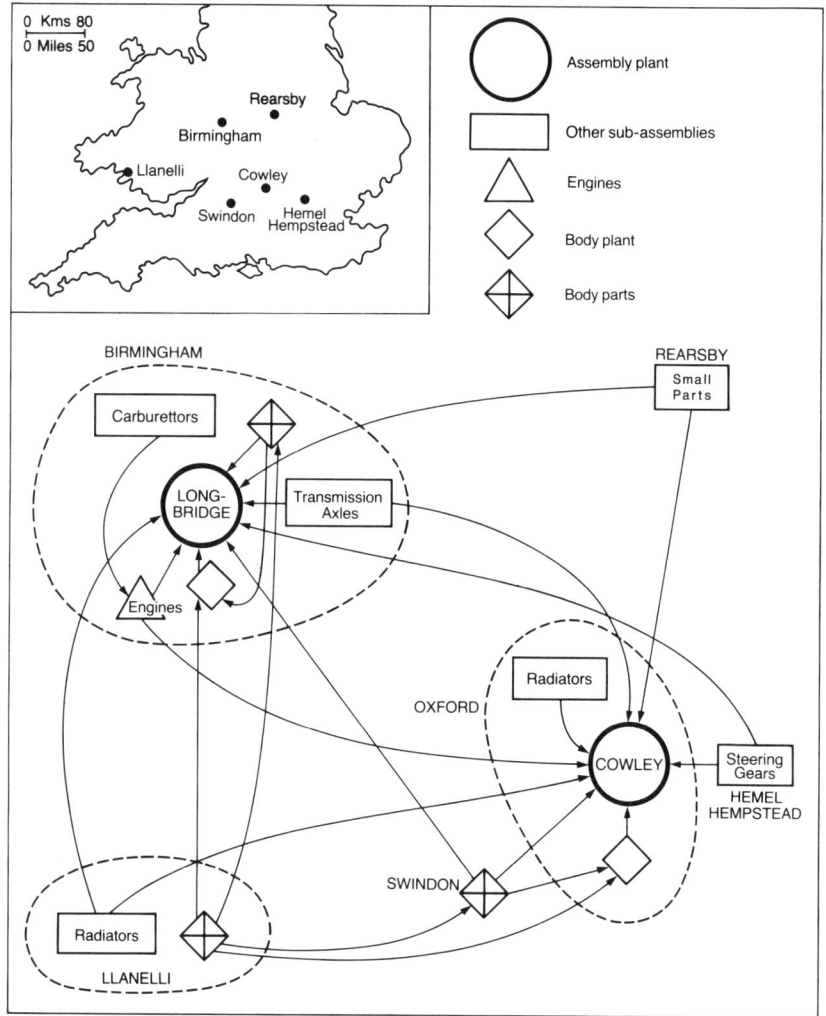

Fig. 6.1 Inter-plant transfers in British Leyland (BL). The pattern depicted is a simplified successor of the company's previous inter-plant flows which were longer and hence more expensive. Car assembly now takes place at Longbridge and Cowley using inputs from several BL plants: overall the car industry acquired 90% (by value) of its 1968 material inputs from other domestic manufacturers, compared with an equivalent 66% for all UK industry. *Source*: based on Bloomfield (1978).

Pattern

Fig. 6.2a shows the industry's employment geography over 1921-71, with some associated pattern indices (see Chapter 4), while Figs. 6.2b and 6.2c show equivalent distributions of car plants. In both respects two trends stand out: first, an increasing pre-war concentration upon a London–Birmingham axis, and, secondly, a relative post-war dispersal to the peripheries, especially South Wales, Northern Ireland, Scotland and Merseyside. Broadly speaking, the first reflects the growing scale economies of agglomeration, and the second the 'regional' arm of government.

(a) West Midlands This remains the dominant concentration of car producers and component suppliers, with Coventry (BL, Talbot) and Birmingham (BL) supreme in the former field. In the new West Midlands county 18% of all 1971 employment was in vehicles, and in Coventry itself 43%. With over 25% of all jobs in the county tied to car-making in some way, this may be 'the most extreme case of regional industrial specialisation in modern Britain' (Rodgers 1980, p. 224). Although sheet steel is now 'imported' from South Wales, the West Midlands, which has Britain's leading concentration of inter-linked metal and engineering-

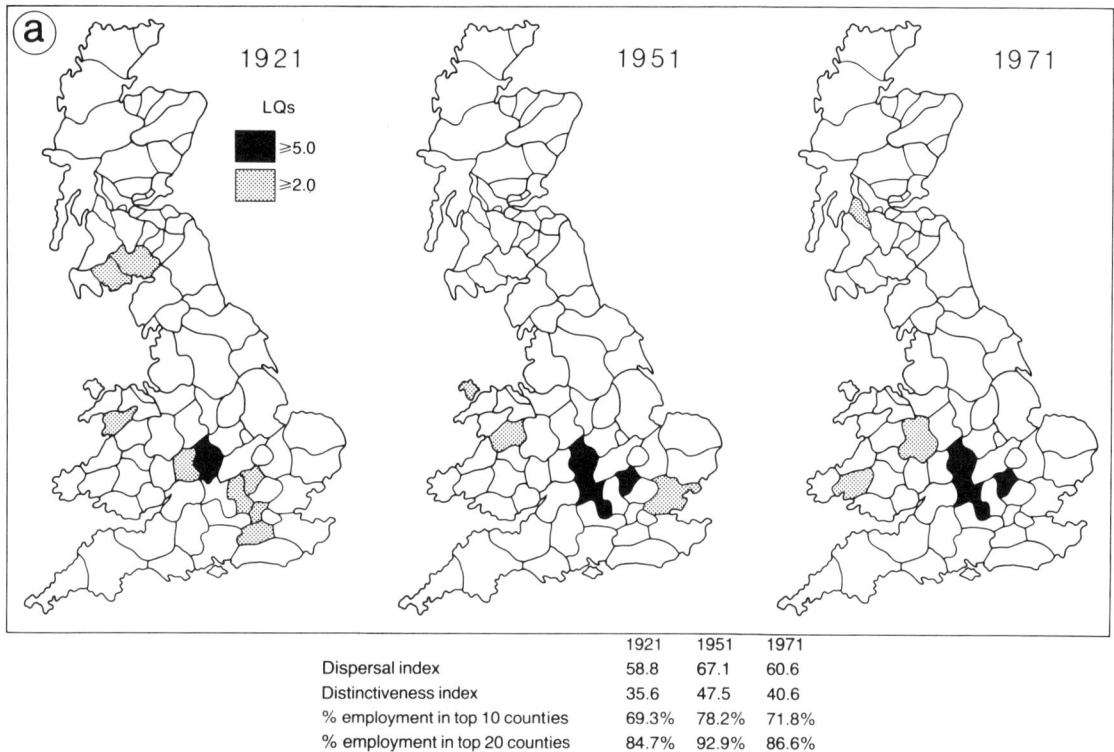

	1921	1951	1971
Dispersal index	58.8	67.1	60.6
Distinctiveness index	35.6	47.5	40.6
% employment in top 10 counties	69.3%	78.2%	71.8%
% employment in top 20 counties	84.7%	92.9%	86.6%

Fig. 6.2 The changing geography of motor car production. (a) All four summary indices (see Chapter 4 and Appendix 1) show the increasing geographical concentration of employment before 1951 and its subsequent spread afterwards. (b) Similarly, factory locations home in on the London-Birmingham axis pre-war, while the current position (c) shows the subsequent dispersal. Most of the 'others' category are specialist producers who seem content to locate away from the main heartlands of car production. *Sources:* (a) calculated from Lee (1979); (b) from Riley (1976); (c) compiled from trade press.

based industries, is the prime source of car components. This has long been so. Car production began in Coventry in 1896 when Daimler switched from cycle manufacture: others did the same from sewing machines and sheep-shearing equipment (Wolseley), finding thereby new outlets for established metal and engineering skills. Symbiotic growth of suppliers and producers then became cumulative, and received a further fillip with the post-war release of aircraft factories suitable for conversion to car production. Recently, though, the industry has experienced severe hiccups: the reduced importance of skilled labour, and competitive troubles leading to a decline of motor vehicle employment in the West Midlands region from 164,000 (1969) to 145,000 (1976).

The 'creaming-off' caused by expansion to the Assisted Areas has contributed too, although some West Midlands producers have escaped this fate, such as Reliant Motors at Tamworth (Staffordshire). Their initial IDC application for on-site extension was rejected in 1962, but after much haggling a revised application for 6 times the original area was granted in 1970. Reliant was most reluctant to move from base, as some 400 suppliers, representing 80% by value of bought-in materials, are within 25 miles of Tamworth, while its modest size by car industry standards would have meant very real problems in splitting production between Tamworth and another site. Perhaps this last factor helps explain why Whitehall eventually relented.

(b) Bedfordshire The house on the south bank of the Thames of a mercenary soldier in King John's reign, one Fulk le Breant, gave its name (Fulk's Hall) to the district of London where the Vauxhall Iron Works was set up in 1857. The first car was produced in 1903, but problems over the lease, and a shortage of space, saw a move to Luton in 1905. There

(b)

1913

21 12 31

1938

(after Riley)

(c)

1980

Car assembly plants	Other major car locations	
F	F	Ford
B	B	British Leyland
T	T	Talbot
V	V	Vauxhall/ General Motors
O		Others

V LINWOOD

BELFAST
De Lorean O V F

BLACKPOOL
O TVR
LIVERPOOL
F V
V O CREWE
Rolls Royce

O TAMWORTH
Reliant
HETHEL O
Lotus
BIRMINGHAM B T
B B T T
MALVERN O T COVENTRY
Morgan Aston O BEDFORD V
Martin O LUTON/
V V DUNSTABLE
LLANELLI OXFORD B V HENDON
B ABINGDON B
BRIDGEND F SWINDON T DAGENHAM
F

V SOUTHAMPTON

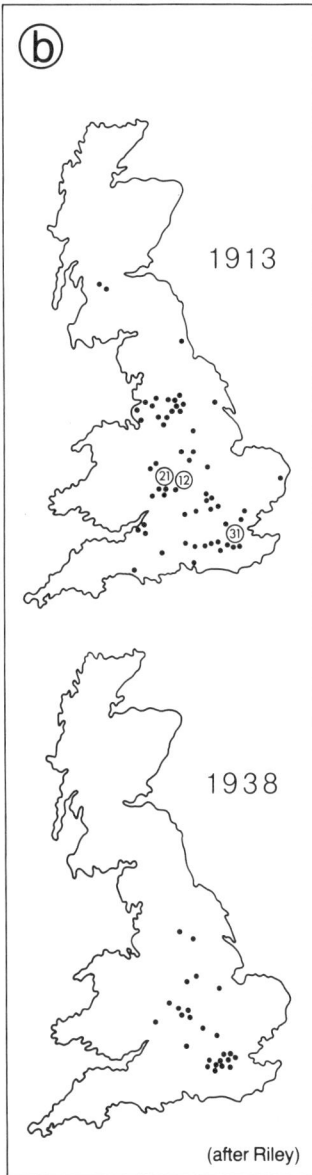

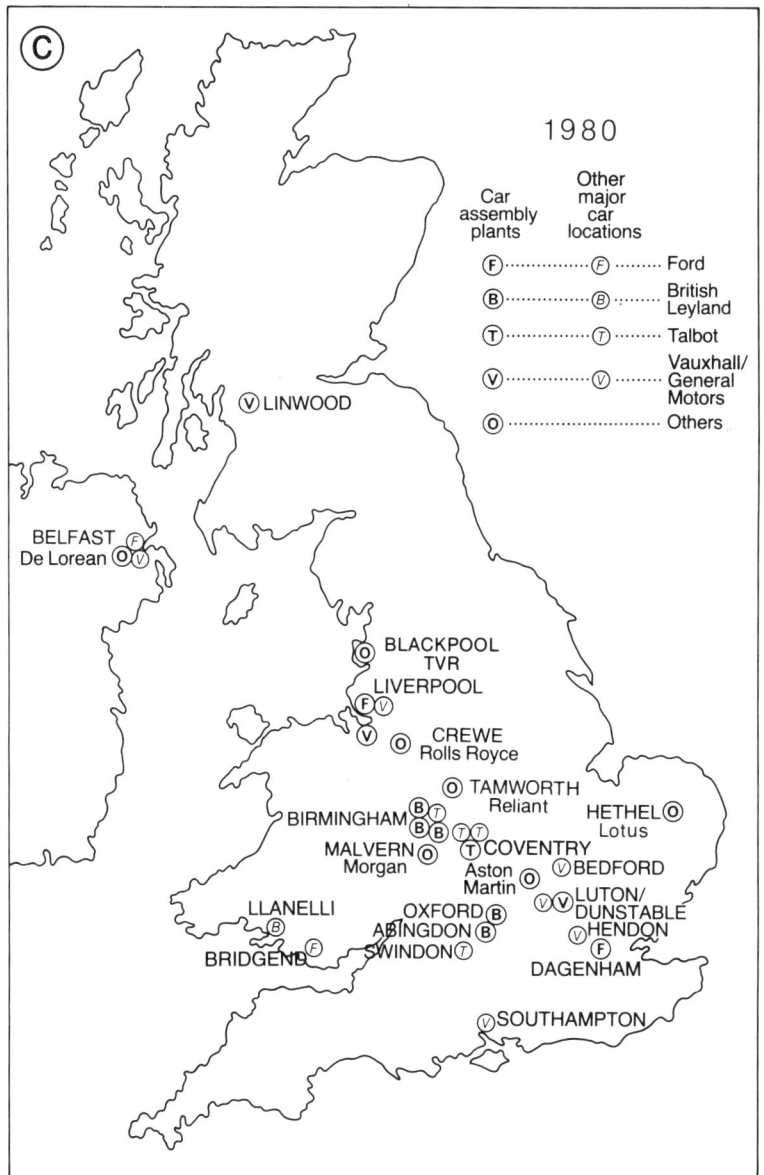

the company changed its name to Vauxhall Motors two years later, and was acquired by General Motors of Detroit in 1925. Perhaps previously agricultural areas like Luton (and Oxford) were more tolerant of the repetitive tasks of mass production than skilled labour areas (Allen 1957). Certainly, expansion at Luton (to 60 acres in 1939, and 318 by 1973) and at nearby Dunstable was dramatic, and has kept the company centred in Bedfordshire, athwart Britain's 'market potential' and routeway axes.

(c) Oxford   Due originally to the enthusiasm and acumen of Oxford bicycle repairer turned car maker, Richard William Morris (Lord Nuffield), production here is now part of the BL complex. Car production began in a hurry (Morris returned from the 1912 Motor Show with an order for 400 cars) and the decision to produce in his home town was a natural outcome. While often seen as a 'chance' location, Oxford offered access to the twin car foci of Birmingham and London.

Expansion saw Morris' works rise from 1% of national production in 1913 to 38% in 1929. It brought some suppliers to Oxford (sheet steel was produced next door from 1927, and radiators elsewhere in Oxford from 1919). Morris also sought supplies elsewhere—from Coventry for castings, and from the United States when British sources failed him. Subsequent expansion, though, limited by restrictive local planning controls, has been hived off to Abingdon and Swindon.

(d) Dagenham   Ford, the world's first mass-market car producer, was established in Manchester in 1911, importing all major needs from Detroit. Shortage of space for expansion eventually led to a search for new premises. In view of the fear of tariffs on car imports to Britain, an 'all-British' car seemed the answer, and with the company's preference for self-containment the search was for a large, integrated site. The choice fell on Dagenham, where production began in 1931. This gave access to London's large if not overly skilled workforce, and to tide-water access to coal and iron ore for the company's blast furnaces. Subsequent growth (90,000 cars in 1939, 500,000 in 1973) has made this Britain's largest single car plant and, by the mid-1970s, the largest car engine plant in Europe.

(e) Peripheries   From the late 1950s the major car producers all opened new production facilities in the Assisted Areas. Sometimes this was for 'final assembly' as with Ford at Halewood, Standard Triumph (now BL) at Speke, Vauxhall at Ellesmere Port (all on Merseyside), BMC (BL) at Bathgate for trucks and Rootes (Chrysler) at Linwood (both in Scotland), the last as part of an integrated package deal with a new steel mill. Other moves were for component manufacture, for example Ford and General Motors to Belfast, Rover (BL) to Cardiff, BMC to Llanelli, and Ford to Swansea and Bridgend. Not all were the result of government pressure: Ford's move to Swansea was, in their own words 'a freak of timing and location', as expansion needs at Dagenham coincided with the former Prestcold plant of John Bloom's collapsed washing machine empire becoming available cheaply and with an existing IDC. More often, though, their prestigious, growth-generating image made car companies prime targets for regional policy. Vauxhall's and Rootes' moves just noted, and Ford's to Belfast and Halewood, were all consequent upon IDC refusals 'at base', in the last case this being part of a deal with Whitehall whereby Ford went to Merseyside in return for permission to build a tractor plant at Basildon (Essex).
   The whole exercise has been of questionable value. The new plants often made little direct impact on unemployment, attracted few component manufacturers in their wake, and have had a chequered history. The estimated additional costs consequent upon Chrysler's Linwood location, in relation to their Coventry base (Table 6.1), are typical of many, and exclude the burden of labour there being less efficient than in the West Midlands. After 1974 even the regional planning benefits have been lost, and the company estimated (in 1973) their annual additional cost would be some £3m. 'Where' problems at Linwood become compounded by 'what' ones: Rootes 'Imp' hit severe production problems while Talbot's Avenger and Sunbeam 'commanded' merely 3% of domestic sales in 1981, making the decision to close

	1963–70 £m. p.a.	1974 and beyond £m. p.a.
Regional policy benefits	0.7	Nil
Additional costs compared with Coventry		
Transport of components	0.47	1.25
Launch costs of new site	0.15	Nil
Relocation of staff	0.37	0.03
Travel and communications	0.125	0.2
Duplication of administration	0.375	0.7
Increased stocks size required by isolation from suppliers	0.087	0.2
Distribution to UK market	0.2	0.5
Distribution to export market	0.05	0.12
Total costs	£1.5m. p.a.	£3.0m. p.a.
Costs minus benefits	£0.81m. p.a.	£3.0m. p.a.

Note: estimates as of October 1972

(February 1981) as unsurprising nationally as it was traumatic locally. BL, too, closed at 'peripheral' Speke, presaging the area's designation as an Enterprise Zone. In contrast, Ford finds nearby Halewood dovetails well with Dagenham for national market coverage. When set against other regional handouts and savings any overall cost penalty attributable to location is hard to identify, as this cautious conclusion from a House of Commons Select Committee (drawing partly on its study of the motor car industry) testifies:

'Such figures as we have do not show beyond doubt that a compulsory or near-compulsory move [of car firms] to a development area is bound to bring significantly higher operating costs for an indefinite period' (House of Commons Expenditure Committee 1973, p. 18).

(f) Specialist producers   Specialist firms have taken small shares of the national market, like Rolls Royce (Crewe), Jensen (bankrupt in 1975, West Bromwich), Morgan (Great Malvern) and Aston Martin (Newport Pagnell). As one example of the different locational experiences of such specialists, consider Lotus. This high-status car manufacturer moved from a restricted Cheshunt (Hertfordshire) site to Hethel, 13 km south-west of Norwich, in 1966. Search for 'fresh air and fields' for expansion, in the words of the Chairman, Colin Chapman, led to a survey (by air) of sites within about 160 km of London. Hethel offered space (40 acres) and an airfield, important for the racing side of the business and for pleasure use. The company had existing business interests in the region (a glass-fibre body plant on the Broads) and, being small, did not have its collar felt by Whitehall's regional arm. Some 90% of staff moved with the firm, at 'Cheshunt wages', above the East Anglian average. 'Remoteness' from the West Midlands is no real problem as road links across the country's transport 'grain' to Birmingham/Coventry are 'adequate' and Lotus buys in less from outside than most car producers. It also makes for a non-unionised workforce (unlike the West Midlands or, indeed, Cheshunt). Specialised technical labour is important, though, and Lotus draws on ex-RAF staff from nearby air bases, and benefits from the residential appeal of a pleasant local and regional environment to mobile, skilled, personnel.

Brewing and malting

Brewing has a distinguished ancestry, originating as a commercial enterprise in the mists of antiquity, with local innkeepers making ale for their customers. Inevitably, an industry whose outputs are still oriented towards domestic consumers is dubbed 'market-oriented'. Despite an inter-war sales slump, this market was larger in 1975 than 1919, but with greater production efficiency brewing employment fell over a similar period from 88,000 (1921) to 79,000 (1971).

Characteristics

(a) Why this market orientation?   First, the major input, water, is sufficiently ubiquitous to have no strong localising effect upon the industry. Representing some 90% of the final product weight, it makes brewing a classic 'weight-gain' industry, pulled towards the market. Technical improvements in processing efficiency of other raw materials (hops, barley, sugar, malt) have reduced still further any small localising effects they might have had. Many brewers have extended 'backwards' into these areas to ensure consistency in supply flow and quality.

(b) Location   Localised advantages of water quality in a less scientifically sophisticated age occasionally led to concentrations of breweries in favoured locations, as with light ales at Burton-on-Trent. Here, reputation led to its survival as a major centre once these initial advantages were diluted by advances in the chemistry of brewing.

(c) Transport costs   At 11% of the industry's overall production costs (in 1968) these are noticeably higher than in both our other examples, and in manufacturing as a whole, serving to underline the market pull. Not only is beer a low value : high weight product, costly to move, but its perishability also encourages short delivery 'legs'. Many breweries thus concentrate on their immediate markets, especially for the most perishable products—draught beers, in traditional 'cask' containers. One East Anglian brewery, Greene King, only supplies customers within 50 miles of one of its breweries (Dixon 1978).

(d) Scale advantages   These, particularly at the plant level, may offset the greater transport costs inevitable as larger output requires a wider market area. While not easy to quantify, estimates suggest the minimum economic size of a brewery has risen dramatically, from perhaps 0.07m. barrels per annum in the 1950s to about 1m. in 1971 (Watts 1977). Courage's new 'Berkshire Brewery' outside Reading will have a 1.5m.-barrel capacity to serve southern Britain, and for some beers nationwide demand is met from just one site, as with Allied's Double Diamond plant at Burton.

Two further factors encourage these trends. First, with more efficient delivery networks, unit transport costs have fallen in real terms. Beer can be pumped directly from modern road tankers into tanks, for example, obviating the manhandling of casks and kegs. Breweries abutting modern road networks, as does the Berkshire Brewery the M4, gain an additional advantage. Secondly, a market shift from cask to less perishable keg and bottled beers (the last as home drinking in front of the television grows apace) encourages wider market areas. Bottled beers, too, require expensive bottling plant. These new trends, and the popularity of lager (rising from 3% to 14% of the beer market between 1965 and 1975) have been promoted by major brewers with national publicity beyond the budget of small breweries. Quite what is the cause of what here is not easy to see, but the net effect has been to strengthen the hand of big producers.

Taking over existing breweries has been the main method of achieving these scale advantages. This gives access to a string of tied houses which, in the early part of our period at least, was the major way of expanding sales under prevailing licensing laws. Acquisitions reduced the 2,889 breweries in the Britain of 1920, to 1,418 in 1930 and 885 in 1939 (Hawkins and Pass 1979)—but the rise of a few giant groups is a post-war phenomenon. By 1967, seven companies controlled 73% of beer production and by 1976 91%, bringing the industry under the eagle eye of the Monopolies Commission to see whether, in the absence of import competition, this was in the public interest. Mergers were particularly active during 1959-61, following a determined (but unsuccessful) attempt by Charles Clore's Sears Holdings Ltd to take over Watney Mann. This underlined how breweries as a whole were undervalued in financial, 'book-value' terms, and so prey to unwanted outside attention. On the 'better the devil you know . . .' principle many merged for defensive reasons, capitalising on previously informal trading agreements or personal or family ties between Boards of Directors.

Victory in this 'transport cost v. production cost' battle thus favoured the latter. Between 1968 and 1977 the number of brewing and malting firms recorded by the Census of Production fell from 151 to 129 and the number of separate plants from 383 to 210, with the 'plants-to-firm' ratio correspondingly declining from 2.5 to 1.6. The trend is not all one way, though. Soaring oil costs hit both transport costs and the 'energy-intensive' newer beers. The CAMRA real ale campaign, tenacious management of small breweries and a host of 'survival' factors have proved the salvation of small, independent local/regional breweries. Significantly, nine of the ten most profitable breweries in Britain in 1980 were small, local ones like Morrell (Oxford) and Gibbs Mew (Salisbury). Small units of larger breweries have also remained viable propositions. When Vaux took over W.M. Darley's brewery in 1977-8 its Chairman was pleased to announce 'they will go on brewing their good local beer', while Ind Coope's decentralisation programme is reviving operating companies such as Benskins, Taylor Walker and Friary Mew which it previously 'absorbed', a course also followed by Watney Mann (Fig. 6.3). Even a 'big' project like the Berkshire Brewery is a scaled down version of Courage's original much more grandiose scheme.

Pattern

Fig. 6.4 shows the relevant spatial patterns for brewing and malting. Despite a more concentrated organisation the industry is less concentrated spatially than the other three examples, as befits a 'market-oriented industry'. Thus the LQ maps (Fig. 6.4a) are characterised by their emptiness, the only 'over 5.0' case being the tiny ex-county of Clackmannan, where Alloa has been a major brewing town since the 1820s at least.

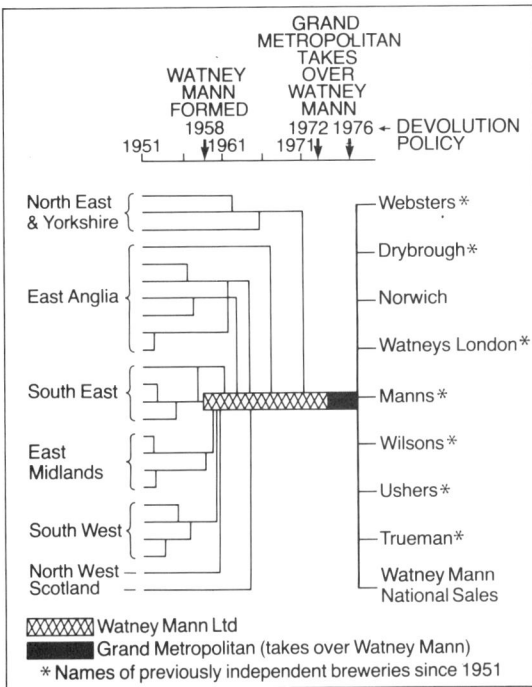

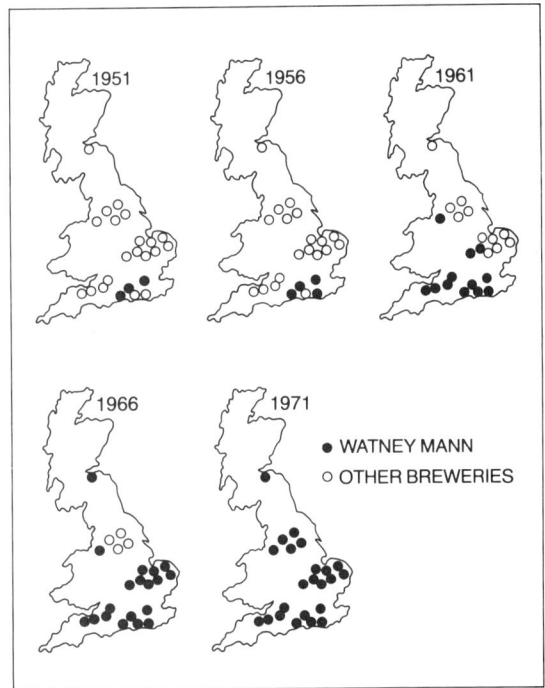

Fig. 6.3 Geographical expansion of the Watney-Mann empire. Corporate growth follows a clear pattern of spatial colonisation from a base region, although the company was swallowed up in its turn by Sir Maxwell Joseph's Grand Metropolitan chain, whose other interests include Berni Inns, Mecca Bookmakers and Express Dairies. *Source:* based on Watts (1977).

The dot maps (Fig. 6.4b) demonstrate the reduction in brewing locations. Fine details of the survival or disappearance patterns owe much to company growth strategies. Whitbread's decision to expand in the South West in 1962 found only three plants available for purchase of which one (at Tiverton) was retained and the other two (at Exeter) closed (Riley 1976). Expansion at another date would probably have found a different set of options to be considered. Watney Mann absorbed 25 independent 1951 breweries in two decades by means of 11 mergers. Their family tree (Fig. 6.3a) shows the importance of the early 1960s (following the Clore incident) and their progressive extension from a south-eastern base. By 1971 the company was truly national (Fig. 6.3b). The organisation growth of other large breweries shows similar geographical extensions from territorial bases (Riley 1976; Hawkins and Pass 1979; Donnachie 1979) but many, like Vaux, are still regional rather than national in character.

Watts' (1977) analysis of take-overs, closures and survivals identified some important geographical characteristics. First, take-overs led to increased dominance of metropolitan-based companies (like Watney Mann) over those based in smaller centres, perhaps because the former could glean scale economies at lower transport cost penalties than those in lower-density beer-drinking areas. Related to this, the survival rate of 'large-town' breweries was also greater than those in small centres. Breweries in 'remote' markets, shielded by transport penalties from metropolitan competition, also have a high survival rate. Expanding brewers swallowed up 'close' breweries first before turning further afield. Once so absorbed, these plants had a smaller chance of survival than did those remaining independent, partly because the latter operated on satisficer–survival criteria unacceptable to the more demanding large companies.

Adaptability in the face of change has also been important. The growing demand for lager has led some companies to switch product lines

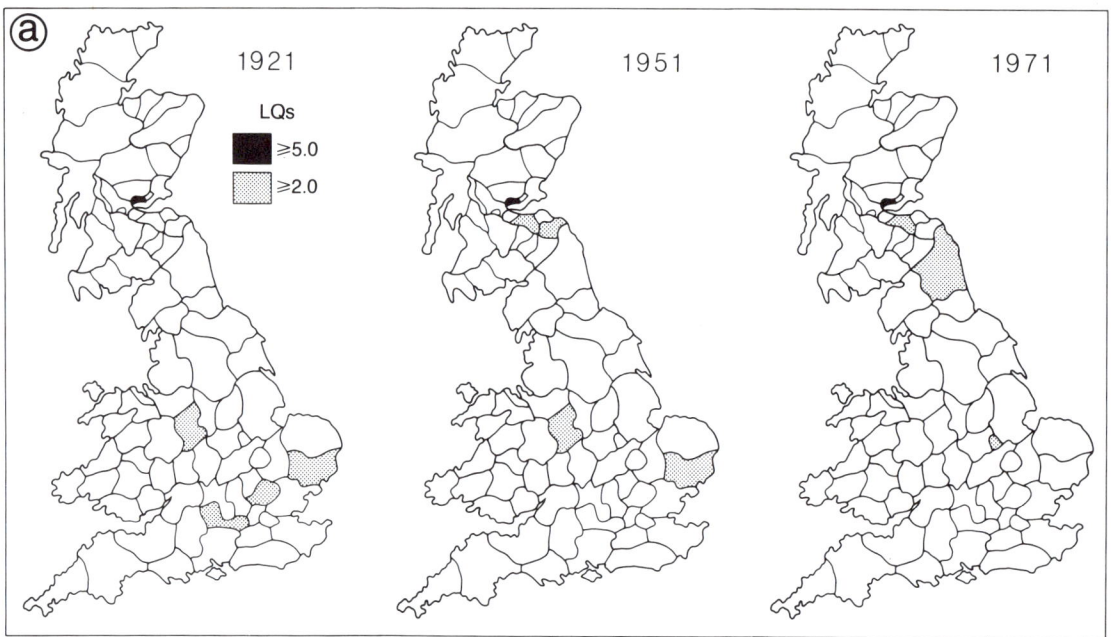

	1921	1951	1971
Dispersal index	55.6	55.4	56.5
Distinctiveness index	20.4	19.5	19.8
% employment in top 10 counties	62.2%	61.1%	58.5%
% employment in top 20 counties	80.1%	80.2%	80.9%

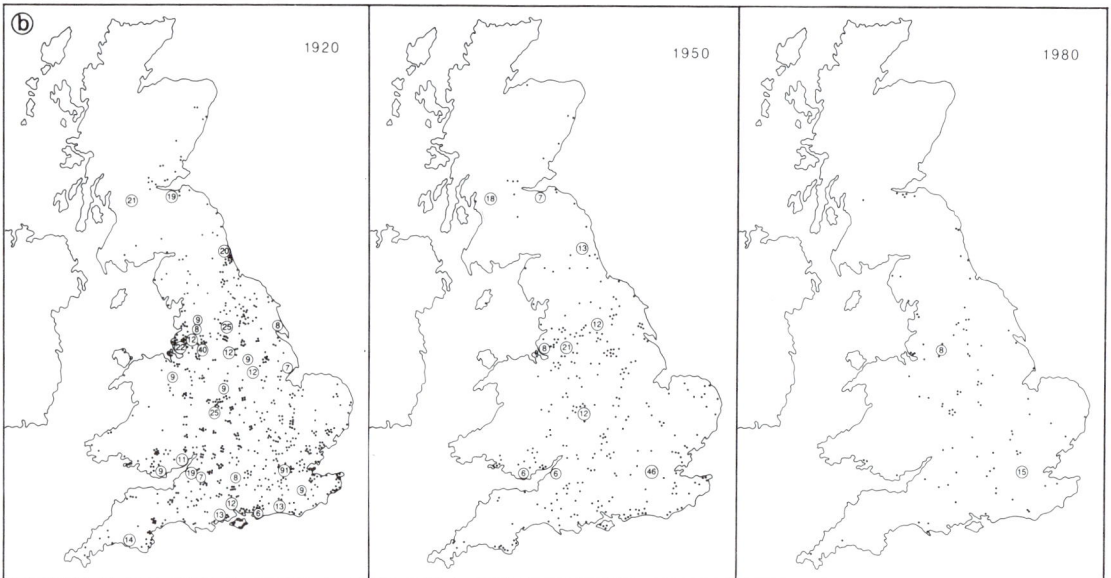

Fig. 6.4 The changing geography of brewing since 1918. (a) The summary indices are all lower than their equivalents in the other case studies, showing how comparatively widespread is the industry's employment. (b) But despite the apparent stability of (a)'s indices and maps, production sites show a dramatic decline over 60 years. *Source:* (a) calculated from Lee (1979); (b) compiled from Kelly's Directories (International Publishing Corporation).

at existing breweries (as with the Bass Charrington at Tadcaster), while others have built new lager breweries at Alton (Courage) and Northampton (Watney Mann/Carlsberg). Faced with rapidly appreciating city-centre sites and with their high-transport-cost product increasingly pinned down by traffic congestion, many companies have closed inner-city breweries in favour of suburban or greenfield sites. Courage have hived off a bottling unit from their central Bristol brewery, and have closed completely their central Reading one, while opening their out-of-town Berkshire Brewery. Redevelopment plans for the Reading site have run into planning approval problems, but other companies have been able to realise the capital value of inner-city locations to finance new investments elsewhere. Thus Whitbread sold their 250-year old Chiswell Street brewery (London) as part of a £40m. redevelopment scheme to fund new breweries at Luton, Magor (South Wales) and Samlesbury (Preston) where, in the Chairman's words:

'We can brew beer and serve our customers needs far more efficiently than from the congested heart of London.'

Electronics'

Electronics is a much newer and more elusive industry than the others in this chapter. Essentially concerned with controlling and harnessing flows of electrons in recording, storing and transmitting information, the electronics industry encompasses such a wide range of materials, products and processes that conventional 'product-based' SICs fail to provide an unequivocal definition of it in official statistics. Growth has been recent and rapid, one definition showing it to have the seventh fastest rate of growth among 108 minimum list headings (MLHs) in Britain between 1959 and 1968 (Keeble 1976, p. 191). Its base, though, is in longer-established industries, notably the radio, TV and telecommunications arms of electrical engineering. From here three generations of electronics developments have been traced: first, valves, secondly, semi-conductors (transistors) and lastly, micro-electronics, where electronic components are manufactured on a silicon chip. Each phase also passes through a hierarchy of markets. Initially produced for governmental (usually military) use, innovations then develop an industrial/commercial application, finally moving into domestic uses like stereo sets, colour TVs and video games. Major companies active in electronics include the British-owned GEC, Plessey, Pye and Ferranti, and foreign giants like Philips, ITT, IBM, Fairchild and Texas Instruments. In semi-conductors foreign companies control 85% of 'British' production (Sciberras 1977). With this rapid pace and diffusion of new electronics products the industry always has something 'new' on offer, sustaining its impressive growth. Correspondingly, though, competition is fierce and death rates high. Closures like Thorn at Skelmersdale (1,400 jobs lost) and Rank Radio International at Bradford (200 losses) show electronics brings no guaranteed prosperity. Rapid progress also affects the geographical requirements of electronics firms.

Characteristics

(a) **Research and development**   R & D spending among electronics firms in Britain is second only to aerospace as a proportion of output. Some of this is subcontracted, 'applied', research, some is pure research that generates later manufacture by researchers who 'go it alone'. Either way, the advantage of 'research-rich' regional environments is obvious (Fig. 2.6). Alternatively, 'in house' research protects commercial secrets, but is such a massive long-term expense as to encourage the dominance of giant corporations. In the scientific and industrial instrument industry, which overlaps into electronics, most important research is 'in house', with universities and research centres used just for 'low-level' information (Oakey *et al.* 1980).

(b) Labour skills   Electronics firms require a supply of qualified labour, the more so if 'in house' research is carried out. Keeble (1976 p. 192) suggests they employ more highly trained scientists and technologists than any other single industry. Thus an environment already rich in such labour (with universities, R & D centres, or established electronics personnel) or one where they can readily be attracted is advantageous. Oakey finds 'labour' is the dominant locational consideration among his sample: labour poaching may encourage relocation but staff reluctance to move house restrains the length of such migration. Once products move into mass production, though, locations with dexterous but cheap labour are favoured, as labour forms a particularly high percentage of electronics production costs (36% in 1968, substantially above the other three examples).

(c) Transport costs   As electronics is a high value : low weight industry its transport costs are predictably low (0.9% of production costs in 1968), and not an important locational force as such. However, the complexity of input requirements may encourage supplier proximity for security reasons. Detailed input–output data for 1968, though, show the industry to be a major customer of its own products, implying that many input requirements may be from secure, inter-plant but intra-firm sources.

(d) Market contacts   These are important both early and late in the electronics 'product cycle'. At an early stage, when prototype items are being developed for government customers 'continuous customer feedback' is essential. Later, at the consumer market stage, new electronic gadgets are offered first in the biggest, richest and most sophisticated markets. Either way the 'centre' wins.

(e) Government policy   At the international scale government policy has helped bring many multinationals to Britain through its 'national preference policy' in purchasing electronics. Thus Texas Instruments was attracted to Britain in 1957, as its first investment venture outside the US, while AUX, an American capacitor manufacturer, located in Britain (first at Aldershot, then at Coleraine) as the Ministry of Defence's BS9000 contract system requires some manufacture and all final testing to be done within this country.

(f) Organisational geography   Not all electronics firms are large. Between 1968 and 1977 the average number of plants per firm in the British electronics industry fell from 1.28 to 1.11, reflecting the high 'birth rate' characteristic of this young industry. But electronics still has more than its fair share of 'large' firms (Keeble 1976). Many are multi-national. The usual consequences follow: companies switch investment internationally, watering down the impact of national regional policy; major locational decisions are taken at base (often abroad) according to global investment strategies; inter-plant linkages are often high (and local 'spin-offs' therefore 'disappointing'); and multi-plant reorganisation for aspatial reasons has profound spatial effects. Massey and Meegan (1979) argue that among electronics firms reorganisation has been undertaken either to achieve scale economies or to increase marketing 'muscle', leading to a wide range of losses (closures, contractions, 'deskilling' and lost decision-making power) in certain locations and gains (the reverse) in others. One of their examples shows the complex outcome 'on the ground' (Fig. 4.18).

Pattern

Adopting the definitions of Fig. 6.5a the 1961-71 electronics geographies show an initial south-eastern clustering declining somewhat over the decade, with the rise of the Edinburgh region as a major outlier. All four indices confirm this. Dot maps of 1971-81 'electronic instrument' changes (Fig. 6.5b) show the continuing spread of the south-eastern core, although for this particular sub-group Scotland seems no more attractive than the West Country, the South Coast, or the Manchester/Cheshire area.

(a) South-eastern dominance   Here four reasons appear important:

1   This region is the major generator and attractor of technically skilled labour.

2   The region contains the major relevant markets, namely government departments and electronics-oriented consumer markets. Radio broadcasting began in London in 1922 and television in 1936, respectively 3 and 13 years before any other region.

3   Success breeds security: a proved operating environment is more able to attract high-risk electronics investment.

4   Unrivalled international communications are offered.

Evidence of intra-regional shifts in plant patterns (Fig. 6.6b) may represent the search for cheap (female) labour for mass-production lines (as in coastal towns like Worthing) and the residential appeal of the South East outside London.

(b) Peripheral advantages   These are nowhere more apparent than in Scotland, where electronics employment grew from an estimated 2,000 in 1949 to 43,000 in 1974. Most firms have settled in the Edinburgh/Fife region, although New Towns like East Kilbride have also been successful, as latterly have the Border counties. Ferranti's move to Edinburgh in 1943 spawned a number of 'splinter' companies, but the influx of US corporations since the 1950s has also been crucial. Again, a number of 'causes' are suggested:

1   cheap, abundant and non-unionised labour for 'mass production'

2   regional policy incentives

3   an attractive environment for American executives (EMIHUS, for example, cites nearness to the Royal and Ancient links as influencing their 1960 investment in Glenrothes)

4   vigorous industrial promotion by the Scottish Council and County of Fife

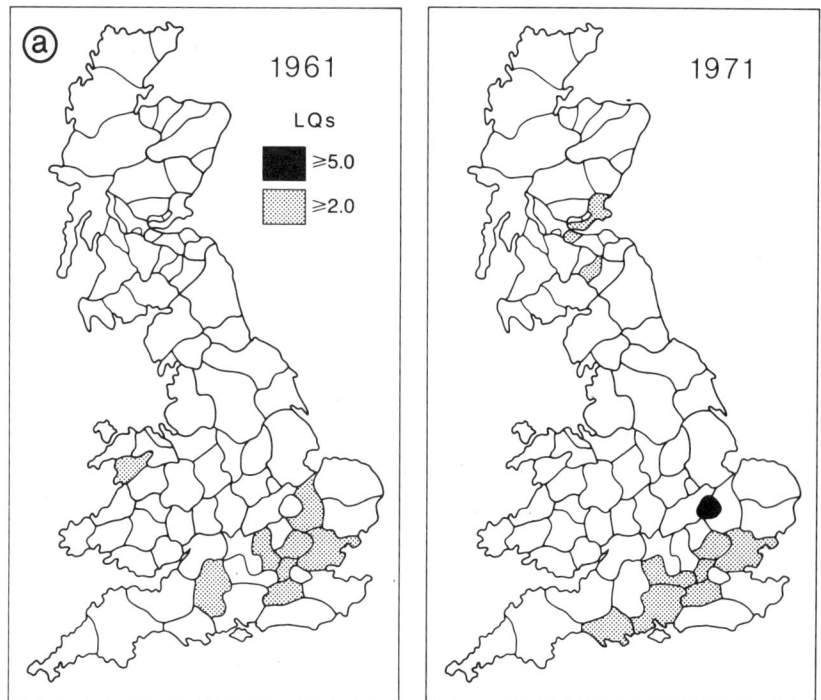

Fig. 6.5 The changing geography of electronics production. (a) Employment data, only available since 1961, show a middling degree of concentration compared to the other examples, and a trend to a more widespread distribution on all four indices, partly attributable to the growing colony in Scotland. In some counties high LQs may represent just one firm (e.g. Sinclair in Huntingdonshire in 1971?). (b) Electronics firms are not easy to define as a coherent group from trade directories, and the example mapped shows the slackening hold of London, though not the importance of Scotland. *Sources:* (a) calculated from Lee (1979); (b) compiled from Kompass Directories (International Publishing Corporation).

	1961	1971
Dispersal index	62.4	58.2
Distinctiveness index	41.1	34.6
% employment in top 10 centres	71.3%	66.7%
% employment in top 20 centres	87.8%	83.6%

5 skilled labour from, and research expertise at, Edinburgh and Herriot-Watt universities (with the former's Department of Electrical Engineering being a particular draw), and

6 the 'snowball' effect of success.

Of this list (1) and (5) (both labour-oriented) seem the most important in peripheral electronics growth in Scotland and beyond (for instance, Texas Instruments at Plymouth, Philips at Durham) (Keeble 1976, Sciberras 1977). Regional policy, in contrast, appears a minor factor, often being the 'icing on the cake' of decisions taken on other grounds. It may well be a self-cancelling device for multi-nationals within Western Europe, offering small returns in real terms, and easy to combat via 'threatened withdrawal' tactics, or circumvent by acquisitions in non-policy regions (Sciberras 1977). Electronics growth in the 'regions' reflects more their suitable labour and the 'goodwill' so achieved with Whitehall, crucial to winning public-sector contracts.

Whatever the 'behind the scenes' reasons, though, regional clamouring for such prestigious new investment is a major public issue, and nowhere more so than with the row over INMOS. This British-born but now American (Colorado)-based microprocessor company is 72% owned by the NEB. Armed with government infusion of £25m., its 'development centre' was established (1979) in Bristol to protests from the North West and elsewhere, where MPs believe:

'The research centre... has gone to Bristol because senior executives

want to live in the Cotswolds, and they feel that this is far too subjective a reason for such a major decision' (*Guardian*, 11 January 1979).

Yet INMOS originally plumped for Colorado for just these 'psychic income' reasons; one of its founders declared:

'We are looking for people of singular talent... that is why we chose the location for headquarters of our United States operations so deliberately: Colorado Springs... in the Rocky Mountains. It is a place the people of INMOS can refresh their spirits and imaginations. It is a place our families will find stimulating' (*The Times*, 11 July 1980).

Other reasons, such as easy road and rail access to Heathrow, important university contacts, Bristol's cultural and education facilities, also had an airing. Its subsequent selection of Bristol for the first production location (for similar reasons, plus the need for contact between company units on an integrated site) brought down the wrath of almost every Assisted Area in Britain (with cries of 'broken promises' from MPs in the North East) on the company, the NEB and the Department of Industry, on whose second influx of £25m. this next stage depended, and who initially approved this decision. After much shadow-boxing and threats from INMOS of withdrawal, the company decided that changing economic circumstances made an Assisted Area location more attractive and settled on Newport (October 1980). The government responded by confirming its

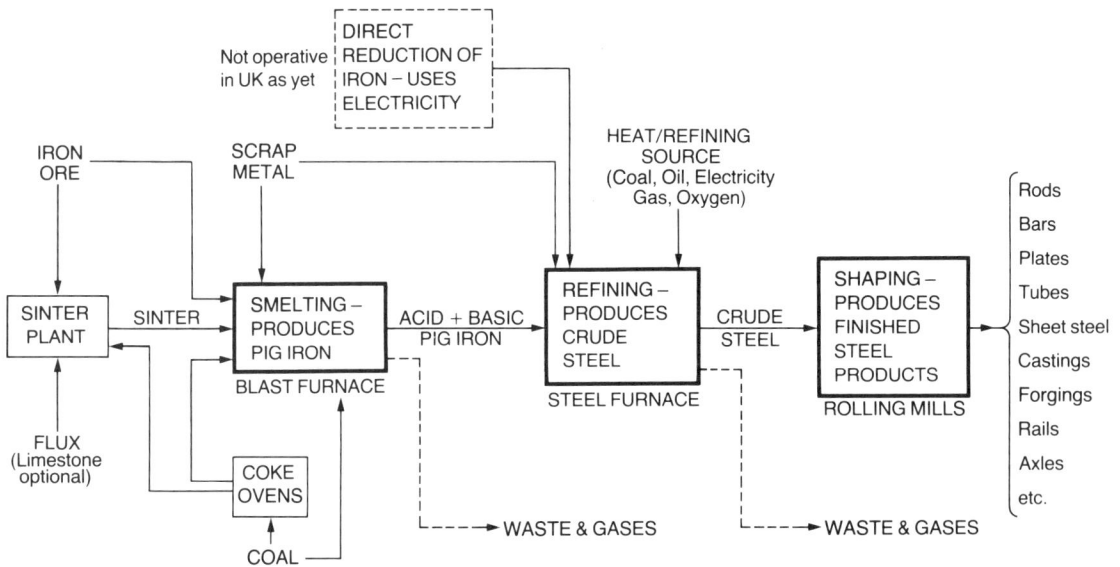

Fig. 6.6 Stages in the modern production of steel. The quantity of inputs necessary to generate a given output has fallen dramatically in the study period: in 1920 1 ton of pig iron required 1.4 tons of coke and 2.4 tons of iron ore, while in 1980 the corresponding figures were 0.66 and 0.45 tons. At the output end, 72% by value of the industry's output went to other domestic manufacturers in 1968, compared with a UK manufacturing average of 50%.

own financial contribution to the company. At Newport, INMOS is just 32 km from Bristol, receives its £25m., plus 'regional' cash from London and Brussels, and makes an ostentatious presence in a problem region (where it will probably do little directly for the unemployed, though perhaps rather more indirectly). And the executives can still live in the Cotswolds if they want.

Iron and steel

Iron and steel vies with motor vehicle manufacturing as Britain's most talked- and written-about modern industry. Records of iron making in Britain date from 800 BC, but its transformation in the eighteenth century to a coalfield-based industry, and the addition of steel after 1850 made it perhaps *the* foundation stone of the Industrial Revolution. Most modern steel output goes to industrial users, so much so that a sick steel industry is often taken as a sign of a sick economy.

The industry consists of three inter-linked stages (Figure 6.6). Integration of two adjacent blocks, or of all three, is commonplace, partly to save costly reheating of materials between stages, and partly to make full use of by-products. Table 6.2 summarises the major technological processes relevant to the geography of British steelmakers since 1918. Note how the early processes discriminated among iron ores in terms of their phosphorous content, and how the role of ferrous scrap metal, widely available in heavy industrial centres, has increased. With the phasing out of the last 'open hearth' furnace in 1980 steel in Britain is

Table 6.2 Major steel-making processes.

'Acid' Bessemer (1856)	Requires use of iron ores of low phosphorus content
Gilchrist–Thomas ('Basic Bessemer') (1878)	Allows use of iron ores of higher phosphorus content ($\geq 2\%$)
Siemens–Martin ('Open Hearth') (1860s–1870s)	Uses scrap metal (for up to about 50% of load) and low phosphorus ores.
LD Converter ('Basic Oxygen') (*c.* 1950)	Scrap for *c.* 25–35% of load
Electric Arc	Allows 100% scrap load

now (1982) produced solely by the 'Basic oxygen (BOS)' and 'electric arc' methods, responsible respectively for 60% and 40% of crude steel output.

Characteristics

(a) Material orientation Materials and fuels feature prominently in the industry's cost structure (some 69% in 1968). In 'weight' terms, too, the same material orientation applies, so that the industry is often depicted as a classic 'weight-loss' industry, with corresponding locational pulls towards material sources. Since 1918 this view has been subject to qualification. First, technological advances, especially in iron-making, have whittled away the inputs needed for a given output, so lessening the geographical pull of materials. Secondly, coal's domination among the inputs in the last century has dwindled in comparison with iron ore, encouraging steel firms to look towards ore fields for economic locations, at least before 1945. Thirdly, the increasing use of scrap has meant that major metal-using centres can be both material and also market locations for steel firms.

Finally, domestic sources of coal and iron ore have weakened, as compared with overseas sources. A long history of working domestic sources has taken its toll in quality, quantity and cost terms, while technological improvements have reduced the real cost of mining vast overseas mineral deposits and transporting them by sea. In the 1950s 10,000-ton carriers were the rule, but 150,000-tonners were commonplace by the 1970s. Until 1969 the largest ships capable of unloading in Britain were of 40,000 tons, and even now only Port Talbot, Hunterston and Redcar can handle those over 100,000 tons. Yet the potential savings are substantial. In 1967 coking coal from Australia could be delivered to the Bristol Channel for £2.25 per ton less than 'local' Welsh coal! Small wonder that modern steel works in Britain and in Western Europe have been drawn to tide-water 'break-of-bulk' locations. Between 1949 and 1969 the component of Britain's iron-making capacity officially classified as 'coastal' rose from 37% to 47% (Warren 1973, p. 81), while the British ores supplied only 19% of the industry's iron ore imports in 1979 compared with 76% in 1930. As these import costs vary little within coastal Britain, this adds to the potential pull of 'the market' over the location of steel plants, as do the growing importance of scrap metal in electric arc furnaces (where weight loss is negligible) and the relatively higher domestic freight rates on steel products than on inputs. Some 25% of Britain's steel consumers are in the non-steel-producing South East, while Scotland, Wales and the North produce 60% but consume only 20% (Warren 1969). Already, continental steelmakers sell in this southern market (some 20% of steel used in Britain is now produced abroad) and have shown interest in opening plants there.

(b) Scale economies Steel firms are large. The economies of scale obtainable in the various processes has encouraged plants of steadily increasing size (Table 6.3). Before 1945 the average blast furnace in Britain produced 60,000 tons of pig iron per annum; by 1976 this was 250,000 tons. The complex nature of an integrated steel works means that the eventual size is a compromise among the optima of the individual

Table 6.3 Indices of variations in unit cost of production with changing scale of output. *Source:* Open University (1972).

	Output (000 tons per annum)					
	100	250	500	1,000	2,000	4,000
Blast furnaces	120	100	94	89	85	82
Steel furnaces	125	100	90	82	78	75
Finishing	137	100	82	68	56	47
Total	128	100	89	79	72	67

Note: raw material costs are included at the stage of steel-making when they are introduced, e.g. iron ore is included as a cost for blast furnaces and steel scrap as a cost of steel furnaces, but the costs exclude the cost of materials transferred from the preceding process, e.g. the costs for steel furnaces exclude the costs of pig iron. Unit costs per ton for a plant with a capacity of 250,000 tons = 100.

components. Two important implications of large size arise. First, extensive, flat and extendable sites are preferable for modern steel plants (like Newport and South Teeside, but unlike constricted valley sites at Ebbw Vale and Stocksbridge (Yorkshire)). Secondly, unless multiplier linkages attract other manufacturers, steel mills can dominate the local economy, creating dangerously vulnerable one-industry towns, especially as the relationship between output and employment is changing. Thus replacing many 'open hearth' furnaces by just two BOS ones at Port Talbot in 1970 turned 2,000 jobs into 500 (Keeble 1976, p. 167). However, 'mini-mills' of up to 0.5 tons output per annum can still be economic when using scrap for electric arc furnaces, as with the privately-owned Sheerness (Kent) plant.

(c) Stability   Reluctance of the geography of steel to follow the principles of the previous sections arises because steel is 'the most inflexible of the manufacturing industries in its geographical location' (Alexandersson 1967, p. 33). Partly this reflects the 'inertia' side of locational stability. The British steel industry since 1918 has contained several independent companies. Often ultra-conservative, with ownership passing from father to son, they have fought tooth and nail to preserve their family name. Thus the South Durham company was dominated by Benjamin Talbot, of whom the company's historian wrote:

'He lacked flexibility on argument and when he sank his large head between his massive shoulders it was evident that no concession or adjustment of his views would be forthcoming. He was in many respects an uneasy bedfellow for his fellow iron and steel manufacturers, being disposed to follow an independent line if this offered immediate advantage to his group.'

After 1945 he successfully reconstructed his West Hartlepool works in defiance both of building and labour licence regulations and of a report of the industry's 'governing' federation recommending its closure; he justified his action in terms of employment generation in a 'problem region'. This same British Iron and Steel Federation exercised such a tame 'live and let live' policy in general over its members that such independent company survival was all the easier.

On the positive, 'momentum', side adaptation to changing times through 'how', 'what' and 'how much' decisions also encourages locational stability. Indeed, Britain's leading 'steel geographer', Kenneth Warren, has commented, 'there seem to be so many escape routes through a variety of technical devices from the consequences of an apparently bad location '(1970, p. viii). As elsewhere, then, *in situ* expansion is the preferred component of change for steel firms. This is especially so in integrated plants, since, as not all units wear out together, there are strong economic pressures to replace worn-out parts on site while the remainder still have life left in them.

One might think that nationalisation would free steel from the locational shackles of its history, but this has not proved to be the case. First, after its establishment in 1967 BSC was run internally along geographical lines—a Midland division, a South Wales division and so on. This was partly to smooth the road to take-over for the proud independents, but it also provided them with a lever with which to maintain their own locations. The subsequent switch to a product-based division has been a response to this and the needless duplication of investment it generated. Secondly, the social costs of plant closure weigh heavily on a nationalised company, whose parliamentary masters may depend on the votes of steelworkers. Many steel towns are in Assisted Areas where unemployment is already well above national levels (Figure 6.7b).

These factors also contributed to British steel's lack of competitiveness internationally, through a heritage of over-capacity, under-investment, low productivity and small plant size (Warren 1976). In the mid-1960s, for example, only 23% of Britain's steel output came from '2m. tons per annum plus' plants, compared with 33% in the EEC, 42% in Japan and 48% in the USA. Coupled with a long and varied steel-making history, and a dispersed resource base (Fig. 2.2) this also meant Britain's steel was widely scattered geographically. Only 22% of output came from the leading region (South Wales) in 1970 compared with 60% of West Germany's and France's respectively from the Ruhr and Lorraine (Warren 1975, p. 193). This bore fruit in conflicting regional claims for such new steel investment as there was.

(d) Government action The steel industry has become a political shuttlecock since 1945. Nationalisation featured in the victorious Labour Party's election manifesto in 1945 and followed in February 1950, only to be abandoned and steel interests sold, often to former owners, in 1953 by the Conservatives. After the present nationalisation of 14 major companies in 1967, subsequent Labour governments have taken a closer interest in its geography than the Conservatives, who have preferred to set general economic targets, leaving the details, geographical and otherwise, to BSC.

Patterns

Fig. 6.7a shows the employment-based distributions and indices for steel. Despite a slight tendency towards dispersal, the main features are its high geographical concentration by county and its lack of change over half a century, despite great changes in technology, products and ownership. At present, some 7 steel areas of importance can be identified (Fig. 6.7b), whose fortunes have changed dramatically over time (Fig. 6.8).

(a) West Midlands This region was already an iron-producer based on charcoal, and its subsequent 'Black Country' image followed the slow

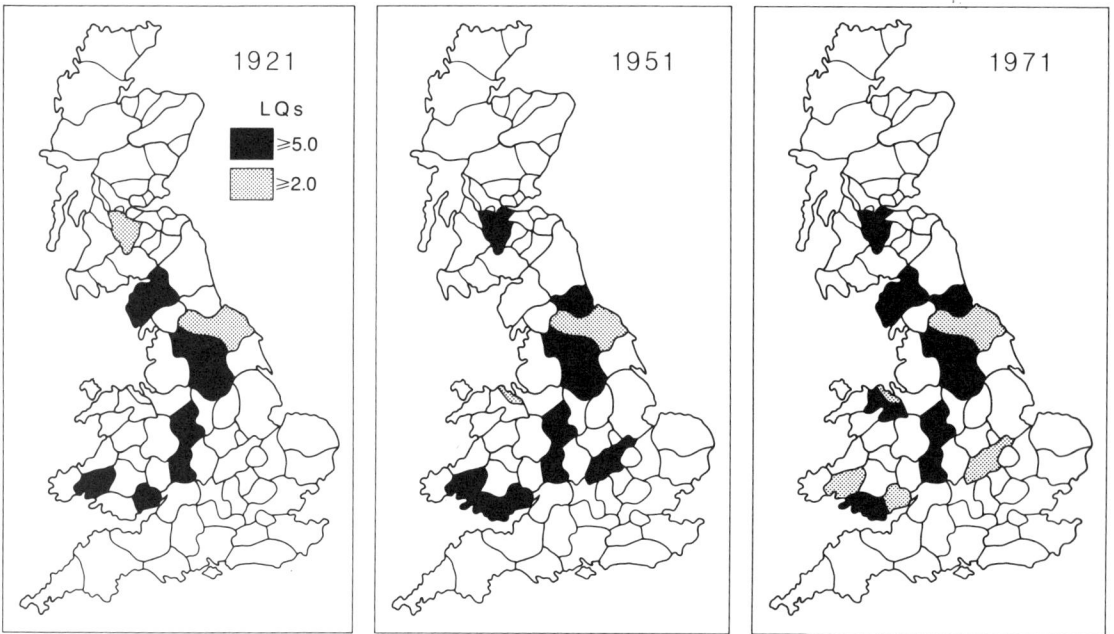

	1921	1951	1971
Dispersal index	75.6	71.7	70.2
Distinctiveness index	61.9	61.9	61.9
% employment in top 10 counties	89.9%	83.6%	80.6%
% employment in top 20 counties	98.5%	96.6%	95.0%

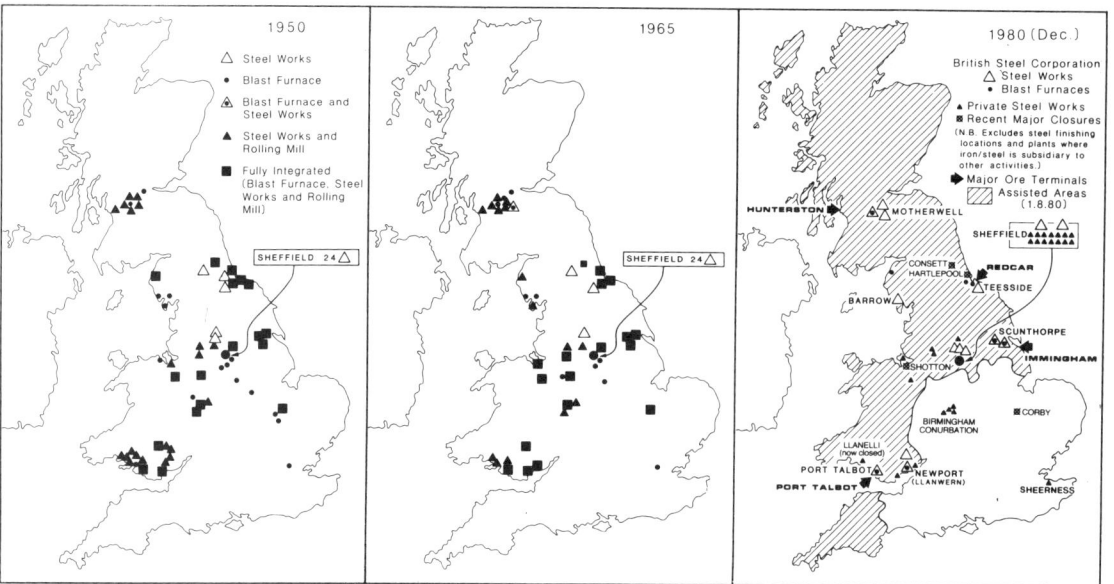

Fig. 6.7 The changing geography of steel production. (a) Steel employment consistently shows a number of major concentrations (high LQs) over the 50 years, while the indices point to the highest levels of concentration among the case studies and only marginal reductions over time. (b) While the specific processes they undertake may vary over time the geographical continuity of specific locations on the ground is very impressive. The 'post-BSC' map shows the close association between steel and the problem regions. *Source:* (a) calculated from Lee (1979); (b) Annual statistics of the iron and steel industry.

Fig. 6.8 Regional crude steel production, 1920-69. When seen in terms of their share of national output few dramatic changes occur, although Scotland, and to a degree the North East, have declined and Lincolnshire risen markedly. Separate figures for 2 regions are unavailable before 1940 and the regional classification used for statistical purposes was drastically overhauled in 1969. *Sources:* (i) Roepke, H. G. (1956) *Movements of the British Iron and Steel Industry—1720 to 1951* (University of Illinois Press, Urbana); (ii) British Iron and Steel Federation: various annual statistics and statistical Year Books.

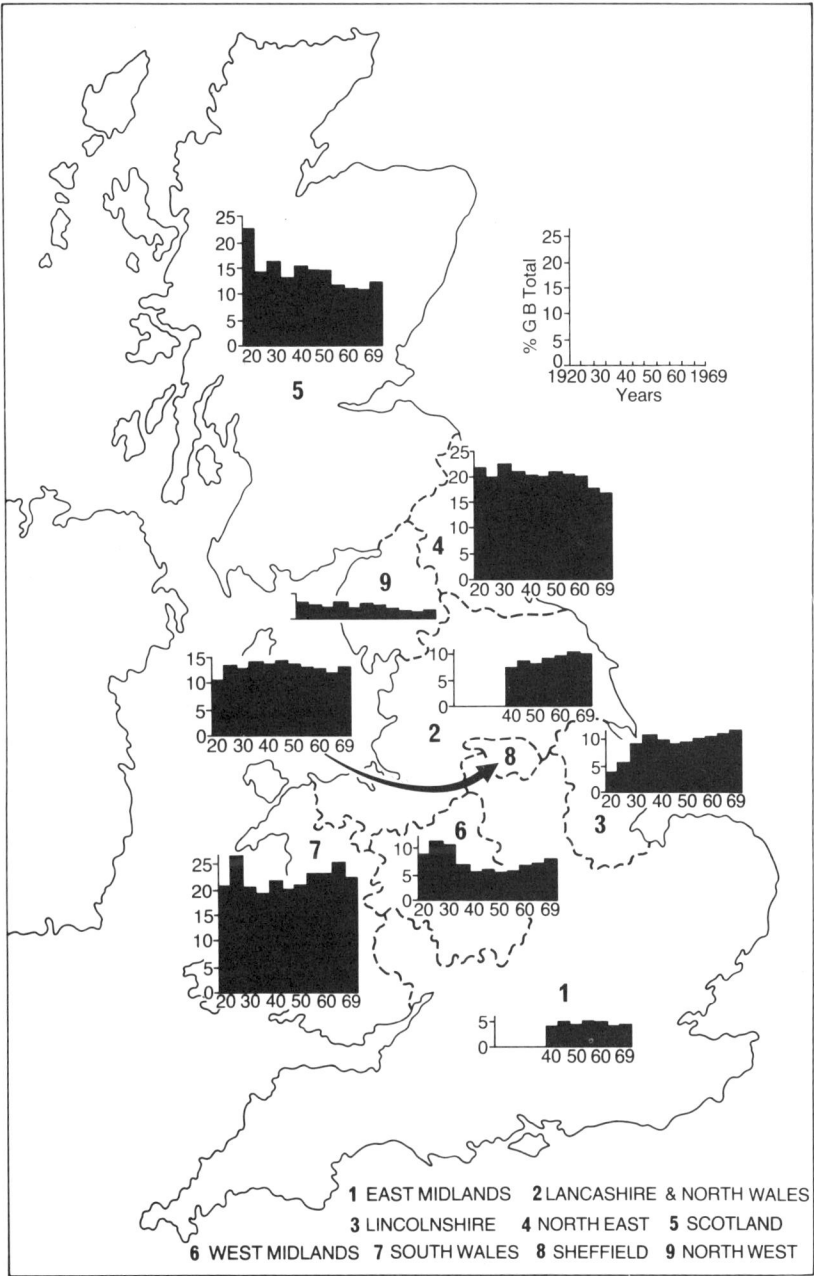

1 EAST MIDLANDS   2 LANCASHIRE & NORTH WALES
3 LINCOLNSHIRE   4 NORTH EAST   5 SCOTLAND
6 WEST MIDLANDS   7 SOUTH WALES   8 SHEFFIELD   9 NORTH WEST

diffusion of Abraham Darby's innovation of smelting iron with coal (coke) at Coalbrookdale (1709). It produced almost 50% of Britain's iron by 1788 using local, interbedded 'blackband' iron and coal, and stimulated a host of iron-using trades including, ultimately, motor cars. Local ores became exhausted. By the 1920s some ore was 'imported' (from the East Midlands), as was all ore and some coal (from South Yorkshire) by 1950. Many iron works closed and one major firm, Lysaghts, left Wolverhampton amidst much local recrimination for Newport (1898) and Lincolnshire (1910). Such as remain reflect the use of local scrap for electric arc furnaces, and successful resistance to closure threats.

(b) North Wales/Lancashire Here is a similar story of past glory, although one that reached its peak later than the West Midlands. Local coal and ores were again the initial trigger, while the importance of the acid Bessemer process here by 1869 suggests the use of Cumbrian high-grade haematite ores too. Upon decline, though, there was no strong metal-working base for scrap. Irlam (Manchester) became Lancashire's major works after its rebuilding in 1934 on the Manchester Ship Canal to receive foreign ores. The other main works is that of John Summers, a Manchester clog-maker turned nail-maker turned Stalybridge iron-master. By 1900 expansion needs took him to Hawarden Bridge (Shotton) on the Dee Estuary, but its shallowness made this an 'inland' plant by 1918, dependent on Staffordshire and Lancashire coal, and ore imports through the Mersey. Though it is well placed to serve the West Midlands market for its major output, sheet steel, in other respects this is now a questionable location for a large steel mill.

(c) South Wales Its rise to be Britain's dominant modern steel region has been an interesting one, geographically. The joint occurrence of iron and coal on the north-eastern outcrop of the region's coalfield brought iron works to the zone between Blaenavon and Hirwaun by 1790. Many blast furnaces were rebuilt here in the Great War, but by 1918 interior sites had become unattractive. The industry's centre of gravity shifted from the coalfield to the coast, though for the most part through the 'births' and '*in situ* expansion' components of change. The Dowlais Iron Works opened a coastal plant (at Cardiff), but was the only interior company so to do. Reasons for the coastwards shift are complex. Watts (1968) lists 28 factors that contributed to it; the exhaustion of local ore, and the need for imported high grade ores for acid steel were particularly important. The major exception was at Ebbw Vale where a steelworks closure in 1929 was followed by the opening of a new sheet mill in 1938. With the use of expensive-to-transport Midlands ore in a constricted valley site, this was anything but an optimal location economically, but a substantial government loan, the Prime Minister's intervention, and pressure to recognise its social obligations caused Richard Thomas and Co. to divert investment from Lincolnshire to its 'home' region, where its chairman had declared two years before 'it would be absurd and against the national interest to build modern works' (Pitfield 1974, p. 164)!

Since 1945, rationalisation and closure have advanced apace (Table 6.4), and two major investments have re-emphasised the coast. First, in 1951 Richard, Thomas and Baldwin opened their Abbey strip mill at Port Talbot. Here iron-making had existed since the 1750s and the important Margam plate works since 1915. Jobs for the contracting workforce at Margam, the momentum of the going concern, plus proximity to major sheet steel markets in the tinplate industry tipped the decision for Port Talbot against other locational claimants. In 1951 and 1956 new tinplate

Table 6.4 South Wales iron and steel contraction.

	Number of production locations		
	Blast furnaces	Steelworks	Tinplate works
1950	4	17	35
1975	4	7	3
1982	2	3	3

works were opened nearby at Trostre and Velindre in high-unemployment areas, and the new ore terminal (1969) removed a major obstacle to ore supply. Coal, as throughout the region's steel history, was 'local'.

Secondly, in 1963 the same company opened its Llanwern (Newport) works on a greenfield site. Access to the region's best coking coal pits, and proximity to West Midlands car firms made this the company's preferred site by 1957 even though ore is supplied through Port Talbot. However, MPs and the TUC in Scotland argued the need for a new mill to revive the Scottish economy generally and its steel specifically. Consequently the Prime Minister, Harold Macmillan, announced in the House on 18 November 1968, that the new strip mill investment would be split, with half going to Colville's existing but landlocked site at Ravenscraig (Lanarkshire)—a decision heralded as 'politics before economics' by a contemporary leader in *The Times* (Warren 1973, pp. 274-7).

(d) Sheffield   Sheffield steel is a prime example of locational momentum. Like all the previous areas, it was an important iron centre before the Industrial Revolution focused attention on local coal. Iron ore deposits have been worked out, and almost all blast furnaces have now disappeared too. During World War I, however, Sheffield developed a reputation for and near-monopoly in high-grade, high-speed steels, including alloy steels, whose demand grew rapidly after 1918. Local scrap proved of growing importance, and by 1924 Sheffield had 80% of Britain's electric arc furnaces. Today, continuing research and development, its reputation, available scrap and local coal have maintained this as a steel (though not iron) centre; Sheffield steel is often produced in small-scale plants. By 1979 Sheffield had 49 of Britain's 82 privately-owned steel furnaces and 60 of its grand total (private and nationalised) of 94.

(e) North-east England   Two important steel centres developed here: Consett based on local coal and iron, and Teesside where basic steel was produced from the 1870s half-way between Jurassic ores and Durham coke. By 1937 this was the country's leading steel region. Determined on-site re-investment allowed Consett to survive the closure of local mines as coal production moved coastwards and imported ore via the Tyne became necessary, entailing a long and expensive overland haul to the works at some 900 ft above sea-level. Locationally, the site was as bad as they come. Teesside's estuarine sites, in contrast, are more suited to using imported ores, now through the modern Redcar ore terminal. Expansion by the Dorman Long company on the southern shore, as at Redcar/Lackenby, has maintained this as a major steel centre in the post-war period.

(f) Scotland   Interbedded 'blackband' ores again stimulated early developments here, and the nineteenth-century rise of Clyde shipbuilders provided a ready market. The inevitable switch to imported ores came later than in South Wales, but with no parallel 'movement' to the coast. Shipbuilding's decline, an interior location and the legacy of small non-integrated plants foretold decline since 1945. By 1951 it was the only area wholly dependent on imported ore (and non-local pig iron) and local coke supplies were also becoming scarce. The one major post-war investment (Ravenscraig) has been noted already, but distance from its dominant market among car producers, especially with Linwood's closure, suggests this is now a marginal plant in a problem area. Plans for an integrated tide-water site at Hunterston next to a new ore terminal opened in 1979 would probably prove the final blow to it. (See also p. 72.)

(g) Jurassic iron field The Èast Midlands ore field represents the newest of the major steel regions. At the Lincolnshire end pig iron manufacture accelerated after the Gilchrist–Thomas process encouraged steel-making near Scunthorpe from high phosphoric ores, from 1890. Alone among the regions, it supplied an increasing share of British steel between 1920 and 1932, using coal from Yorkshire and Nottinghamshire, but by 1951 the most economic open-cast local ores were scarce, and imported ore was making a contribution, a trend helped in 1973 by a new terminal at Immingham.

Further south, steel spread to Corby in 1935 when Stewart and Lloyds opened a basic Bessemer works. Many workers were brought in from the company's base, Glasgow, to a new town in this previously agricultural area. Whatever the case for such 'social engineering', Corby economically was an excellent site (Pitfield 1974). An official report of 1936 found the Northamptonshire ore field the cheapest location for steel in the country, in complete contrast to the almost contemporaneous Ebbw Vale. More recently, local ores have been supplemented from overseas, while coal now comes from a variety of British areas.

1967 and beyond

The British Steel Corporation is the second biggest manufacturing employer in Britain, employing in 1979 250,000 staff and producing 55% of steel consumed in Britain. Given the problems identified earlier, the 39 plants it inherited in 1967 were clearly ripe for 'rationalisation'. In its 1972 Heritage Plan (Figure 6.9), hailed as a 'blueprint for survival', BSC planned to invest in good existing locations, including the integration of separate plants as with Scunthorpe's Anchor project, and cut out weak ones. No totally new sites were indicated, even at attractive tide-water locations like Immingham.

In the event, this plan has had mixed fortunes. Irlam closed in 1974, but in February 1975 the Labour government approved Lord Beswick's review of the Heritage Plan, whereby closure of 17 plants was deferred for 2 to 4 years. One was reprieved, with new electric arc investment at Shelton Bar, and only Ebbw Vale was to close its steelworks (with tinplating to continue). The subsequent Conservative government has been less interventionist. Complete closures have followed at East Moors (1978) and Consett (1980), and partial ones at Corby, Shotton and Hartlepool and Workington. Rationalisation elsewhere (such as 18,000 out of 39,000 jobs at Port Talbot and Llanwern between January 1980 and May 1981) meant that the total BSC workforce was reduced to 111,000 by June 1981.

For a company making a loss of £668m. in 1980/81, with an estimated 22% over-capacity and under strict instructions from Whitehall to balance the books, such cuts seem justified as a general principle, but in

Fig. 6.9 BSC's Heritage Plan (1972), styled 'Heritage' as it continued the role of well-established steel centres, without precluding new developments within them. The scale of this plan shows what is possible and necessary when a large corporation assumes responsibility for an industry with strongly-inbuilt forces of inertia. *Sources:* contemporary newspaper accounts.

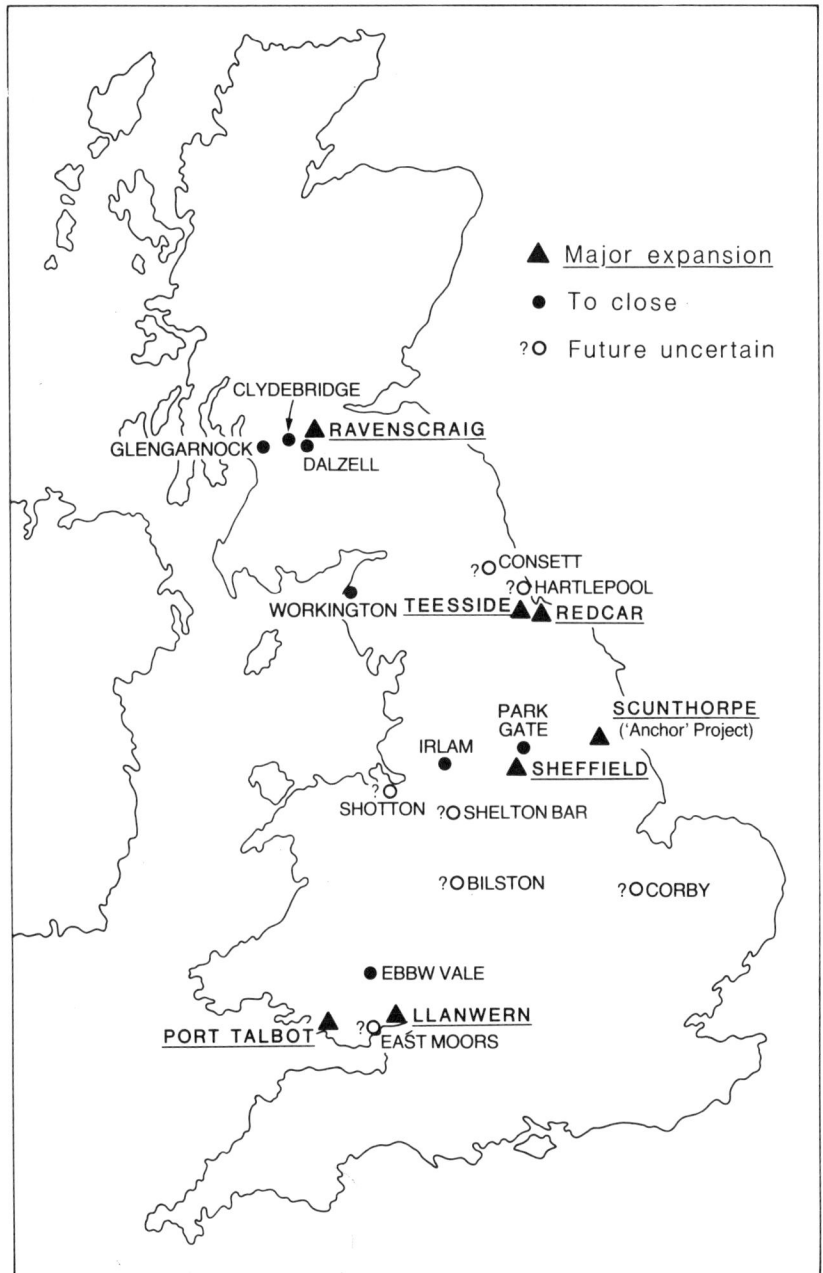

△ Major expansion

● To close

?○ Future uncertain

CLYDEBRIDGE
▲ RAVENSCRAIG
GLENGARNOCK
DALZELL

?○ CONSETT
?○ HARTLEPOOL
WORKINGTON TEESSIDE ▲▲ REDCAR

SCUNTHORPE
('Anchor' Project)
PARK GATE
IRLAM
▲ SHEFFIELD
SHOTTON ?○ SHELTON BAR

?○ BILSTON   ?○ CORBY

● EBBW VALE
PORT TALBOT ▲ ▲ LLANWERN
?○ EAST MOORS

practice the arguments for and against are very complex in particular cases, such as Corby (Table 6.5). But whether the cuts were right or wrong, steel employment has fallen here from 10,000 (January 1980) to 3,000 (May 1981) and the area, like Shotton, has been given Assisted Area status.

This example of one plant in one firm in one industry illustrates nicely the conflict in Britain's contemporary industrial geography between economic, wealth-orientated goals linked to the 'driving forces' of Chapter 2, and those of welfare objectives working through the social and political constraints of Chapter 3.

Table 6.5 Should Corby steelworks be closed?

The case for

1   Corby is at best a marginal site economically, and with out-dated plant and low-grade local ore, this will not improve.

2   Switching production to Redcar, thus enabling the latter to run at lower unit cost, will save £42m. p.a. on a Corby operation.

3   Regional planning assistance, plus infrastructural and promotional work by BSC's industrial development 'arm', will provide new jobs.

The case against

4   If done differently, the 'sums' reduce the Redcar–Corby gap from £42m. to £6m. p.a.

5   Redcar will import both iron ore and coal, the first raising the national import bill by a further £12m. p.a. and the second endangering NCB's viability and mining jobs.

6   Corby redundancy costs will be about £27m.

7   Some 5,000–6,000 unemployed steelworkers raises the spectre of local unemployment of 30% plus, in a one-industry town. 'Remedial measures' planned (3, above) are unlikely to provide more than 300 jobs.

8   Existing problems of poor and abandoned housing, rising crime, broken homes, etc., will become worse as the local authority loses £1m. p.a. in rateable income on the closure, and the image of a 'ghost town' deepens.

Appendix 1

Quantitative indices

Quantitative measures of industrial activity are kept to a minimum in this book, but two are used.

1
Location
Quotient

This measures the extent to which an activity is concentrated in an area or, conversely, an area specialises in an activity, compared with what would be expected on 'fair-share' grounds, knowing the overall role of the activity and of the area in the national economy. Fig. A.1 shows how the LQ is calculated for any given activity/area pair.

2
Gini
Coefficient

This versatile coefficient provides a measure of the similarity between two different percentage distributions when seen over the same set of observation units. These distributions may be employment in two different industries measured over a set of regions, or in two geographical areas over a set of industries. In each case the index has the value of 0 when the two distributions are identical, and 100 when dissimilarity is maximised. Calculation is as below.

Observation unit (i)	Distribution 1 $(p1)$	Distribution 2 $(p2)$	$[p1\text{-}p2]$ (neglecting sign)
1	50%	5%	45
2	15%	15%	0
3	15%	30%	15
4	10%	20%	10
5	10%	30%	20
			Total 90

$$\text{Gini} = \frac{1}{2} \Sigma_i [p1_i - p2_i]$$

Where $p1(2)_i = $ % of distribution 1(2) in observation unit i

and $\Sigma_i = $ Sum of, over all i cases

$$\text{Gini} = \frac{1}{2} (45 + 0 + 15 + 10 + 20)$$
$$= 45$$

Fig. A.1 Calculation of
location quotients. A simple
technique suitable for a wide
range of geographical
applications, and used
extensively in Chapters 4, 5,
and 6.

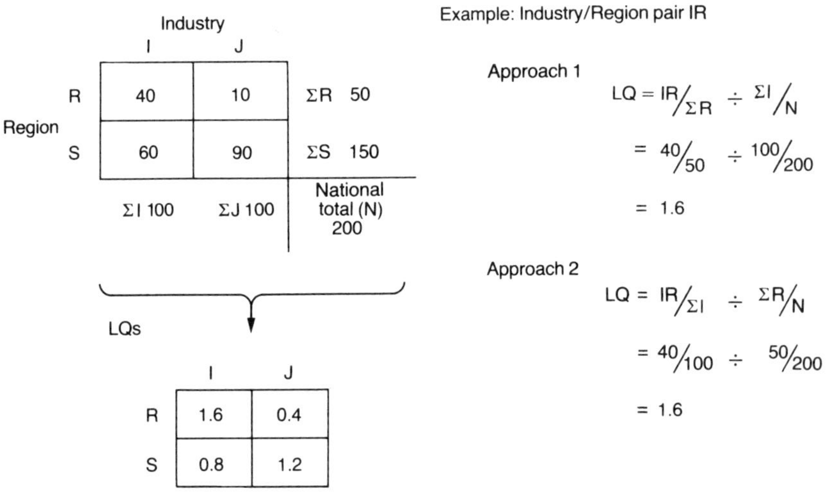

Industry

	I	J	
Region R	40	10	ΣR 50
S	60	90	ΣS 150
	ΣI 100	ΣJ 100	National total (N) 200

LQs

	I	J
R	1.6	0.4
S	0.8	1.2

Example: Industry/Region pair IR

Approach 1

$$LQ = \frac{IR}{\Sigma R} \div \frac{\Sigma I}{N}$$

$$= \frac{40}{50} \div \frac{100}{200}$$

$$= 1.6$$

Approach 2

$$LQ = \frac{IR}{\Sigma I} \div \frac{\Sigma R}{N}$$

$$= \frac{40}{100} \div \frac{50}{200}$$

$$= 1.6$$

Four Gini variants are used in the book, defined thus:

Index	Distributions compared	Observation units
1 *Regional specialisation*		
(a) Diversification	R_i and Even$_i$	Individual industries (i)
(b) Distinctiveness	R_i and National$_i$	
2 *Industrial localisation*		
(a) Dispersal	I_r and Even$_r$	Individual regions (r)
(b) Distinctiveness	I_r and National$_r$	

when

R_i = % regional manufacturing employment in industry i

Even$_i$ = 100/Number of i industries

I_r = % industrial employment in region r

Even$_r$ = 100/number of r regions

National$_i$ = % Great Britain manufacturing employment in industry i

National$_r$ = % Great Britain manufacturing employment in region r

Appendix 2

Evolution of regional policy: the main features

Year	Policy	Description
1928	Industrial Transference Board	To assist migration of unemployed with modest loans and grants.
1934	Special Areas Act	First attempt to bring industry to high unemployment areas (see Fig. 3.10) under guidance of Special Area Commissioners who were given limited financial powers.
1936	Trading Estates	A small number established in the Special Areas (e.g. Treforest, Team Valley).
1937	Special Areas (Amendment) Act	Extension of financial incentives offered by Special Area Commissioners.
1940	Report of the 'Royal Commission on the Distribution of the Industrial Population' under Sir Montague Barlow	Identified the social, economic and political/strategic problems of industrial congestion, and the ways in which these were related to the problems of the 'regions'. Influenced much post-war legislation.
1945	Distribution of Industry Act	Post-war Labour government extended 'Special Areas' to 'Development Areas' (DAs) with much extended financial incentives available, and wider geographical coverage (see Fig. 3.10).
1946	Resettlement Scheme	General assistance for migration of unemployed, with additional provision for movement of 'key staff' employed by firms moving to DAs.
1946	New Towns Act	Made provision for establishment of New Towns. Most were designated on intra-regional planning grounds (Chapter 5) but also played a role in long-distance industrial migration to DAs.
1947	Town and Country Planning Act	Established legal control of local government in wide range of land use issues (Chapter 3) and set up Industrial Development Certificate (IDC) system for all new and extended factories over a specified threshold size (originally 5,000 sq.ft but much altered later) Separation of the 'key staff' aspect of 1946 Resettlement Scheme into a distinct aspect of policy.
1958	Distribution of Industry Act	Extension of DAs' incentives to high-unemployment centres; elsewhere the 'DATAC' areas (see Fig. 3.10).
1960	Local Employment Act	A number of measures, chief amongst which was replacement of DAs by fragmented pattern of 'Development Districts' designated (and de-designated) depending on whether local unemployment exceeded 4½%.
1963 (Budget)		Replaced capital loans and grants by 'free' depreciation, permitting firms to choose the rate they claimed depreciation allowances on plant against taxation.

1963	White papers on two assisted areas— Central Scotland and north-east England.	Advocated 'growth centre' (central Scotland) 'growth zone' (N.E.) policy for intra-regional planning.
1964	Intra-regional planning machinery	Department of Economic Affairs established eight Economic Planning regions in England, each with a Council of non-elected regional worthies, and a 'Board' of Civil Servants. These had no decision-making powers but one of their main tasks became the preparation of intra-regional (strategic) plans (see Chapter 5).
1963	Location of Offices Bureau	Established to offer advice to offices thinking of leaving London.
1965	Control of Office and Industrial Development Act	Established Office Development Permits (ODPs), similar to IDCs. These restricted office expansion in the South East and other prosperous areas but offered no attractive 'carrots' to entice decentralising offices to the assisted areas, in contrast to the combined 'stick' and 'carrot' policies operating for factories.
1965	Highlands and Islands Development (Scotland) Act	Established the Highlands and Islands Development Board with wide-ranging powers to assist economic development in Northern Scotland.
1966	Industrial Development Act	Replaced Development Districts by much less fragmented 'Development Areas' and 'free' depreciation incentives by capital investment grants.
1967	Finance Act	Established a rebate for manufacturers in the DAs, based directly on labour-force strength. The first substantial assistance offered by regional policy to running costs rather than fixed costs.
1967	Special Development Areas (SDAs)	SDAs established for parts of the DAs with particularly high unemployment levels. Incentives set at levels above those prevailing in the DAs (see Fig. 3.10).
1969	Commission on the Intermediate Areas chaired by Sir Joseph Hunt	Examined the regional problems of areas outside the DAs and SDAs. While far from fully implemented, a new tier of Assisted Areas, the 'Intermediate ('Grey') Areas', was established, with incentives levels generally below those in the DAs (see Fig. 3.10).
1970	October 'Mini-Budget'	Relaxation of IDC and ODP thresholds and restoration of 'free' depreciation in place of capital grants as the main 'carrot'.
1972	Industry Act	Reversion to capital grants as basis for regional incentives, introduction of selective ('Section 7') assistance, ending of IDCs for DAs and SDAs, plus a variety of other measures.
1973	Office incentives	Increased incentives in Assisted Areas for service firms in rent and removal expenses.
1973	European Economic Community	Britain's entry made her eligible for existing EEC regionally-based funds, and encouraged a rethink and upgrading of EEC regional policy as a whole. All of the UK's assisted areas became designated as 'peripheral' in EEC terms, with no ceiling on the level of regional incentives supplied by national governments.

1973	Hardman Report	Assessed the scope for decentralising civil service jobs, and recommended some 30,000 could be moved from London.
1975	EEC Regional Development	Regional Development Fund set up to offer investment grants on a quota basis to member states in addition to national regional planning incentives.
1976	Scottish and Welsh Development Agencies	Established with wide powers to build, lease and sell advance factories, to manage industrial estates, to offer industrial finance, to publicise industrial opportunities in Wales and Scotland, and to reclaim and improve derelict land.
1976	Service incentives	Extended regional incentives to service industry firms.
1977	Regional Employment Premium	REP abandoned in Great Britain (but continued in modified form in Northern Ireland), as required by the financial support for Britain offered by the International Monetary Fund in 1976.
1977	Industrial Strategy	Introduced a sectorally-based approach to revive national manufacturing, and reduced the relative attractions of regional incentives.
1979	Conservative Government's July Package	Reduced the levels of incentives available to the assisted areas, drastically cut the areas so designated, abolished ODPs, raised the threshold for IDCs to an unprecedented 50,000 sq.ft, and abolished the Regional Economic Planning Councils.
1981	House of Commons debate on the West Midlands	Government announced its decision to abandon remaining IDC controls throughout the country.

Notes

Chapter 1

A comprehensive review of trends in the United Kingdom economy is provided by the latest available edition of Prest, A.R. and Coppock, D.J. (eds.) *The U.K. economy: a manual of applied economics* (Weidenfeld and Nicolson, London).

Chapter 4

For further discussion of regional economic growth theory the following reviews may prove useful:

Armstrong, H.W. and Taylor, J. (1978) *Regional economic policy and its analysis* (Philip Allen, Deddington, Oxford) Ch. 2.
Glasson, J. (1978) *An introduction to regional planning*, 2nd edition (Heinemann, London) Ch. 1.
Keeble, D.E. (1967) Models of economic development. In Chorley, R.J. and Haggett, P. (eds.) *Models in geography* (Methuen, London), Ch. 8.
Richardson, H.W. (1978) *Regional and urban economics* (Penguin, Harmondsworth) Part 1.

And for further discussion of regional economic trends in Britain since 1918, including those in non-manufacturing sectors, see:

Law, C.M. (1980) *British regional development since World War 1* (David and Charles, Newton Abbot).

Chapter 5

For further study of the economic and planning structure of London and the South East see:

Ash, M.A. (1972) *A guide to the structure of London* (Adams and Dart, Bath).
Hall, J.M. (1976) *London: metropolis and region* (Oxford University Press, Oxford).
Hall, P.G. (1963) *London 2000* (Faber, London).
Keeble, D.E. (1980) Ch. 4-6 in Manners, G. *et al.*, *Regional development in Britain*, 2nd edn (Wiley, Chichester).

And on the inner-city debate in Britain see:
Cameron, G.C. (ed.) (1980) *The future of the British conurbations* (Longman, London).
Coursey, R. (1977) *The debate on urban policy* (RPA, Corbridge).
Evans, A. and Eversley, A. (eds.) (1980) *The inner city: employment and industry* (Heinemann, London).
Lawless, P. (1981) *Britain's inner cities: problems and policies* (Harper and Row, London).

Chapter 6

Data for the employment distribution maps for the four case study industries were defined as follows:

Population Census Industrial Classifications

Motor vehicles	(Fig. 6.2a) 174-7 (1921)	MLH 80 (1951)	MLH 381 (1971)
Brewing and malting	(Fig. 6.4a) 380-2 (1921)	MLH 163 (1951)	MLH 231 (1971)
Electronics	(Fig. 6.6a)	MLH 364 (1961)	MLHs 364, 366, 367 (1971)
Iron and steel	(Fig. 6.8a) 111-14 (1921)	MLH 41, 44 (1951)	MLH 311, 312 (1971)

A detailed review of the British iron and steel industry for the inter-war and immediate post-World War II period is supplied by Roepke, H.G. (1956) *Movements of the British iron and steel industry 1720-1951* (University of Illinois Press, Urbana).

Bibliography

Alexandersson, G. (1967) *Geography of manufacturing* (Prentice-Hall, Englewood Cliffs, N.J.).

Allen, D.E. (1968) *British tastes: an enquiry into the likes and dislikes of the regional consumer* (Heinemann, London).

Allen, G.C. (1957) *British industries and their organisation* (Longman, London).

Armstrong, H.W. (1978) Community regional policy: a survey and critique. *Reg. Stud.* **12**, 511–28.

Armstrong, H.W. and Taylor, J. (1978) *Regional economic policy and its analysis* (Philip Allen, Deddington, Oxford).

Ashcroft, B. and Taylor, J. (1979) The effect of regional policy on the movement of industry in Great Britain. Ch. 2 in Maclennan, D. and Parr, J.B. (eds.) *Regional Policy: past experience and new directions* (Robertson, Oxford).

Bale, J. (1976) *The location of manufacturing industry* (Oliver and Boyd, Edinburgh).

Bayliss, B.T. and Edwards, S.L. (1970) *Industrial demand for transport* (HMSO, London).

Bloomfield, G. (1978) *The world automotive industry* (David and Charles, Newton Abbot).

Blunden, J.R. (1975) *The mineral resources of Britain: a study in exploitation and planning* (Hutchinson, London).

Boal, F.W. (1969) Territoriality and the Shankill-Falls divide. *Irish Geogr.* **6**, 30–50.

Board of Trade (1968) *The movement of manufacturing industry in the United Kingdom, 1945–1965* (HMSO, London).

Boon, G. (1974) A household survey of unemployment in Ashington and Bedlington. *Reg. Stud.* **8**, 175–84.

Brown, C. (1966) The industry of the New Towns of the London region. Ch. 11 in Martin, J.E. *Greater London: an industrial geography* (Bell, London).

Burgess, J.A. (1982) Selling places: environmental images for the executive. *Reg. Stud.* **16**, 1–17.

Busteed, M.A. (1974) *Northern Ireland* (Oxford University Press, Oxford).
    (1976) Small-scale economic development in Northern Ireland. *Scott. Geogr. Mag.* **92**, 172–81.

Buswell, R.J. and Lewis, E.Q. (1970) The geographical distribution of industrial research activity in the United Kingdom. *Reg. Stud.* **4**, 297–306.

Cambridge Information and Research Services Ltd (1980) *Industrial Development Guide* (Cambridge Information and Research Services Ltd, Cambridge).

Cameron, G.C. and Evans, A.W. (1973) The British conurbation centres. *Reg. Stud.* **7**, 47–55.

Camina, M.M. (1974) Local authorities and the attraction of industry. *Prog. in Plann.* **3**, 83–182.

Canning Town Community Development Project (1975) *Canning Town to North Woolwich: the aims of industry* (Canning Town CDP, London).

Centre for Inter-Firm Comparison (1977) *Management policies and practices and business performance* (Centre for Inter-Firm Comparison, London).

Chapman, K. (1976) *North Sea oil and gas: a geographical perspective* (David and Charles, Newton Abbot).

Chisholm, M. (1966) *Geography and economics* (Bell, London).

Chisholm, M. and O'Sullivan, P. (1973) *Freight flows and spatial aspects of the British economy* (Cambridge University Press, Cambridge).

Clout, H.D. (ed.) (1981) *Regional development in Western Europe* (2nd edn, Wiley, Chichester).

Corden, W.M. and Fels, G. (eds.) (1976) *Public assistance to industry: protection and subsidies in Britain and Germany* (Macmillan, London).

Cowan, P. (1969) *The office: a facet of urban growth* (Heinemann, London).

Crum, R.E. and Gudgin, G. (1977) *Non-productive activities in UK manufacturing industry* (Regional Policy Series No. 3, Commission of the European Communities Regional Policy, Brussels).

CSO (Central Statistical Office) (1973) *Input–output tables for the United Kingdom* (Studies in Official Statistics No. 22, HMSO, London).

Dennis, R. (1978) The decline of manufacturing employment in Greater London. *Urban Stud.* **15**, 63–73.

Department of Commerce (of Northern Ireland) (1978) *Facts and figures on the Northern Ireland economy* (Department of Commerce, Belfast).

Department of Employment (1978) *British labour statistics 1976* (HMSO, London).

Department of the Environment (1973) *Strategic planning in the South East: a first report of the Monitoring Group* (Department of the Environment, London).

(1977) *Inner area studies, Liverpool, Birmingham and Lambeth: summaries of consultants' final reports* (HMSO, London).

Department of Industry (1981) *Industrial movement in the United Kingdom, 1966–1975* (HMSO, London).

Department of Trade and Industry (1973) *Expenditure committee (Trade and Industry Sub-Committee) Minutes of evidence 4 July, 1973* (Session 1972–3, HMSO, London).

Dicken, P. and Lloyd, P.E. (1978) Inner metropolitan industrial change, enterprise structures and policy issues: case studies of Manchester and Merseyside. *Reg. Stud.* **12**, 181–97.

Dixon, C. (1978) The changing structure of the British brewing industry. *Geography* **63**, 108–13.

Donnachie, I. (1979) *A history of the brewing industry in Scotland* (John Donald, Edinburgh).

Drewett, R., Goddard, J.B. and Spence, N. (1976) Urban Britain: beyond containment. Ch. 3 in Berry, B.J.L. (ed.) *Urbanisation and counterurbanisation* (Sage Publications, Beverley Hills).

Economist Intelligence Unit (1964) *A survey of factors concerning the location of offices in London* (Economist Intelligence Unit, London).

Edge, G. (1973) The suburbanisation of industry. In *The city as an economic system* (Open University Social Sciences second-level course, DT 201, Unit 13), pp. 119–49 (Open University, Milton Keynes).

Edwards, S.L. (1970) Transport costs in British industry. *Jl Transport Econ. and Policy* **4**, 1–19.

Eversley, D.E. (1965) Social and psychological factors in the determination of industrial location. In Wilson, T. (ed.) *Papers in regional development* (Blackwell, Oxford).

Fordham, R.C. (1970) Airport planning in the context of the Third London Airport. *The Economic Journal* **80**, 307–322.

Fothergill, S. and Gudgin, G. (1979) In defence of shift–share. *Urban Stud.* **16**, 309–19.

Frost, M. (1977) The influence of the state in determining patterns of economic activity. *Geography* **62**, 291–6.

George, K.D. (1974) *Industrial organisation: competition, growth and structural change in Britain* (Allen and Unwin, London).

Glasson, J. (1978) *An introduction to regional planning* (2nd edn, Hutchinson, London).

Gleave, M.E. (1965) Some contrasts in the English brick-making industry. *Tijdschr. Econ. en Soc. Geogr.* **56**, 54–62.

Goddard, J.B. (1975) *Office location in urban and regional development* (Oxford University Press, Oxford).

Goddard, J.B. and Smith, I. (1978) Changes in corporate control in the British urban system 1972–1977. *Environ. and Plann. A* **10**, 1073–84.

Gould, P.R. and White, R.R. (1968) The mental maps of British school leavers. *Reg. Stud.* **2**, 161–82.

Green, D.H. (1977) Industrialists' information levels of regional incentives. *Reg. Stud.* **11**, 7–18.

Gudgin, G. (1978) *Industrial location processes and regional employment growth* (Saxon House, Farnborough).

Gudgin, G., Brunskill, I. and Fothergill, S. (1979) *New manufacturing firms in regional employment growth* (Research Series 39, Centre for Environmental Studies, London).

Hall, J. (1970) Industry grows where the grass in greener. *Area* **3**, 40–6.

Hall, P.G. (1962) *The industries of London since 1861* (Hutchinson, London).

(1978) The South East: Britain's tarnished golden corner. *New Society* 28 July, 228–31

Harris, C.D. (1954) The market as a factor in the localisation of industry in the United States. *Annals Assoc. Amer. Geogr.* **44**, 315–48.

Hawkins, K.H. and Pass, C.L. (1979) *The brewing industry: a study of industrial organisation and public policy* (Heinemann, London).

Heal, D.W. (1974) *The steel industry in post-war Britain* (David and Charles, Newton Abbot).

Hoare, A.G. (1973) The spheres of influence of industrial location factors. *Reg. Stud.* **7**, 301–14.

(1974) International airports as growth poles: a case study of Heathrow Airport. *Trans. Inst. Geogr.* **63**, 75–96.

(1975) Linkage flows, locational evaluation and industrial geography: a study of Greater London. *Environ. and Plann. A* **7**, 41–58.

(1978) Industrial linkages and the dual economy: the case of Northern Ireland. *Reg. Stud.* **12**, 167–80.

(1981) Why they go where they go: the political imagery of industrial location. *Trans. Inst. Br. Geogr.* NS **6**, 152–75.

157

(1982) Problem region and regional problem. Ch. 8 in Boal, F.W. and Douglas, J.N.H. (eds.) *Integration and division* (Academic Press, London).

Holland, S. (1976) *The regional problem* (Macmillan, London).

House, J.W. (ed.) 1977 *The UK space* (Weidenfeld and Nicolson, London).

House of Commons Expenditure Committee (1973) *Regional development incentives, second report* (Trade and Industry Sub-Committee, Session 1973–4, HMSO, London).

Johnston, R.J. (1979) *Political, electoral and spatial systems* (Oxford University Press, Oxford).

Keeble, D.E. (1969) Local industrial linkage and manufacturing growth in outer London. *Town Plann. Rev.* **40**, 163–8.

(1971) Employment mobility in Britain. Ch. 2 in Chisholm, M. and Manners, G. (eds.) *Spatial policy problems of the British economy.* (Cambridge University Press, Cambridge).

(1976) *Industrial location and planning in the United Kingdom* (Methuen, London).

(1978) Industrial decline in the inner city and conurbation. *Trans. Inst. Br. Geogr.* NS **3**, 101–14.

Keeble, D.E. and Hauser, D.P. (1972) Spatial analysis of manufacturing growth in outer south-east England 1960–67, 2: method and results. *Reg. Stud.* **6**, 11–36.

Kirby, A. (1978) *The inner city: causes and effects* (RPA, Corbridge).

Knox, P.L. (1973) *Social well-being: a spatial perspective* (Oxford University Press, Oxford).

Law, D. (1964) Industrial movement and locational advantage. *Manchester Sch. Econ. and Soc. Stud.* **32**, 131–54.

Lambert, J. (1979) Manufacturing employment change in the Bristol travel-to-work area. Unpublished paper, Department of Industry, Bristol.

Lee, C.H. (1979) *British regional employment statistics* (Cambridge University Press, Cambridge).

Leigh, R. and North, D. (1978) Regional aspects of acquisition activity in British manufacturing industry. *Reg. Stud.* **12**, 227–45.

Lever, W.F. (1972) Industrial movement, spatial association and functional linkages. *Reg. Stud.* **6**, 371–84.

Lewis, E.W. (1971) The location of manufacturing industry in the western home counties. Unpublished M. Phil. thesis, University of London.

Luttrell, W.F. (1962) *Factory location and industrial movement*, Vol. 1 (National Institute for Economic and Social Research, London).

McCallum, J.D. (1979) The development of British regional policy. Ch. 1 in Maclennan, D. and Parr, J.B. (eds.) *Regional policy: past experience and new directions* (Martin Robertson, Oxford).

McCrone, G. (1969) *Regional policy in Britain* (Allen and Unwin, London).

Mackay, R. (1979) The death of regional policy—or resurrection squared? *Reg. Stud.* **13**, 281–95.

Marshall, J.N. (1979) Ownership, organisation and industrial linkage: a case study of the northern region of England. *Reg. Stud.* **13**, 531–58.

Martin, J.E. (1966) *Greater London: an industrial geography* (Bell, London).

Massey, D. and Meegan, R.A. (1979) The geography of industrial reorganisation: the spatial effects of the restructuring of the electrical engineering sector under the Industrial Reorganisation Corporation. *Prog. in Plann.* **10**, 155–237.

Matthew, R.H. (1964) *Belfast regional survey and plan 1962: a report* (HMSO, Belfast).

Miller, R. (1978) *Attitudes to work in Northern Ireland* (Research Report No. 2, Fair Employment Agency, Belfast).

Moore, B. and Rhodes, J. (1976) Regional economic policy and the movement of manufacturing firms to Development Areas. *Economica* **43**, 17–31.

Moore, B., Rhodes, J. and Tarling, R. (1978) Industrial policy and economic development: the experience of Northern Ireland and the Republic of Ireland. *Cambridge Jl Econ.* **2**, 99–114.

Mounfield, P. (1977) The place of time in economic geography. *Geography* **62**, 268–85.

Moyes, A. (1975) Second world war manufacturing industry and its significance in north Staffordshire. Ch. 15 in Phillips, A.D.M. and Turton, B.J. (eds.) *Environment, man and economic change* (Longman, London).

Murie, A.S., Birrell, W.D., Hillyard, P.A.R. and Roche, D.J.D. (1973) A survey of industrial movement to Northern Ireland between 1965 and 1969. *Econ. and Soc. Rev.* **4**, 231–44.

Myrdal, G.M. (1957) *Economic theory and under-developed regions* (Duckworth, London).

Nelson, D. and Potter, D. (1982) *A survey of employees in the manufacturing sector in the South West* (Government Economic Service Working Paper No. 50, Department of Industry, London).

NIESR (National Institute of Economic and Social Research) (1977) *The United Kingdom economy* (Heinemann, London).

NIHE (Northern Ireland Housing Executive) (no date) *Belfast household survey 1978* (NIHE, Belfast).

North, D.C. (1955) Location theory and regional economic growth. *Jl Polit. Econ.* **63**, 243–58.

Northcott, J. (1977) *Industry in the development areas: the experience of firms opening new factories* (Broadsheet 573, Political and Economic Planning, London).

Northern Ireland Office (1974) *Finance and the economy* (HMSO, London).

Nunn, S. (1980) *The opening and closure of manufacturing units in the United Kingdom 1966–1975* (Government Economic Service Working Paper No. 36, Department of Industry, London).

Oakey, R.P., Thwaites, A.T. and Nash, P.N. (1980) The regional distribution of innovative manufacturing establishments in Britain. *Reg. Stud.* **14**, 235–53.

Open University (1972) The iron and steel industry. In *New trends in Geography II* (Open University Social Sciences second-level course DT 281, Block II, Unit 8), pp. 87–118 (Open University, Milton Keynes).

Phillips, G.A. and Maddock, R.T. (1973) *The growth of the British economy 1918–1968* (Allen and Unwin, London).

Pitfield, D.E. (1974) Regional economic policy and the long run: innovation and location in the iron and steel industry. *Business Hist.* **16**, 160–74.

Pocock, D. and Hudson, H. (1978) *Images of the urban environment* (Macmillan, London).

Pollard, S. (1969) *The development of the British economy 1914–1967* (2nd edn, Edward Arnold, London).

Prais, S.J. (1976) *The evolution of giant firms in Britain* (Cambridge University Press, Cambridge).

Quigley, W.G.H. (1976) *Economic and industrial strategy for Northern Ireland: report by the review team* (under the chairmanship of Dr Quigley) (HMSO, Belfast).

Rees, J. (1969) *Industrial demand for water: a study of south-east England* (Research Monographs No 31, London School of Economics, London).

Richardson, H.W. (1969) *Elements of regional economics* (Penguin, Harmondsworth). (1978) *Regional and urban economics* (Penguin, Harmondsworth).

Riley, R.C. (1976) *Industrial geography* (Chatto and Windus, London).

Rodgers, B. (1980) The West Midlands and Central Wales. Ch. 8 in Manners, G. *et al.* (eds.) *Regional development in Britain* (2nd edn, Wiley, Chichester).

Rogers, P.B. and Smith, C.R. (1977) The local authority's role in economic development: the Tyne and Wear Act 1976. *Reg. Stud.* **11**, 153–63.

Schiller, P. (1978) Companies little affected by 'troubles'. *Business Location File* (April/May), 40.

Sciberras, E. (1977) *Multinational electronics companies and national economic policies* (JAI Press, Greenwich, Connecticut).

Simon, H.A. (1957) *Models of man, social and rational* (Wiley, New York).

SEJPT (South East Joint Planning Team) (1971a) *Strategic plan for the South East: studies volume 1* (population and employment) (HMSO, London). (1971b) *Strategic plan for the South East: studies volume 5* (report of Economic Consultants Ltd) (HMSO, London).

Smith, D.H. (1933) *The industries of Greater London* (P.S. King, London).

Spooner, D.J. (1972) Industrial movement and the rural periphery: the case of Devon and Cornwall. *Reg. Stud.* **6**, 197–215.

Steed, G.P.F. (1967) Locational changes: a 'shift and share' analysis of Northern Ireland's manufacturing mix, 1950–1964. *Tijdschr. Econ. en Soc. Geogr.* **58**, 265–70. (1968) The changing milieu of a firm: a case study of a shipbuilding concern. *Annals Assoc. Amer. Geogr.* **58**, 506–24. (1974) The Northern Ireland linen complex, 1960–1970. *Annals Assoc. Amer. Geogr.* **64**, 397–408.

Taylor, M.J. (1968) Hidden female labour reserves. *Reg. Stud.* **2**, 20–49.

Taylor, M.J. and Wood, P.A. (1973) Industrial linkage and local agglomeration in the West Midlands metal industries. *Trans. Inst. Br. Geogr.* **59**, 129–54.

Taylor, T.G. (1979) Changes in the Northern Ireland textile industry 1945–1975. Unpublished MSc. thesis, University College, Swansea.

Thrift, N. (1979) Unemployment in the inner city. Ch. 5 in Herbert, D. and Johnston, R.J. (eds.) *Geography and the Urban Environment,* Vol. 2. (Wiley, Chichester). (no date) *An introduction to time geography* (CATMOG No. 13, Geo Abstracts, Norwich).

Tiebout, C. (1956) Exports and regional economic growth. *Jl Polit. Econ.* **64**, 160–4.

Townroe, P.N. (1971) *Industrial location decisions: a study of management behaviour.* (Occasional paper No. 15, University of Birmingham Centre for Urban and Regional Studies, Birmingham).

Toyne, P. (1974) *Organisation, location and behaviour: decision-making in economic geography* (Macmillan, London).

Turner, G. (1963) *The car makers* (Eyre and Spottiswoode, London).

Walker, R. and Storper, M. (1981) Capital and industrial location. *Prog. in Human Geogr.* **5**, 473–509.

Warnes, A.M. (1980) A long-term view of employment decentralisation from the larger English cities. Ch. 1 in Evans, A. and Eversley, D. (eds.) *The inner city: employment and industry* (Heinemann, London).

Warren, K. (1969) Recent changes in the geographical location of the British steel industry. *Geogrl J.* **135**, 343–64.

(1970) *The British iron and sheet steel industry since 1840* (Bell, London).

(1973) The location of British heavy industry—problems and policies. *Geogrl J.* **139**, 76–83.

(1975) *World steel: an economic geography* (David and Charles, Newton Abbot).

(1976) British steel: the problems of rebuilding an old industrial structure. *Geography* **61**, 1–7.

Watts, D.G. (1968) Changes in location of the South Wales iron and steel industry 1860–1930. *Geography* **53**, 294–307.

Watts, H.D. (1970) The location of aluminium reduction plant in the United Kingdom. *Tijdschr. Econ. en Soc. Geogr.* **61**, 148–156.

(1977) Market areas and spatial rationalisation: the British brewing industry after 1945. *Tijdschr. Econ. en Soc. Geogr.* **68**, 224–40.

(1981) *The branch plant economy: a study of external control* (Longman, Harlow).

Whitehand, J. (1967) The settlement morphology of London's cocktail belt. *Tijdschr. Econ. en Soc. Geogr.* **58**, 20–7.

Wise, M.J. (1950) On the evolution of the jewellery and gun quarters in Birmingham. *Trans. Inst. Br. Geogr.* **15**, 59–72.

Wood, P.A. (1976) *The West Midlands* (David and Charles, Newton Abbot).